# China's Civil Service Reform

As part of China's overall reform process, China's civil service has also been reformed, beginning in the late 1970s, undergoing a major change in 1993 with the implementation of a new civil service system, with the reforms continuing to unfold thereafter. The creation of a modern, clean, competent and merit-based civil service is extremely important to enable China to regulate and manage its increasingly complex economy and society. This book, based on extensive original research, outlines the civil service reforms and assesses their effectiveness. It shows how recruitment and promotion, now based on merit, control by policy-makers and overall effectiveness have all been improved, with this being attested to by citizens acknowledging that the civil service now does a better job. The book concludes by discussing how China's civil service reforms can serve as a model for other Asian countries.

**Wang Xiaoqi** is a Research Assistant Professor in the Department of Politics and Public Administration, University of Hong Kong. Her research interests include Chinese politics, public governance and management, institutional analysis, coordination and collaboration, comparative public policy and state-society relations. Her articles have appeared in *The China Quarterly* and *International Social Science Journal*.

**Comparative development and policy in Asia series**
Series Editors:
Ka Ho Mok
(*Faculty of Social Sciences, The University of Hong Kong, China*)
Rachel Murphy
*(Oxford University, UK)*
Yongjin Zhang
*(Centre for East Asian Studies, University of Bristol, UK)*

1  **Cultural Exclusion in China**
   State education, social mobility and cultural difference
   *Lin Yi*

2  **Labour Migration and Social Development in Contemporary China**
   *Edited by Rachel Murphy*

3  **Changing Governance and Public Policy in East Asia**
   *Edited by Ka Ha Mok and Ray Forrest*

4  **Ageing in East Asia**
   Challenges and policies for the twenty-first century
   *Edited by Tsung-hsi Fu and Rhidian Hughes*

5  **Towards Responsible Government in East Asia**
   Trajectories, intentions and meanings
   *Edited by Linda Chelan Li*

6  **Government and Policy-Making Reform in China**
   The implications of governing capacity
   *Bill K.P. Chou*

7  **Governance for Harmony in Asia and Beyond**
   *Edited by Julia Tao, Anthony Cheung, Martin Painter and Chenyang Li*

8  **Welfare Reform in East Asia**
   Towards workfare?
   *Edited by Chak Kwan Chan and Kinglun Ngok*

9  **China's Assimilationist Language Policy**
   Impact on indigenous/minority literacy and social harmony
   *Edited by Gulbahar H. Beckett and Gerard A. Postiglione*

10 **The Emergent Knowledge Society and the Future of Higher Education**
Asian perspectives
*Deane E. Neubauer*

11 **China's Civil Service Reform**
*Wang Xiaoqi*

# China's Civil Service Reform

Wang Xiaoqi

LONDON AND NEW YORK

First published 2012
by Routledge
2 Park Square, Milton Park, Abingdon, Oxfordshire OX14 4RN
Simultaneously published in the USA and Canada
by Routledge
711 Third Avenue, New York, NY 10017
First issued in paperback 2014

*Routledge is an imprint of the Taylor and Francis Group, an informa business*

© 2012 Wang Xiaoqi

The right of Wang Xiaoqi to be identified as author of this work has been asserted by her in accordance with sections 77 and 78 of the Copyright, Designs and Patents Act 1988.

All rights reserved. No part of this book may be reprinted or reproduced or utilized in any form or by any electronic, mechanical, or other means, now known or hereafter invented, including photocopying and recording, or in any information storage or retrieval system, without permission in writing from the publishers.

*Trademark notice*: Product or corporate names may be trademarks or registered trademarks, and are used only for identification and explanation without intent to infringe.

*British Library Cataloguing in Publication Data*
A catalogue record for this book is available from the British Library

*Library of Congress Cataloging in Publication Data*
Wang, Xiaoqi, Ph. D.
China's civil service reform/Wang Xiaoqi.
  p. cm. – (Comparative development and policy in Asia series; 11)
  Includes bibliographical references and index.
  1. Civil service reform–China. I. Title.
  JQ1512.W295 2012
  352.6′3–dc23
              2011042493

ISBN 978-0-415-57748-9 (hbk)
ISBN 978-1-138-81559-9 (pbk)
ISBN 978-0-203-12150-4 (ebk)

Typeset in Times New Roman
by Wearset Ltd, Boldon, Tyne and Wear

**To my husband Yang and our adorable son Shijun**

# Contents

*List of figures*     xi
*List of tables*     xii
*Acknowledgments*     xiv

**1 Introduction**     1
   *Research questions and importance* 1
   *Existing literature and gaps* 6
   *Theoretical framework and research design* 8
   *Structure of the book* 17

**2 Civil service scope, structure and context for reforms**     20
   *The civil service: scope, size and structure* 20
   *Political and organizational context for managing civil servants* 32
   *Legal context for civil service reforms* 36
   *Problems of the old cadre system* 37

**3 Civil service reform policy and implementation**     41
   *To discover more information* 42
   *To align the incentives* 49
   *Wage reform* 52
   *Discipline policy* 63

**4 Local implementation of civil service reforms**     67
   *Civil service reforms in Haidian* 67
   *Civil service reforms in Ningbo* 76
   *Civil service reforms in Changchun* 81
   *Discussion* 83
   *Conclusion* 91

## 5 Control of the bureaucracy and reform outcomes 93
*Decentralization of personnel management 94*
*Programs of the civil service reforms to reassert control 97*
*Intra-party reforms and anticorruption measures 103*
*Public service delivery and citizen satisfaction 107*
*Conclusion 117*

## 6 Implications for Asian developing countries 118
*Summary of China's reform experience 119*
*Initial conditions of the five countries 120*
*Patterns of civil service reforms in four countries 122*
*Discussion 134*

## 7 Conclusion 138
*Summary of research findings 139*
*Policy implications 142*
*Limitations 144*
*Future research agenda 145*

**Appendices** 146
*Appendix 1 The empirical database 146*
*Appendix 2 Protocol for the 90 in-depth interviews 150*
*Appendix 3 Haidian citizen satisfaction survey questionnaire 154*
*Appendix 4 Fieldwork questionnaire 166*

| | |
|---|---|
| *Notes* | 168 |
| *Bibliography* | 173 |
| *Index* | 185 |

# Figures

| | | |
|---|---|---|
| 2.1 | Relationships between the four concepts | 23 |
| 2.2 | Overview of civil service scope extension, 1978–2008 | 29 |
| 4.1 | Number of civil servants and their educational level in Haidian, 1991–2000 | 74 |
| 4.2 | Number of civil servants and their educational level in Ningbo Education Commission, 1991–2001 | 79 |

# Tables

| | | |
|---|---|---|
| 2.1 | Number and distribution of civil servants by administrative level, 1998 | 24 |
| 2.2 | Number and distribution of civil servants by rank, 1998 | 24 |
| 2.3 | Number employed by government agencies, party organs, social organizations and public service units, 1978–2008 (thousands) | 26 |
| 2.4 | Public sector employment for various provinces, 2008 | 27 |
| 2.5 | Administrative expenses, 1978–2008 | 28 |
| 2.6 | Position and grade structure change | 31 |
| 3.1 | Number of vacancies and applicants for centrally managed civil service positions, 1994–2009 | 44 |
| 3.2 | Chinese civil service position and grade structure | 57 |
| 3.3 | Composition of 2006 wage system (responsibility wages (*zhiwu gongzi*)) | 58 |
| 3.4 | Composition of 2006 wage system (grade wages (*yuan*)) | 59 |
| 3.5 | Wage bill and average year wage in various provinces, 2007 | 63 |
| 3.6 | 'Wet' functions | 65 |
| 4.1 | Transfer method in Haidian, 1997 | 69 |
| 4.2 | Haidian civil servants selection, 1995–2002 | 70 |
| 4.3 | Demobilized soldiers transferred into Haidian, 1995–2001 | 71 |
| 4.4 | Number of civil servants, their education level and age in Haidian Personnel Bureau, 1991–2000 | 75 |
| 4.5 | Ningbo absorption of demobilized soldiers, 1997–1999 | 78 |
| 4.6 | Number of civil servants, their education level and age in Ningbo Environmental Protection Bureau, 1996–2000 | 80 |
| 4.7 | Position classification in Changchun, 1996 | 81 |
| 4.8 | Perception that pay and performance are linked, Haidian and Changchun (number of interviewees) | 85 |
| 4.9 | Training hours | 89 |
| 5.1 | Number and distribution of leading cadres, 1979–1998 | 98 |
| 5.2 | Environmental performance scores, 1994 and 1999 | 108 |
| 5.3 | Perception that bureau performance has improved (percent) | 109 |

| | | |
|---|---|---|
| 5.4 | To what extent citizens are informed about government policy and activities ($N=501$) | 113 |
| 5.5 | Through what channels citizens know of the policies and activities ($N=501$) | 114 |
| 5.6 | General evaluation of educational performance compared with five years ago (%) | 115 |
| 5.7 | Evaluation of Haidian education performance by gender, age, education and income ($N=450$) | 115 |
| 5.8 | Citizens' evaluation of Haidian educational performance ($N=501$) | 116 |
| 5.9 | Evaluation of government policy responsiveness | 116 |
| 5.10 | Evaluation of government responsiveness by gender, age, education and income ($N=482$) | 117 |
| 6.1 | Overview of economy, 2007 | 121 |
| 6.2 | Corruption Perception Index 2009 | 121 |
| 6.3 | Public service employment in Vietnam, 2002 | 124 |
| 6.4 | Profile of the Lao civil service, 1995, 2002 | 127 |
| 6.5 | Number of civil servants in Indonesia, 2005 | 129 |
| 6.6 | Profile of the Philippine civil service, 1997–2001 | 133 |
| A.1 | Profile of interviewees | 147 |
| A.2 | Profile of interviewees | 148 |
| A.3 | Profile of interviewees | 149 |

# Acknowledgments

A number of wonderful people and institutions deserve thanks for their help and service over the course of the research effort culminating in this book. First, I am immensely grateful to John Burns, my doctoral supervisor, who has showed me how a great scholar should have passionate devotion to his field. His insightful guidance, constant encouragement and kind support enabled the fulfillment of this research. I am also deeply indebted to Wai-Fung Lam, who has been a great source of inspiration and challenge. With a sharp and critical mind, superb analytical skills and good humor, Wai-Fung Lam sets an example of both excellent scholarship and marvelous mentorship. I am particularly grateful to Ka-Ho Mok for encouraging me to publish my dissertation as a book and giving me invaluable suggestions.

I benefited greatly from the comments on the earlier drafts of this book from many other scholars, including James Perry, Guy Peters, Melanie Manion, Lynn White, Anthony Cheung, Tom Liou, Richard Hu, Peter Cheung, Ian Thynne and Bill Chou.

I have been fortunate enough to be a recipient of several research and conference grants from the University of Hong Kong. I would like to thank the Urban China Research Network of the State University of New York at Albany for a Graduate Student Research Grant. I also thank the Hong Kong Association of University Women for supporting my fieldwork with the HKAUW Thomas H. C. Cheung Scholarship.

I am also grateful to the people I interviewed and the people who helped me during my fieldwork in Beijing, Ningbo and Changchun between 2004 and 2008. Many of the local civil servants I interviewed were very open-minded and helpful. I also wish to thank my editors at Routledge, Peter Sowden and Jillian Morrison, for guiding me through the publication process.

I wish to thank my parents and three elder sisters for providing me with endless love and caring. Most importantly, I wish to thank my husband Yang and our adorable son Shijun for their love. My husband has been a staunch supporter of my writing from the very beginning. His intellectual and emotional support has been an enduring source of stimulation and insight and has always given me the strength to go through challenging times. I became a new mother just as the book was finalized. All parents will understand how exciting and overwhelming this was. My son has really enriched my life. His company has introduced a new perspective on life and also inspired me to work particularly hard for this book. I would like to dedicate this book to my husband Yang and our son Shijun.

# 1 Introduction

The Chinese economy and society have undergone tremendous changes in the past three decades. In general, a market economy has emerged and a more liberal society has taken shape. These developments have brought great challenges to the outdated governance structure and personnel management system. To improve the decision-making process within the government and reshape the management system amidst a more complex economy and society, post-Mao authorities have implemented a number of administrative reforms including the civil service reform, which had an emphasis on selecting and promoting public officials based on their capability and work performance. In particular, with the promulgation of the *Provisional Regulations on State Civil Servants* in 1993, the government of China announced that it was establishing a new civil service system[1] to manage the 5.3 million or so white-collar workers who were employed as 'civil servants' by the government. The purpose of the change, broadly speaking, was to improve the efficiency, capacity and integrity of the civil service and strengthen policy-makers' control over the bureaucracy. The reforms have been implemented nationwide since 1993 and thousands of positions have been filled under the new rules and procedures. On 27 April 2005, the new *Civil Service Law* of the People's Republic of China was approved by the National People's Congress and has been implemented to manage the whole civil service of the country since 2006. Accordingly, it now presents a timely opportunity to investigate the impact that the civil service reforms had on the Chinese government and politics. This book will examine the implementation and performance of the ongoing civil service reforms in China. It will study the efforts of the Chinese authorities to modernize the government personnel system from the late 1970s with a focus on the 1993 reform.

## Research questions and importance

Modern governments are very much dependent upon civil servants, who exercise considerable power and influence in the discharge of executive functions and the delivery of public services. This makes the civil service system a basic constituent part of the modern government and a key analytical unit of public administration research. In recent years, Western governments and international

2   *Introduction*

development agencies have embarked on a new agenda of 'good governance'[2] and this search for good governance has become a high priority on the political agenda of Asian countries as well (Cheung 2005; Mok and Forest 2008; Painter 2004; Turner 2002). The emerged-out trend in Asian countries is to build or rebuild robust governance structures and institutions to counter the tensions between the increasingly liberalized economy and the partially reformed (and usually fragile and weak) institutions. Given that a competent, clean and merit-based civil service is crucial to further economic reform and social development, various authorities in Asia seek to design civil service reforms that will affect the behavior of government employees and, thus, improve administrative performance. In the effort to make the bureaucracy more meritocratic, authorities in China are no exception. Given the country's global stature, China's efforts in searching for good governance and a meritocratic civil service demand rigorous analysis.

Dating from the late 1970s and strengthened by the new civil service regulations in 1993 and by the implementation of the *Civil Service Law* in 2006, China's reforms introduced more open and competitive selection processes, tighter monitoring mechanisms and greater incentives to reward performance. China's civil service reforms were based on a logic that over-simplified the relationship between superiors and subordinates while leaving in place elements of an organization culture that condoned illegal behavior such as corruption. The establishment of the civil service system in China tried to abolish the inflexible, over-centralized cadre personnel management system by introducing a rational management system based on categorization. The civil service reform was of far-reaching significance for the development of China's political system since the new system also introduced a certain degree of public participation and legal elements into public personnel management practices. Management and administration in contemporary China are now performed largely in accordance to the law. Moreover, government rebuilding and changes in governance had important impacts on the welfare of Chinese citizens. Admittedly, reform is an ongoing process and many events are still gradually unfolding. Studies of this process will contribute not only to a general understanding of China's political development, but also an in-depth understanding of public administration and management practices.

Civil service reforms in China had the potential to make a departure from the established structure of the cadre personnel management system that was developed by the Chinese Communist Party (CCP) during the Communist revolutionary period (Wu 2009: 14–16). However, scholars observed that the new reforms had done little to undermine the old cadre system despite several years of policy development (Chan and Li 2007). Is this true? Or does this conclusion over-simplify the complicated implementation of the reforms? This book, based on extensive original research, will outline the civil service reforms and assess their effectiveness. Adopting a principal–agent framework, I find that the effectiveness of the reform initiatives was mixed. In general, the civil service reforms in China successfully addressed some adverse selection problems while failing to adequately address incentive alignment issues. On one hand, the current Chinese civil service recruitment relies heavily on examinations and competitions. Thus, the process of selecting and promoting civil servants in China today is undoubtedly more open, transparent and competitive than it was under the cadre personnel management system. This book will show how recruitment and promotion, which is now based on merit, control by policy-makers and overall effectiveness were improved, as attested by citizens who acknowledged that the civil service now does a better job than before. On the other hand, formal policy instruments (to align the incentives of superiors and subordinates) such as pay and promotion did not serve as effective motivators for the rank-and-file civil servants. Ironically, it was found that the real motivation came from informal incentive alignment measures: superiors and their subordinates collaborated in illicit activities such as the buying and selling of government posts. That is to say, the official policy to align the incentives of principal and agents in China's civil service reforms failed while the informal or illegal motivators successfully aligned the incentives of corrupt superiors and their subordinates. This suggests that discipline is now emerging as an urgent issue for the civil service in reform.

To evaluate the policy outcomes of a series of reforms, we should first be clear about the policy problems the reforms are intended to address. In this book, the main research questions are based on my understanding of the managerial and political goals of the civil service reforms and of the evolving process that policy-makers in China have come to adopt in the current civil service system. Personnel system reforms are a popular means to improve government performance. In their performance management movement, most OECD countries have adopted new approaches to manage government employees based on the belief that more effective management of people in areas such as recruitment, promotion, pay, training, performance evaluation and job satisfaction will lead to more effective and efficient government (OECD 1994, 1996a, 1996b, 1996c). One of the objectives of introducing a civil service system in China was to improve government performance, as clearly stated in a series of official documents. For example, the *1993 Provisional Regulations on State Civil Servants* (hereafter *1993 Provisional Regulations*) stated that the objectives of these regulations were to optimize the civil service workforce, curb corruption and improve administrative performance (*xiaoneng*).[3] *The Notice for the Implementation Plan for the Civil Service System* pointed out that the establishment of a civil service system was an important step to promote the abilities and skills of the civil service workforce and improve government efficiency.[4]

While the above understanding points to the managerial goals of the civil service reforms in China, the reforms also had political goals. To understand the political goals, we need to understand the evolving process in which policy-makers have come to adopt the current civil service system. The leadership shifted the focus of China's development strategy to the economy from the late 1970s. They saw political institutional reform as a means to promote and implement economic restructuring (Shirk 1993, 1994; Whiting 2000). However, the cadre personnel management system became incompatible with this new situation. To tailor China's management to its more complex economy, the post-Mao authorities were forced to select administrative leaders from professionals and specialists based in part on their work performance and problem-solving ability rather than, as in the Mao era, on political credentials alone (Bo 2002; Burns 1999a; Chow 1991; Dong 1994; Liou 1997; Liu 2001).

Reform of the cadre system had been considered since the late 1970s. Deng Xiaoping called for the separation of the Party from the government (*dang zheng fen kai*) and put reform of the cadre system on the Party's agenda in his August 1980 address to the Politburo (Deng 1984: 302). At the 13th national congress in October 1987, the CCP endorsed a program of political reform. The aim was to separate the functions of the Party and the government and give to the latter more autonomy over the management of its own staff. Establishing a civil service system served as one of the tasks of the political reform (Burns 1989a, 1989b). Zhao Ziyang (the former General Secretary of the CCP) announced plans to divide the cadres within the government organs into 'professional civil servants' (*yewu gongwuyuan*) and 'political civil servants' (*zhengwu gongwuyuan*). The former would consist of officials recruited through open examinations and promoted on the basis of job performance while the latter senior officials would be recommended by the Party to supervise the civil service.

However, the orthodox first generation of the Communist revolutionaries in the Party leadership prevented the inclusion of political reforms in the country's political agenda. They feared that the separation of the Party and the government would take considerable power in terms of personnel allocation away from the Party.[5] The orthodox Li Peng announced the postponement of the introduction of the civil service system soon after he took over the premiership in 1988. The Tiananmen Incident of 1989 further halted the proposed political reform. After this incident, discussions on the separation of the Party from the government were taboo (Lam and Chan 1996a, 1996b).

In the aftermath of the 1989 Tiananmen Incident, the reformers in the top decision-making circle were defensive and a whole series of reform policies were put on hold. In the spring of 1992, Deng Xiaoping made his famous trip to Shenzhen, the leading testing field of economic reform, in order to counter the rise of Leftist ideology and create a momentum for further reform. This helped to launch another round of economic liberalization and administrative reforms in China (Lieberthal 2004: 143–4). At the 14th national congress in October 1992, the CCP reaffirmed its commitment to civil service reforms. The civil service reforms were implemented from October 1993, after the promulgation of the *1993 Provisional Regulations*. This time, the political goals of the civil service reforms changed. Instead of separating the functions of the Party from the government, policy-makers put emphasis on strengthening the control over the bureaucracy and improving the local implementation of central policies. In the *1993 Provisional Regulations*, some radical components of the original plan were deleted. One example was the removal of the division between the political civil servants category and the professional category. The new civil service system had an emphasis on ensuring the Party's overall control of the government personnel system. It aimed to strengthen the control of the bureaucracy by institutionalizing new rules on the appointment, promotion, and exchange and rotation system. By strengthening control over the bureaucracy and building a capable civil service, the leadership hoped to gain or regain legitimacy and public support (Yan 1995).

On 27 April 2005, the *Civil Service Law* was approved by the National People's Congress to upgrade the status of the *1993 Provisional Regulations*. In the new law, the term 'civil servant' was redefined, which expanded the scope of the civil service. The *Civil Service Law* lays down the most detailed employment and human resource procedures under which a civil servant might be recruited, assessed, promoted and rewarded, disciplined or dismissed. In particular, the *Civil Service Law* places great emphasis on competitive selection, performance appraisal, promotion and disciplinary procedures in hopes of improving the transparency and efficiency of the personnel management. A new wage structure was put into place in 2006, shortly after the beginning of the implementation of the *Civil Service Law*. To facilitate the implementation of the new law and wage structure, a national bureau—Civil Service Bureau—was established under the Ministry of Human Resource and Social Security in 2008. The mission of the new bureau was to manage the country's civil service including supervising local governments' management of their employees. This was another illustration of the leadership's attempt to strengthen the central control.

After studying the rationale behind civil service reforms in China, I raise the following questions to be pursued in this study. Did the civil service reforms improve the quality and efficiency of government employees? Did the civil service reforms result in some improvements in routine management? These questions aim to examine whether the managerial objectives of the reforms have been achieved. Besides focusing on the technical issues of public personnel management, civil service reforms in China also sought to reinforce the established norms and foster a closer Party-government employment framework (especially since the *Civil Service Law*). So it needs to be asked whether the central control was strengthened. Further, did the civil service reforms result in some improvements in public service provision and delivery? In other words, what were the consequences of bureaucratic maximization or sponsor control for the quality of public services? These questions aim to examine whether the political objectives of the reforms have been achieved.

When compared with countries of other continents, Asian countries appear to cluster together in terms of the limited scope of the civil service (public sector) reforms and the lower levels of success in achieving various reform objectives such as efficiency, downsizing, privatization and anticorruption (Cheung and Scott 2003). Within Asia, significant variations exist among countries in terms of reform patterns and outcomes (Burns 2007; Cheung 2005; Painter 2004). Four developing countries in Southeast Asia, namely Vietnam, Laos, Indonesia and the Philippines, are selected in this study to constitute a comparative study of civil service reforms in Asia. Governments in these countries are facing the dilemma of how to recruit, retain and motivate skilled employees at an affordable cost. One of the objectives of China's reforms was to strengthen the capacity of the government in order to counter the challenges brought on by the market. Despite the significant decentralization of power and resources to the local governments, the leadership in China resorted to civil service reforms and devised feasible instruments to strengthen control over the bureaucracy. All the governments of the selected countries in this study have also resorted to civil service reforms in order to reinvent structures and systems of operations that can improve bureaucratic competence and performance in public service delivery. What does China's experience reveal? To what extent is China's experience relevant to the selected countries? This book seeks to provide insights on these issues.

In particular, this book aims to answer the following related questions:

- Managerial goal: How did the new sets of rules or initiatives shape the incentives facing civil servants and, thus, influenced the way they exercise their discretion?
- Political goal: How did reforms affect the ability of the Chinese leadership to control the bureaucracy and what were the implications of the reforms for the relationships between the political leadership, the bureaucrats and the citizens?
- Implications for Asian governments: To what extent is China's experience relevant to the selected developing countries in Asia, given that the governments in these countries are facing the dilemma of how to recruit, retain and motivate skilled government employees at an affordable cost?

## Existing literature and gaps

China's government and civil service reforms have been studied extensively; however, prior studies have mainly focused on the description and analysis of changes to specific civil service norms such as retirement and the process of appointment and promotion (Burns 2005, 1994b; Li 1990; Manion 1993, 1985) while leaving the intrinsic characteristics of the bureaucratic organization untouched. With the assistance of the principal–agent logic (which helps to highlight the rationale behind the institutional design through studying the intrinsic characteristics of the bureaucratic organization and individual incentive), this book will analyze the impact of reform policies on the incentive structures and behavior of civil servants and, thus, provides some thoughts in understanding the rationale behind the administrative reforms in China. Findings suggested that some reform efforts did not coincidently just happen. Rather, they were components of incremental changes intentionally made by the Chinese leadership. As such, the civil service reform is part of a much greater transformation that the Chinese authorities will and must go through.

Scholars have also sought to analyze the socioeconomic factors that account for the mobility of Chinese officials (Bo 2002; Walder 1995; Zhou 1995). Few studies, however, have focused on the implementation of civil service reforms and those that do offer conflicting interpretations of the efficacy of the reforms.

On the one hand, scholars such as Tsao and Worthley (1995), Tong et al. (1999) and Chan (2003) have evaluated the reforms positively, but have focused mostly on the process of reform. On the other hand, scholars such as Chou (2009, 2008, 2004) have compared the goals and results of reform and have found them wanting. Indeed, Chou referred to the reforms as an 'implementation failure'. This book will not only provide three case studies of the reforms that were implemented by local governments, but will also assess the impact of these reforms on local governance and performance of public service delivery. Given that reform implementations consume considerable financial and human resources and technology, evaluating the return on this investment is of great importance. Moreover, the ability of different local governments to bear the administrative costs of reform implementations is different. Therefore, investigating the performance changes of local government agencies rather than the policy design of the central government is the direct way to test what and to what magnitude happened in various local governments in China.

This book also contributes to the long-standing debate among students of China studies regarding the ability of central government to control policy implementation by a decentralized bureaucratic system. Some studies showed that bureaucratic non-compliance has emerged as one of the most challenging problems facing the Chinese leadership in contemporary China. Accordingly, it was claimed there is a governance crisis in China and collapse is imminent (Chang 2001; Pei 2006, 1994). On the other hand, a great deal of literature argued that the CCP is capable of great institutional adaptability and that the capacity of the central government to control and monitor lower-level governments and bureaucrats has increased (Burns 1999a; Edin 2003; Yang 2004). This book argues that through the implementation of the civil service system and other administrative monitoring mechanisms, the central leadership has improved its capacity to shape, reward and control local governments and bureaucrats.

Governments in developing countries in Asia are facing the dilemma of how to recruit, retain and motivate skilled staff at an affordable cost (Nunberg 2002, 1995, 1992). Both the quality of their civil service systems and current reform efforts have been weak (Asian Development Bank 2005, 2004, 2001; Kristiansen and Ramli 2006; Painter 2006, 2003a, 2003b; Turner 2002). Their civil services have inadequate systems of establishment control, personnel information management and manpower planning. There are no sufficient incentives to motivate staff performance given that civil service salaries are low and promotions are mainly based on seniority. In addition, appropriate career development and training programs for civil servants are almost non-existent. In general, civil service reform initiatives are undertaken on a limited, pilot basis and are sometimes stymied by difficulties. In contrast, China established a uniformed legislative framework and a centralized institutional arrangement for civil service management and reforms. Management and administration in China are now performed largely in accordance to the law. Positive elements such as openness, transparency and merit-based competition against patronage were incorporated into the processes of civil service recruitment and promotion. The processes to increase both the officials' accountability as well as public participation are now at the beginning stage. These experiences have implications for the selected Asian countries.

## Theoretical framework and research design

Principal–agent theory is chosen as the theoretical framework of this book for its parsimony and considerable relevancy to the analysis of authority relationships (Moe 1984). In government organizations, problems of control occur when subordinates have different interests from their superiors and when the behavior of subordinates is imperfectly monitored. Control mechanisms are designed (and sometimes take the form of reform initiatives) to mitigate such problems by aligning the incentives between the superiors and their subordinates or improving the availability of information. This book explores China's civil service reforms and the impacts within such a principal–agent framework. Because of the information asymmetry and conflict of interest, bureaucratic superiors within the old cadre personnel management system had trouble in obtaining full compliance from their bureaucratic subordinates. But, being rational, the bureaucratic superiors (especially the Chinese leadership) designed rules and institutions to mitigate these problems. The introduction of the civil service system in 1993 to manage government officials was shaped by such thinking. I argue that China's civil service reform policy included mechanisms designed to address agency problems that were associated with the cadre personnel management system. These reform initiatives included measures to foster competition, reduce information asymmetries and align incentives. However, policy design is very different from policy implementation. Whether the implementation of civil service reforms could provide superiors with solutions to agency problems serves as the central question of this inquiry.

From the perspective of principal–agent theory, I assume that civil servants in China are boundedly rational and they are utility maximizers (Brehm and Gates 1999; Frederickson and Smith 2003; Horn 1995; Moe 1984; Peters 2005: 47–70). Generally, this means that civil servants seek to maximize their utilities such as power and income and that the repertoire of civil servant behavior includes working, shirking and sabotage (Brehm and Gates 1999). Here, working means devoting effort toward accomplishing policy goals while shirking means directing effort away from policy goals (e.g., watching DVDs, chatting online and monitoring the stock market or other activities that are unrelated to the job). Sabotage means actively undermining policy goals through acts that lead to delay, hindrance or obstruction. Corruption, which damages the government's reputation, is viewed as a kind of sabotage where civil servants either on their own or in collusion with their superiors defraud the public and, thus, undermine the central government's stated goal of reducing or eliminating corruption.[6] Civil servants in China serve multiple principals, including their immediate superiors, the local government, the central government and the public.

Due to the division of labor and the nature of administrative work, an individual's effort cannot be easily observed and directly measured in government organizations. Subordinates have an information advantage over their supervisors regarding the tasks that are assigned to them and their own abilities and efforts in accomplishing these tasks. This information asymmetry between subordinates and supervisors causes problems, namely adverse selection and moral hazard. From the perspective of principal–agent theory, adverse selection denotes the difficulty that the principal faces in discovering the true nature of the agent before entering into a contract with her. This is commonly found in the labor market. Moral hazard refers to the difficulty that the principal faces in observing the actual effort of the agent. Shirking behavior is an instance of moral hazard (Alchian and Demsetz 1972; Holmstrom and Milgrom 1991). In this study, the supervisor–subordinate relationship within a government organization is identified as a typical principal–agent relationship. To counter agency problems, scholars of the conventional principal–agent theory identified several top-down control mechanisms that supervisors could use to shape the behavior of their subordinates (Jensen and Meckling 1976; Rees 1985). In general, these strategies emphasized the role of the supervisor in inducing subordinates' compliance and the utility of the top-down control mechanisms. The control mechanisms included inducing competition through open, competitive selection procedures; information discovery through screening, monitoring and performance appraisal; and various incentive-alignment mechanisms such as performance-based rewards systems (Baiman 1990, 1982; Horn 1995; Milgrom and Roberts 1992; Tirole 1986). I will turn to each of these mechanisms below.

The conventional principal–agent model argues the principal should design optimal incentive contracts and compensation arrangements in organizations to induce desirable actions from the agent (Baiman 1990, 1982). The two parties' interests could be aligned through institutional innovations, such as a risk-sharing contractual arrangement. This incentive-compatible mechanism lies in the belief that the agent will share the interests of the principal if his reward, like the principal's, is directly linked to the performance of their entity. The agent may receive a bonus or suffer a loss contingent on the final output. Other administrative procedures such as rewards and punishments can also help the principal shape the agent's behavior. Under this arrangement, agents that work hard are rewarded and poor conduct and deviant behavior are punished.

Monitoring refers to putting into place various monitoring devices, such as reporting routines and inspection teams. These devices allow the principal to observe more aspects of the agent's behavior. Focusing on monitoring is intended to partly address the information asymmetry problem. Constant monitoring may be effective in reducing the agency losses, but it is too costly to implement in reality and vulnerable to collusion between the agent and the monitoring agent (Tirole 1994, 1986). Moreover, administrative work is difficult to monitor. Given that the mission of any government bureau is abstract, the task of implementing or enforcing rules for the individual bureaucrat is far from simple and easy. He needs to make numerous discretionary decisions to apply general rules to specific situations or to work out solutions for specific problems (Simon et al. 1991). No monitoring could make sure that every discretionary decision made by the bureaucrat was for the benefit of the bureau as a whole. In other words, no monitoring could make sure that the bureaucrat is not directing his efforts to private benefit.

Usually, a hierarchical layer involves one principal and many agents. Launching competition among the agents can be one effective control mechanism for the principal. Competition can be instilled by evaluating and then compensating an agent's performance relative to that of other agents. By using ordinal measures of performance rather than cardinal measures, competition ensures that principals will honor contracts even when the verification of absolute performance is difficult. However, competition schemes will fail when the agents collude with one another against the principal (Tirole 1994, 1986).

As we will see, elements of these strategies can be found in China's civil service reforms. However, reforms based on the ideas of conventional principal–agent theory are doomed to face serious implementation problems. This is because the conventional model puts too much emphasis on the role of supervisor and top-down control mechanisms. Scholars of the conventional model believe that subordinates will work hard and refrain from shirking and sabotage in the presence of the elementary top-down arrangements (incentive-alignment, monitoring and competition) of public management. They neglect the role of the subordinate to a successful supervisor-subordinate relationship and fail to investigate agency problems from the subordinate's stance. Thus some very important potential factors that determine subordinate behavior and organizational compliance are overlooked. Scholars of organization theory and the behavioral paradigm have explicitly criticized the conventional principal–agent model. In their opinion, the conventional principal–agent theorists consider individual subordinates as units of a large machine and will follow instructions automatically. Such an assumption of the subordinate is far from realistic (Simon 1985, 1981). Through studying the psychological foundation of organizational compliance, scholars of the behavioral paradigm have incorporated useful elements into the conventional principal–agent model and made it be able to provide sound explanations for political phenomena. First, the subordinate has his own preference; and that preference influences his choice of behavior. Simon's concept of authority could help us understand the role of the subordinate's preference. Simon stressed that the authority relation is not characterized by command or fiat, as classical organization theorists suggest, but rather is two-way. The nature of authority relation and whether or how well it works depend upon both parties to the agreement. That is because the subordinate has a 'zone of acceptance' within which he willingly allows the supervisor to direct his behavior (Simon 1947).

The conventional principal–agent model assumes complete rationality of individuals. They can fully comprehend the whole situation in which their actions are embedded. This model demands superhuman cognitive abilities to work (Wildavsky 1975). Research in bounded rationality has pointed out the limitations of human cognition, and highlighted their implications for decision-making and management in organizations (Gigerenzer and Selten 2001; Simon 1985, 1981). The individual is boundedly rational. His access to information and knowledge is limited, and so is his computational ability and skills to perform cost-benefit calculus. These cognitive limits prevent him from forming a comprehensive understanding of the whole situation and from making every decision in a fully deliberate manner. Scholars of the behavioral paradigm point out that human behavior is often produced without conscious thought, but propelled by habit, emotion, take-for-granted custom, conditioned reflex, unconditioned reflex, posthypnotic suggestion and unconscious desire. The boundedly rational actors are in most circumstances unable to comprehend the environment and to make decisions in a deliberate manner; instead they adopt various heuristics or mental models that help them economize on their limited cognitive ability and hence enhance their problem-solving efficiency. These heuristics might include the 'consistency of behavior' and 'seeking social proof' (Brehm and Gates 1999).

Following Brehm and Gates (1999), I argue that the conventional principal–agent model over-emphasizes the capacity of supervisors to control their subordinates because the relationship is much more complex than the conventional theory allows. Moreover, the conventional perspective neglects the aspect of learning where subordinates learn from their peers or they become aware of informal norms of what is appropriate behavior, which plays a significant part in determining subordinate behavior.

*Supervisors as credible leaders*

The notion that supervisors in the bureaucracy are able to *control* subordinate compliance is, Barnard (1938) wrote, 'a fiction'. The amount of work (which requires delegation and, therefore, is difficult to monitor), the nature of public output (which is difficult to measure), the nature of civil service rules and regulations and subordinates' own preferences all operate to frustrate supervisory control (Brehm and Gates 1999). Simon (1947) argued that authority relations are not characterized by command or fiat, but as a two-way relationship. The nature of authority relations and whether or how well it works depend upon both parties in a relationship. That is, subordinates have a 'zone of acceptance' within which they willingly allow their supervisors to direct their behavior.

Hierarchical control is never complete (Miller 1992). For any given incentive scheme, the agents still have some room to pursue their own interests including shirking or engaging in sabotage. Because supervisors cannot expect compliance from subordinates just by command (Alchian and Demsetz 1972), organizational leadership is required. Bianco and Bates (1990) focused on the role of managers as leaders to induce compliance among agents in an environment with repeated contact between principals and agents. Compliance and conformity among subordinates vary with the capabilities of leaders in their model. Effective leadership can inspire agents to forgo narrow self-interest and align their own goals to that of the organization (Kreps 1990; Miller 1992; Tirole 1994). One manifestation of leadership is the inculcation of trust among agents/subordinates, that is, instilling the belief that the commitment from the principal/supervisor is credible. Breton and Wintrobe (1986, 1982) showed the necessity of trust and credible commitment. Supervisors can act as educators in helping subordinates to identify more efficient ways to accomplish what is in the interests of both parties. In this study, I understand that although supervisors do not in any sense control subordinate compliance, they can influence it when the leadership is credible.

### Subordinate learning

Research on bounded rationality has pointed out the limitations of human cognition and has highlighted their implications for decision-making and the management of organizations (Simon 1985, 1981; Gigerenzer and Selten 2001). Individuals are boundedly rational: they have limited computational capacity for processing information and acquiring knowledge. These cognitive limits prevent individuals from attaining a comprehensive picture of the whole situation and from making every decision in a fully deliberate manner. Unable to make deliberative decisions in many circumstances, individuals adopt various heuristics or mental models that help them to economize their limited cognitive ability and, in turn, enhance their problem-solving efficiency. These heuristics include 'consistency of behavior' and 'seeking social proof' (Brehm and Gates 1999). Civil servants learn from one another what is appropriate behavior and, through this process, informal norms emerge. Reforms that run counter to informal norms are likely to come across difficulties in implementation or may even be defeated. I argue that China's civil service reforms neglected organization culture, especially the informal norms that allow or actively encourage sabotage such as corruption (Walder 1986).[7] The conventional principal–agent theory focuses on formal top-down control mechanisms; neglects the underlying culture of public organization. Scholars find reforms that target formal structures but neglect the underlying culture of public organization always end in failure (Peters 2005).

The mission of government bureaux is abstract; therefore tasks to fulfill the mission are shaped by a process of trial and error. For an individual bureaucrat, implementing or enforcing rules is far from simple and easy. He needs to make numerous discretionary decisions to apply general rules to specific situations or to work out solutions for specific problems (Simon *et al.* 1991). In addition, a high degree of uncertainties is always a part of the process of government work. Under conditions of uncertainty, individuals learn from others and look for 'social proof' for their own actions. By asking 'what are others like myself doing', bureaucrats develop a heuristic for imitation. Imitation is a very simple and direct information shortcut for conditions when formal rules are ambiguous (Brehm and Gates 1999). In other words, bureaucrats with bounded rationality will learn from one another within a government organization about appropriate behavior when they face unforeseen contingencies.

Learning from peers constitutes the process for informal rules within an organization to emerge and evolve. Scholars help us understand how the informal rules of an organization emerged when the peer subordinates learn from one another; and how these informal rules lead to a particular organization's culture (Kreps 1990; Miller 1992). They argue that organizational culture offers a set of principles for dealing with unforeseen contingencies and establishes a code of conduct between supervisors and subordinates (principal and agents). The structure of organizational cultures could have tremendous consequences for the attainment of compliance. Conformity that stems from organization culture can either induce or impede compliance with superiors. Bureaucratic supervisors will experience considerable difficulties in implementing policies that run counter to organizational norms. On the other hand, compliance will be very high in cases where the organizational culture reinforces the superior's request. At the micro level, the structure of organization cultures can have implications for the acceptance for individual instructions from the leadership. At the macro level, the structure of organization cultures can affect the prospects of reforms.

The principal–agent framework has been extensively applied to studies of Chinese politics and reforms. This book also chooses the principal–agent model as the theoretical framework because it provides a more sound explanation of China's civil service reforms. A review on prior studies will help to justify this point. The application of the principal–agent framework has driven the debate over the political implications of the post-Mao reforms and the adoption of new management practices at various levels of government in the interests of economic development (Kwong and Lee 2000), local agenda compliance (Whiting 2000) and other scenarios of administration. While research on these topics is highly relevant to the general literature on development economics, central–local relations, and public management reforms in post-Communist countries, recent scholarship suggests that unique mechanisms have been developed to address the form of agency problems that are intertwined with the particular conditions of China, an authoritarian state in a rapidly modernizing society.

A much-debated aspect of China's development concerns the degree of control the central government retains over local officials. Opinion is divided on the extent to which the regime structure has become decentralized following more than three decades of reforms. Walder (1995) and Wang and Hu (1999) contend that centralized control in China has been considerably compromised by the growth of local autonomy on economic and policy matters. Their observations highlight a typical manifestation of the agency problem as the central government had to reinvent the tools for controlling local officials, as they could exploit the newly obtained autonomy from the central government in pursuit of activities that are incompatible with national policy objectives (Edin 2003). In China, the introduction of motivational techniques associated with the new public management movement (Whiting 2000) is innovatively combined with personnel management practices inherited from the pre-reform era (Huang 2002). By linking the income and career prospects of local officials to their performance, the central government employs extrinsic incentives to encourage compliance to national policy goals, ranging from economic growth and industrial production to birth control and social harmony. A degree of civic engagement at the local level is encouraged so that more information can be revealed to the political principal (O'Brien and Li 1999). Appointing successful local officials to high-level positions and rotating officials between positions also increase the central government's access to local-level officials, which keeps top local actors under the close inspection of their political principal (Li 2004). Similarly, the increase in provincial fiscal autonomy (Wedeman 1999) and the diversity of interests and the staggering size of the Chinese bureaucracy (Huang 2002) are well contained using similar tools available to the central government.

The fact that such measures are widely adopted indicates that public administrators in contemporary China perceive local autonomy to be potentially detrimental and are actively adopting a mixed set of new and existing mechanisms to increase policy compliance among local officials. While some scholars consider the unraveling of centralized coordination as the cause of ineffectual policy implementation (Bernstein and Lu 2000), an increase in centralized control through effective principal–agent control mechanisms is admittedly difficult to translate into effective implementation due to conflicting priorities. Indeed, the problem of fragmented control of agents in China re-emerges in the case of the sovereign wealth funds, where competing ministerial interests fail to provide a unified leadership (Eaton and Zhang 2010). Managers of sovereign funds are prone to agency problems under arrangements where ownership and control are separated. Since the political regime of contemporary China has become more fragmented over time (Lieberthal 1995), the option of placing the sovereign wealth funds under direct control by the political principal becomes infeasible. The difficulty in monitoring the sovereign funds is compounded by the lack of transparency and reliable information. Eaton and Zhang (2010) argue that a 'tournament' system in which separate funds operate as competitors to promote better alignment of interests between the fund managers and their political principal should be created. The career prospects and income of fund managers are linked to their performance in the 'tournament'. Rather than using internal mechanisms, the Chinese government relies on external competition between the sovereign wealth funds to overcome agency problems.

In the study of local economic development, the case has been made that the rise of successful township and village enterprises (TVEs) is enabled by the alignment of interests (Kwong and Lee 2000). The incentive structure of the workers and managers of the TVEs is affected by the ill-defined property rights and the collective ownership of these organizations. Lacking well-developed property rights institutions, the TVEs may not contribute to the local economy because there is no formal residual claimant of the profits. The use of profits for local purposes and linking rewards with the performance of the TVEs alleviate the agency problem and successfully mitigate the problem of interests misalignment—in fact, they offer an alternative to privatization in a transitional economy that is institutionally ill-adapted to the incentive structure that requires well-developed property rights protection.

The legacy of Communist rule and the authoritarian nature of China's governance create unique problems at various levels. Internal conflicts between factions (Eaton and Zhang 2010), unreliable and insufficient information (Eaton and

Zhang 2010; O'Brien and Li 1999), unclear property rights definitions (Kwong and Lee 2000) and the rise of local autonomy (Walder 1995) render many of the established tools for agency problems ineffectual. In enforcing national policy agendas at localities, the central government combines new public management techniques with personnel practices inherited from the pre-reform era to increase compliance. Economic development is sustained in townships and villages through profit-sharing in the shadow of underdeveloped property institutions. As the cost of direct control and monitoring is unjustified in the absence of reliable information and unified leadership, external mechanisms encouraging competition are adopted to prevent the fund managers from exploiting their position for personal gains. While the principal–agent framework has served the purpose of exploring and articulating the nature of the myriad administrative and governance challenges that occur in contemporary China, it also highlighted that agency problems in China are the unique consequence of its Communist past, the authoritarian institutions in force today, and the ongoing reform and adoption of new techniques of public management under rapid modernization and social change.

*Research design*

Three urban areas—Beijing's Haidian district, Changchun city and Ningbo city—are selected for field study. They are different from each other in terms of administrative rank, geographic location and the level of economic development. Beijing's Haidian district is a prefecture-level unit of the capital, which itself is a municipality directly administered by the central government while Changchun and Ningbo are vice-provincial-level cities. Changchun (with a population of 3.5 million) in the less developed northeast is the poorest of the three sites (annual GDP per capita was RMB39,341 in 2007) while Ningbo (with a population of 2.2 million) in the south is the richest (annual GDP per capita was RMB74,458 in 2007) (National Bureau of Statistics 2008: 125).[8] Haidian has a population of two million people. The annual GDP per capita was RMB64,988 in 2007, which situates it somewhere in between the other two cities.[9] The structure of their economies also varies. The tertiary sector is the most developed in Beijing where it contributes about 71 percent to the total local GDP compared to 42 percent and 40 percent for Changchun and Ningbo respectively. Primary industry contributes the most to Changchun (9 percent of GDP) compared to 5 percent in Ningbo and 1.25 percent in Beijing (National Bureau of Statistics 2008: 133). I make no claim that the experience of the field sites is representative of the country as a whole. I chose them in order to examine the impact of civil service reform in several urban contexts. Accessibility is another important factor in the selection of field research sites. Examining different field sites allows for the detection of variations in the implementation of civil service reform and I speculate that the variations may be explained by proximity to power, level of economic development and historical circumstance.

Environmental protection and education bureaux are selected for field research. I anticipate that the bureaux in these two different policy areas would

16  *Introduction*

provide an interesting contrast. Education bureaux have existed for a very long time in China, have a relatively high bureaucratic rank and have been staffed by generalists with a background in education. Indeed, education bureaux have recruited their staff from school teachers. By contrast, environmental protection bureaux are relatively recent establishments (mostly set up in the 1980s) and until recently have had a comparatively lower bureaucratic rank and should be staffed by specialists (Jahiel 1998; Lo *et al*. 2000). Generally, city education bureaux (sometimes called commissions) are two to three times larger than environmental protection bureaux. In this study, environmental protection bureaux range from 28 to 30 employees. In spite of the variations in the number of residents, the environmental protection bureau in Changchun with twice as many people is the same size as the bureau in Ningbo. Education bureaux or commissions, by contrast, vary in size from 64 employees in Changchun to 90 or more in Ningbo and Beijing's Haidian.[10] That is, the government of the poorer and more populous Changchun appears to have been comparatively under-resourced in the areas of environmental protection and education. Moreover, the functions of the bureaux in the two policy areas are somewhat different. While both the environmental protection and education bureaux carry out inspections and provide services to clients, the education bureaux also allocate resources to schools that are under their control.

A variety of research methods were employed in this study, including comparative case studies for data analysis and documentary research, in-depth interviews and questionnaire survey for data collection. To examine the implementation of the reforms, fieldwork research was conducted. In particular, a questionnaire survey and in-depth interviews were used to gather information on reform implementation of the three local governments concerned in this study. The empirical data set of this study included three main parts.[11] First, we interviewed a total of 90 officials in education and environmental protection bureaux of the three local governments and a selection of their clients (e.g., school principals for education policy; factory managers for environmental protection policy) in 2001. The interviews were designed to elicit perceptions of how well the bureaux were performing and to identify those factors (including civil service reform) that contributed to their performance (Wang 2006).[12] The 40 officials were selected from a pool of 388 officials. To increase the comprehensiveness of the response, we selected them from various bureaucratic ranks.[13]

Second, we conducted a questionnaire survey to examine how citizens evaluated government performance in the Haidian district of Beijing between January and March 2003. A random sample of 728 adults in Haidian was generated using the probabilities proportional to size sampling method. First, 25 urban residential committees (*juweihui*) were randomly chosen. Second, 29 households were randomly chosen from each of the 25 urban residential committees, producing a total of 728 households. Third, one individual aged between 18 and 66 was randomly chosen from each of the 728 households as the interviewee. During the survey, a fieldworker took the questionnaire to the randomly chosen individual respondent and conducted the interview. An interview took 45 minutes on average. Upon completion, the fieldworker brought the questionnaire back to the survey center. As a result of this effort, a total of 501 permanent urban residents aged between 18 and 66 were interviewed. The response rate was approximately 69 percent. The demographic information of the interviewees is shown in Appendix 1.

Third, we followed up with a second round of interviews with 52 officials in Haidian and Changchun in 2004 (a profile can be found in Appendix 1). The interviews focused on the implementation of civil service reforms and performance measurement in local government bureaux. The interviewees who were civil servants were employed at the district level in Haidian and at the city level in the case of the two cities. Admittedly, the focus on the education and environmental protection bureaux rather than town and township officials in the field sites might have biased the results toward urban concerns. However, given the importance of cities and the trend toward increasing urbanization in China, the picture of the impact of the reforms that this book presents, though quite limited, is still significant.

## Structure of the book

This book will examine several important issues including the interaction between institutions and individual incentives in reform implementation, the control by the policy-makers over the bureaucracy and the feasibility of transferring a country's reform experience to other contexts with similar cultural values and initial conditions to undertake reform initiatives. The book is divided into seven chapters. Chapter 2 examines the scope and structure of the Chinese civil service and the context for reforms. An analysis on the scope, size, cost and structure of the Chinese civil service can inform our examination of the implementation and problems of the reforms. China has witnessed an expansion of scope in its civil service in the past two decades. Initially, the authorities tried to establish a separate personnel management system for government (narrowly defined) employees in the early 1990s. The civil service experienced rapid expansion as government expenditure took up an increasing share of the GDP and more resources were allocated to payroll expenditures and administrative activities in the public sector. Chapter 2 also offers an analysis of the political, organizational and legal contexts for the reforms. In particular, the role of the Party, the authority of the *nomenklatura* and several important organizations that were involved in civil service personnel decision-making and management at both the central and local levels are reviewed. The old cadre personnel management system and its problems are analyzed at the end. In general, the cadre system suffered from serious defects. It was a highly centralized and undifferentiated approach to personnel management. The management methods were outdated and simplistic. There were vague guidelines for promotion, performance appraisal and training. In addition, poor performance was tolerated while incentives for performance were insufficient to motivate cadres.

Chapter 3 examines the reform policy and nationwide implementation. It focuses on the impacts of the reforms on the incentive structure and behavior of the civil servants. It argues that China's civil service reform policy included mechanisms designed to address the agency problems that were associated with the cadre personnel management system. The reform initiatives included measures to foster competition, reduce information asymmetries and align incentives. Specifically, Chapter 3 is divided into four sections. The first section reviews the reform programs that aimed to address the problem of information asymmetry. The second section focuses on reform programs related to the incentive alignment issues. The third section discusses the wage reforms. The last section elaborates on the enforcement of discipline. Chapter 3 presents a mixed picture on the effectiveness of civil service reforms. On one hand, some new measures to obtain additional information were effective. For example, open, competitive selection and promotion led to positive outcomes as critical information about the job candidates was made available through standardized test procedures. On the other hand, other measures to improve information availability were unsuccessful. For example, performance appraisal for individual civil servants was ineffective and the monitoring system remained weak. As for the incentive alignment measures, formal policy instruments such as pay and promotion did not serve as motivators for the rank-and-file civil servants. Considering that the important objectives of wage reforms were to motivate performance, eliminate financial mismanagement of local governments and tackle regional gaps of civil service welfares, the implementation of wage reforms fell short of their promises. Ironically, the real motivation came from informal incentive alignment measures: superiors and their subordinates collaborated in illicit activities such as the buying and selling of government posts. In other words, the official policy to align the incentives of the principals and agents in China's civil service reforms failed while the informal or illegal motivators successfully aligned the incentives of corrupt superiors and their subordinates. This indicated a failed implementation of discipline policy in civil service reforms.

Decentralization is a common characteristic of many policy areas in China including the public personnel management. The Chinese leadership is responsible for outlining the general personnel management reform framework through the CCP Central Committee and its Organization Department, State Council, the Ministry of Personnel and other concerned ministries. Provincial and subprovincial governments are not only charged with the responsibility to adapt the framework to local realities, but also to design and implement the concrete programs. In other words, local governments have a certain degree of autonomy in the implementation of central policies. As a consequence of this autonomy, local leaders are able to direct the programs either towards or away from the stated policy goals. It is necessary, therefore, to examine how various local governments implement civil service reforms in China. Chapter 4 provides three case studies on the local implementation of these reforms. Given the size of the country and the uneven development among its regions, conditions for implementing policies in China varied significantly. Balancing the requirement for uniformity in the civil service reforms with the wide diversity in regional circumstances and among the different levels of government was extremely challenging. The reform experiences of the three local governments are compared in the discussion section in Chapter 4. Findings showed that each local government's ability to bear the financial and administrative costs of implementing reforms was different from one another. In addition, without the necessary political support from local leaders, the implementation process was slow and arduous.

Chapter 5 examines the ability of the central leadership to control policy implementation by a decentralized bureaucratic system. It analyzes how the upper echelons of the Party-government exercised control over lower-level bureaucrats through competitive appointment and promotion, performance evaluation, rotation and avoidance. Other related initiatives such as administrative monitoring, intra-party reforms and anticorruption measures are also analyzed in this chapter. This chapter suggests that the implementation of the civil service reforms and other related programs helped the central leadership in China to strengthen its control over the local governments and bureaucrats. The tightened control brought about improvement in public service delivery. Both statistical data and case studies of public service delivery illustrated this improvement. The improvement was also attested by citizens who acknowledged that the civil service does a better job now than before.

Chapter 6 provides a comparative analysis of civil service reforms in Asia and identifies the implications of China's reform experience to other Asian countries. In particular, it examines the contents and trajectories of civil service reforms in four developing countries in Southeast Asia including Vietnam, Laos, Indonesia and the Philippines. These countries are selected as their governments are facing the dilemma of how to recruit, retain and motivate skilled staff at an affordable cost. However, a review of the reform processes and outcomes suggested that they varied in many areas such as the initial capacity of systems to undertake modernization programs, the contextual conditions of politics and receptivity to external administrative models as well as their reform trajectories and problems. China's experience in managing and reforming its civil service could serve as a model for these countries. First, to establish and maintain a competent, efficient and professional civil service bureaucracy, a uniformed legislative and institutional framework for civil service management should be established. Second, civil servants should be recruited, promoted and managed according to merit and competition. Governments should pay attention to cultivating performance culture in the civil services. Third, an effective system of establishment control, personnel information management and manpower planning should also be constructed. Finally, in addition to increasing the openness and transparency of the public personnel management system, both the officials' accountability as well as public participation should be strengthened.

Chapter 7 is the concluding chapter of this book and it provides a summary of the empirical findings. Several policy implications resulting from the analysis are identified. Subsequent to a discussion on the limitations, the chapter closes with further directions for research.

# 2 Civil service scope, structure and context for reforms

China has witnessed an expansion in the scope of its civil service over the past two decades. It is, therefore, important for us to have a clear understanding of the current definition of 'civil servants' and know exactly to which group of employees the personnel management reforms are applicable. Initially, the authorities tried to establish a separate personnel management system for government (narrowly defined) employees in the early 1990s. Subsequently, the civil service underwent rapid expansion as government expenditure took up an increasing share of the GDP and more resources were being allocated to payroll expenditures and administrative activities in the public sector. An analysis on the scope, size, cost and structure of the Chinese civil service can inform our examination of the implementation and problems of the reforms. In this chapter, I offer an analysis of the political, organizational and legal contexts for the reforms. In particular, the role of the Party, the authority of the *nomenklatura* and several important organizations that were involved in civil service personnel decision-making and management at both the central and local levels will be reviewed. Finally, an analysis of the old cadre personnel management system and its problems will follow accordingly. In general, the cadre system suffered from serious defects. It was a highly centralized and undifferentiated approach to personnel management where its management methods were outdated and simplistic. Not only were there vague guidelines for promotion, performance appraisal and training, poor performance was tolerated while incentives for performance were insufficient to motivate cadres.

## The civil service: scope, size and structure

Any discussion of the civil service system and reform in China needs to take into consideration a number of key political and administrative concepts and terms that are peculiar to Chinese politics. These concepts include 'cadres' (*ganbu*), 'officials' (*guanyuan*), 'civil servants' (*gongwuyuan*), 'staff and workers of the state organs' (*guojia jiguan gongzuo renyuan*) and 'public employees supported by the state budget' (*caizheng gongyang renyuan*). Scholarly literature on Chinese politics often used these concepts and terms interchangeably (for example, Chou 2009). The reason is that although the civil service system has been established for more than a decade, many government agencies and other state organs have not yet started to classify their employees according to the civil servants category when they compile their personnel data. In the official Chinese archives, the term 'staff and workers of the state organs' (which is frequently referred as 'officials' by the media and the public) and the term 'cadres' are used more frequently than the term 'civil servants'. The number of public employees supported by the state is frequently reported in the official Chinese statistics.

I will begin with a discussion of the important terms 'cadres' and the 'cadre personnel management system' (*ganbu renshi guanli zhidu*). During the Communist revolutionary period, the term of 'cadres' referred to leaders, in contrast to the masses, who were the followers in a revolution. After the Chinese Communist Party (CCP) became the ruling party, the term 'cadres' came to include all those who were paid from the state budget, but did not engage in productive manual labor in China (Lee 1991: 4). Correspondingly, scholars described cadres as those who had a certain level of education (initially secondary school level and above), who had some specialist ability, who carried out 'mental' rather than 'manual' labor (Burns 2001: 85) and who held leadership positions and authority. In a broader sense, cadres included all political and administrative elites who staffed the huge Party-government hierarchy. Cadres were a privileged group of people since the term 'cadre' represented a status conferred upon an individual by the Party-government. This status helped to distinguish cadres from workers, peasants and ordinary people. The acquisition of the cadre status was a prerequisite for appointment to the public sector (Barnett 1967; Harding 1981; Lee 1991).

Currently, all administrators, managers and professionals are referred to as cadres regardless of their professional affiliation with the Party, the government, the army or the legislative or judiciary organs. The legislative and judiciary organs here include the organs of people's congresses, political consultative conferences, the courts and the procuratorates. Servicemen at or above the rank of platoon leaders (*paizhang*) in the army are called cadres in China. The managerial and professional personnel working in state-owned enterprises, public service units (*shiye danwei*), mass organizations (*renmin tuanti*), social organizations (*shehui tuanti*) and the eight democratic parties are also called the cadres. The CCP established a personnel management system for all cadres from the Communist revolutionary period (Wu 2009: 14–16). The system remained in use after the establishment of the People's Republic of China (PRC) (Barnett 1967; Harding 1981; Lee 1991; Schurmann 1968). The cadre personnel management system targeted the whole cadre corps, which included all political and administrative elites in China. It should be recognized that employees whose jobs differed in nature required different methods of management. Yet, the management methods applied under the cadre system were undifferentiated, simplistic, vague and unscientific. Thus, the authorities started to reform the cadre system in the late 1970s (Deng 1984). To establish a civil service system that managed government employees was part of the cadre management reforms.

A separate management system (known as the civil service system) has been established for cadres who have worked in the government since 1993. Officially, 'civil servants' were defined as administrators, managers and professionals who worked in the administrative organizations at all levels of the government. Blue-collar workers employed by the government were excluded from the civil service (Article 3, the 1993 Provisional Regulations). Of course, civil servants continued to be classified as cadres. Although the civil servant status was initially reserved for government employees, the civil service system was actually extended to include many other public organizations in the ensuing years. Every year, the CCP would pick several organizations (at both central and local levels) to be managed by reference to the civil service regulations (*canzhao guanli*). Here, the reference management means the personnel management methods, that is, more open competitive recruitment, civil service-type performance evaluation, salaries and benefits pegged to civil service pay and benefits, and so forth would be applied to these organizations too. The civil service management was applied to the CCP itself in 1993 and it was applied to almost all the public organizations such as the people's congresses, the political consultative conferences, the judiciary and the procuratorate as well as mass organizations, social organizations and the eight democratic parties until 2005.[1] Currently, the scope of the civil service is extended to cover not only the executive, but also the legislature, judiciary and political parties.

The passage of the *Civil Service Law*, which became effective on 1 January 2006, confirmed the expansion in the scope of the civil service. The *Civil Service Law* provided a new definition of 'civil servants' and the criteria by which public organizations could be included into the civil service. According to Article 2, 'civil servants' should include all employees who execute state functionaries (*guojia gongzhi*) according to law and who are hired according to the administrative establishment plan (*xingzheng bianzhi*) and paid by the state treasury. Accordingly, three criteria are used to map the scope of the current civil service in China: (1) the performance of public duties such as policy-making, executing supervisory powers over state and public affairs; (2) recruitment according to the administrative establishment plan; and (3) salary payment by the state treasury. Therefore, personnel other than manual workers in the employment of the following seven entities are all currently called 'civil servants': the CCP, people's congresses, government, political consultative conferences, judicial bodies, procuratorial bodies and democratic parties (Chan and Li 2007; Hou 2007: 192). The mass organizations and social organizations such as the Youth League, the Women's Federation, the All-China Federation of Trade Unions and a few others are still under the name of management by reference to the civil service law and regulations. The policy-makers thought that if all the mass and social organizations were made part of the civil service, it would be inappropriate for them to participate in activities of international non-government organizations (Hou 2007: 192).

Accordingly, the scope of the Chinese civil service underwent an expansion from a restricted definition of government employees to cover the personnel of the administrative bureaux of the Party, the people's congresses, the political consultative conferences, the discipline and inspection commissions as well as the judicial and the procuratorate at various administrative levels. This expansion had the effect of undermining the 1993 effort to establish a relatively independent civil service. However, scholars argued that the leverage for the Chinese leadership to control the civil service actually increased as a result of the more extensive definition of the civil service (Chan and Li 2007). This book argued that the central control in China was strengthened not only through the expansion in the scope of the civil service, but also (more importantly) through the implementation of civil service management in the Chinese Party-government hierarchy.

As the above analysis suggested, many government agencies and other state organs did not collect personnel data regarding employees who belonged to the civil servants category. Therefore, it was not easy to approximate the size of the expansion of the civil service using the recently published official statistics. The terms 'staff and workers of the state organs' (referred to as 'officials' by the media and the public) and 'public employees supported by the state' were used frequently in the official Chinese statistics. Figure 2.1 suggests the relationships between the four concepts. In particular, 'civil servants' and staff of the mass and social organizations (whose management referred to civil service regulations) constituted the so-called 'officials' (staff and workers of state organs). The huge 'cadre' corps included 'officials' and the managerial and professional personnel in the state-owned enterprises (SOEs) and public service units (such as schools, hospitals and research institutes) as well as servicemen at or above the rank of platoon leaders in the army. The 'public employees supported by the state budget' included all the 'cadres', the retired cadres and the blue-collar workers who were hired by the state organs such as drivers, guardians and

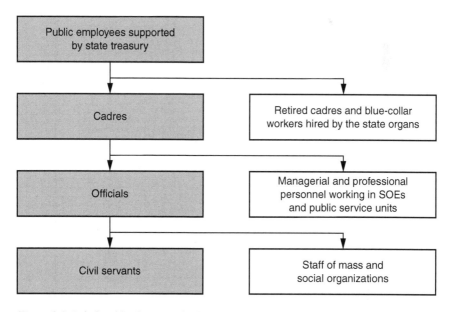

*Figure 2.1* Relationships between the four concepts.

caretakers. Currently, there are approximately 50 million public employees who are supported by the state budget. The corresponding figures for the cadres, officials and civil servants are 36 million, ten million and eight million respectively (Zhu 2008: 63).[2]

The expansion in the scope of the civil service from 1993 to 2005 was expected to lead to a corresponding expansion in the size of the civil service. However, this could not be confirmed since the statistics for the cadres and the civil servants in China remained as classified information. Data on the size and distribution of civil servants were not available with very few exceptions. Table 2.1 and Table 2.2 suggest the profile of the Chinese civil service in 1998.

At that time, most civil servants (about 90 percent) worked in the local governments in China. Only about 10 percent of civil servants worked in the central government. About 11 percent worked in provincial governments, 21 percent at the prefectural level, 41 percent at the county level and 17 percent at the township level governments. As for the administrative rank of individuals, less than 1,000 civil servants were ranked at the minister or provincial governor level while most civil servants held the rank of section chief or deputy chief (35.69 percent) or section member (46.78 percent). Bureau-level officials, employed either in the

*Table 2.1* Number and distribution of civil servants by administrative level, 1998

| Administrative level | Number of civil servants | Percentage |
| --- | --- | --- |
| Central level | 495,022 | 9.28 |
| Provincial level | 592,589 | 11.11 |
| Prefectural level | 1,133,977 | 21.26 |
| County level | 2,186,263 | 40.98 |
| Township level | 926,471 | 17.37 |
| Total | 5,334,322 | 100.00 |

Source: Xi (2002: 29).

*Table 2.2* Number and distribution of civil servants by rank, 1998

| Rank | Number of civil servants | Percentage |
| --- | --- | --- |
| Provincial/ministerial # | 867 | 0.02 |
| Directorate/bureau # | 21,152 | 0.40 |
| County/division # | 295,347 | 5.54 |
| Township/section # | 1,904,020 | 35.69 |
| Section staff level | 2,495,489 | 46.78 |
| Clerical staff | 617,447 | 11.57 |
| Total | 5,334,322 | 100.00 |

Source: Xi (2002: 30).

Note
# The figure includes civil servants at the deputy level.

central government or at the provincial level, constituted less than half a percent of the total while about 5.5 percent of the civil servants were division chiefs (employed in central ministries and in provincial government) or county heads.

With a restricted definition of civil service, Xi (2002) reported that in 1998 there were about 5.33 million civil servants in China. As a result of the expanded scope of the civil service, scholars reported that there were about 6.34 million in 2003 (Chan and Li 2007: 389). Following the definition of the *Civil Service Law*, there were about 6.34 million civil servants nationwide according to the 2003 statistics. About 4.9 million civil servants worked in various levels of government, 720,000 in CCP organs, 120,000 in people's congresses, 60,000 in political consultative conferences, 450,000 in judicial and procuratorial organs and 90,000 in democratic parties.

Table 2.3 suggests the number of personnel employed by government agencies, party organs, social organizations and public service units from 1978 to 2008. I found that in 1978, officials constituted less than 5 percent of the total employment while in 2008, the share increased to more than 11 percent.

Table 2.4 suggests the public employment for various provinces in 2008. In terms of the ratio of officials to the population, the figure for the Anhui province was the smallest while the figure for Tibet was the largest. This meant that for every 100 people, almost three of them were officials in Tibet. This might imply that authorities granted more administrative positions in Tibet for security reasons given its relatively large minority population. As for the ratio of the public sector employees to the total employment, the figure for Shanghai was the smallest while the figure for Tibet was once again the largest. Guizhou had the second highest ratio. In all, it is safe to say that in urban China, one in every five people worked for the public sector.

Table 2.5 suggests the cost of the civil service where the payroll expenditure was included in the item labeled administrative expenses. I found that both the number of administrative expenses and its share in the government expenditure increased from 1978 to 2005. In 2005, almost one fifth of government expenditure was used to cover the cost for personnel and administrative activities in the public sector. I also found that the growth rate of the GDP was bigger than that of government expenditure in the 1980s and early 1990s. The ratio of government expenditure to GDP started to increase drastically from 1997 and it amounted to nearly 21 percent in 2008.

Figure 2.2 suggests the environment in which the scope expansion and cost increase of the civil service took place. I found that from 1978 to 2008, the scope of the civil service expanded from around 5 percent to more than 10 percent of the total employment. The cost of the civil service increased even more drastically (the ratio of administrative expenses to government expenditure increased from 5 percent to 20 percent). The government expenditure as a percentage of GDP increased substantially as well from 1997. The data suggested that the government in China paid its employees very generously and this might explain why a career in the civil service has appeared to be attractive in recent years, resulting in the competitiveness of civil servant recruitment.

Table 2.3 Number employed by government agencies, party organs, social organizations and public service units, 1978–2008 (thousands)

| | 1978 | 1985 | 1993 | 1995 | 1999 | 2000 | 2003 | 2005 | 2007 | 2008 |
|---|---|---|---|---|---|---|---|---|---|---|
| Government (*guojia jiguan*) | NA | NA | 8,790 | 9,390 | 10,171 | 10,221 | 10,569 | 11,216 | 11,633 | 11,933 |
| Party (*zhengdang jiguan*) | NA | NA | 530 | 530 | 515 | 519 | 553 | 581 | 649 | 656 |
| Social organizations (*shehui tuanti*) | NA | NA | 980 | 350 | 198 | 167 | 172 | 186 | 197 | 204 |
| Officials (A) (*guanyuan*) | 4,300 | 7,180 | 10,300 | 10,270 | 10,840 | 10,910 | 11,294 | 11,983 | 12,479 | 12,793 |
| Public service units (*shiye danwei*) | 12,410 | 17,060 | 22,090 | 23,560 | 25,750 | 25,970 | 26,437 | 27,129 | 27,849 | 28,028 |
| Total number employed (B) | 94,990 | 123,580 | 148,490 | 149,080 | 117,730 | 112,590 | 104,920 | 108,500 | 114,270 | 115,150 |
| (A)/(B) (%) | 4.53 | 5.81 | 6.94 | 6.89 | 9.21 | 9.69 | 10.76 | 11.04 | 10.92 | 11.11 |

Source: National Bureau of Statistics, *China Statistical Yearbook* (various years).

Note
The statistics for the period of 1978–2000 are numbers of employees in government agencies, party organs and social organizations. From 2003, the statistics appear under the category of 'public management and social organizations'. This category covers employees in government agencies, party organs, political consultative conferences, democratic parties and non-government organizations.

Table 2.4 Public sector employment for various provinces, 2008

| | Population (A) (thousands) | Officials (B) (thousands) | (B)/(A) (%) | Public sector employees (C) (thousands) | Number of employed (D) (thousands) | (C)/(D) (%) |
|---|---|---|---|---|---|---|
| Beijing | 16,950 | 340 | 2.01 | 1,142 | 5,703 | 20.02 |
| Tianjin | 11,760 | 138 | 1.17 | 470 | 2,006 | 23.43 |
| Hebei | 69,888 | 745 | 1.07 | 1,886 | 5,010 | 37.64 |
| Shanxi | 34,106 | 479 | 1.40 | 1,175 | 3,752 | 31.32 |
| Inner Mongolia | 24,137 | 329 | 1.36 | 842 | 2,448 | 34.40 |
| Liaoning | 43,147 | 493 | 1.14 | 1,308 | 5,108 | 25.61 |
| Jilin | 27,340 | 310 | 1.13 | 882 | 2,620 | 33.66 |
| Heilongjiang | 38,254 | 408 | 1.07 | 1,130 | 4,751 | 23.78 |
| Shanghai | 18,885 | 177 | 0.94 | 692 | 3,772 | 18.35 |
| Jiangsu | 76,773 | 608 | 0.79 | 1,846 | 7,076 | 26.09 |
| Zhejiang | 51,200 | 524 | 1.02 | 1,428 | 7,412 | 19.27 |
| Anhui | 61,350 | 447 | 0.73 | 1,270 | 3,437 | 36.95 |
| Fujian | 36,040 | 295 | 0.82 | 933 | 4,587 | 20.34 |
| Jiangxi | 44,000 | 417 | 0.95 | 1,057 | 2,892 | 36.55 |
| Shandong | 94,172 | 1,005 | 1.07 | 2,546 | 9,014 | 28.24 |
| Henan | 94,290 | 988 | 1.05 | 2,536 | 7,144 | 35.50 |
| Hubei | 57,110 | 544 | 0.95 | 1,519 | 4,703 | 32.30 |
| Hunan | 63,800 | 674 | 1.06 | 1,677 | 4,547 | 36.88 |
| Guangdong | 95,440 | 906 | 0.95 | 2,547 | 10,079 | 25.27 |
| Guangxi | 48,160 | 370 | 0.77 | 1,159 | 2,928 | 39.58 |
| Hainan | 8,540 | 90 | 1.05 | 240 | 768 | 31.25 |
| Chongqing | 28,390 | 227 | 0.80 | 695 | 2,417 | 28.75 |
| Sichuan | 81,380 | 696 | 0.86 | 1,860 | 5,509 | 33.76 |
| Guizhou | 37,927 | 352 | 0.93 | 887 | 2,110 | 42.04 |
| Yunnan | 45,430 | 439 | 0.97 | 1,125 | 3,035 | 37.07 |
| Tibet | 2,870 | 78 | 2.72 | 135 | 203 | 66.50 |
| Shaanxi | 37,620 | 447 | 1.19 | 1,182 | 3,444 | 34.32 |
| Gansu | 26,281 | 346 | 1.32 | 800 | 1,925 | 41.56 |
| Qinghai | 5,543 | 79 | 1.43 | 186 | 470 | 39.57 |
| Ningxia | 6,177 | 76 | 1.23 | 190 | 571 | 33.27 |
| Xinjiang | 21,308 | 324 | 1.52 | 807 | 2,482 | 32.51 |

Source: National Bureau of Statistics (2010: 124–6).

Table 2.5 Administrative expenses, 1978–2008

| Year | GDP (A) (billion yuan) | Government expenditure (B) (billion yuan) | (B)/(A) (%) | Administrative expenses (C) (billion yuan) | (C)/(B) (%) |
| --- | --- | --- | --- | --- | --- |
| 1978 | 365 | 112 | 30.68 | 5 | 4.46 |
| 1980 | 455 | 123 | 27.03 | 8 | 6.50 |
| 1985 | 902 | 200 | 22.17 | 17 | 8.50 |
| 1990 | 1,867 | 308 | 16.50 | 41 | 13.31 |
| 1991 | 2,178 | 339 | 15.56 | 41 | 12.09 |
| 1992 | 2,692 | 374 | 13.89 | 46 | 12.30 |
| 1993 | 3,533 | 464 | 13.13 | 63 | 13.58 |
| 1994 | 4,820 | 579 | 12.01 | 85 | 14.68 |
| 1995 | 6,079 | 682 | 11.22 | 100 | 14.66 |
| 1996 | 7,118 | 794 | 11.15 | 119 | 14.99 |
| 1997 | 7,897 | 923 | 11.69 | 136 | 14.73 |
| 1998 | 8,440 | 1,080 | 12.80 | 160 | 14.81 |
| 1999 | 8,968 | 1,319 | 14.71 | 202 | 15.31 |
| 2000 | 9,921 | 1,589 | 16.02 | 277 | 17.43 |
| 2001 | 10,966 | 1,890 | 17.24 | 351 | 18.57 |
| 2002 | 12,033 | 2,205 | 18.32 | 410 | 18.59 |
| 2003 | 13,582 | 2,465 | 18.15 | 469 | 19.03 |
| 2004 | 15,988 | 2,849 | 17.82 | 552 | 19.38 |
| 2005 | 18,322 | 3,393 | 18.52 | 651 | 19.19 |
| 2006 | 21,192 | 4,042 | 19.07 | NA | NA |
| 2007 | 25,731 | 4,978 | 19.35 | NA | NA |
| 2008 | 30,067 | 6,259 | 20.82 | NA | NA |

Source: National Bureau of Statistics, *China Statistical Yearbook* (various years).

*Scope, structure and context for reforms* 29

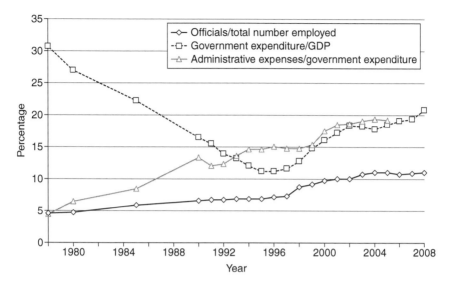

*Figure 2.2* Overview of civil service scope extension, 1978–2008.

## Structure

Different positions require different managing methods in the public sector. The design of the Chinese civil service took this into consideration and it was designed in accordance with the principle of management by categories. With the different nature, characteristics and management requirements, civil service positions are divided into three categories. First, the generalists (*zonghe guanlilei*) are in charge of general management and administrative work and they constitute the largest group in the civil service. The second category of civil servants is the professionals and technicians (*zhuanye jishulei*). The third category of civil servants is officers for regulation enforcement (*xingzheng zhifalei*) (Article 14, *Civil Service Law*). According to the status in the hierarchy, civil service positions are further divided into leading and non-leading positions (Article 16, *Civil Service Law*). Leading positions are spread across ten levels: state-level head and deputy positions, ministerial/provincial-level head and deputy positions, bureau/department-level head and deputy positions, division/county-level head and deputy positions, and section/township-level head and deputy positions. Non-leading positions include clerks, section members, deputy section chiefs, section chiefs, deputy researchers, researchers, deputy inspectors and inspectors (Article 17, *Civil Service Law*). The introduction of non-leading positions is an attempt to alleviate the ever-present pressure to increase the number of leading positions in government. The leading and non-leading positions are effectively the same, but administrative power only comes with the former. In other words, non-leading positions have all the benefits and status associated with the leading positions, but lack administrative power. For example, in terms of administrative rank, inspectors can be considered as equivalent to the bureau-level officials; however, inspectors do not execute administrative power as bureau chiefs do. An official who deserves a promotion but cannot get it because all the leading positions are filled may be promoted to a non-leading position. Non-leading positions also make it possible to retire cadres reaching a certain age from the leading positions to give way to young aspirants (Lam and Chan 1996a). This classification of positions only applies to the generalists. The position classification system for professionals and technicians and regulation-enforcement officers has yet to be developed.

As for the management of professionals and technicians, the *Civil Service Law* specified the possibility of using contract employment in specialized areas. The contract employment method gave various administrative organizations considerable flexibility in hiring special expertise. While it was legally approved in 2005, the contract employment method has actually been in use since the early 1990s. The employment contract usually ranges between one to five years and is preceded by a probation period of six months. The contract includes guidelines on wage, welfare provisions, insurance treatment and breach of liabilities. The contract-based government employees may be exempted from the open recruitment process. Hiring organizations are also granted autonomy in determining salary levels on the condition that decisions are made according to establishment and budget plans. However, using this method requires the approval of the personnel department at provincial level. Moreover, it cannot be applied to positions that involve state secrets.

Currently, civil servants are managed according to the *Civil Service Law* and a number of supplementary regulations and directives. The *Civil Service Law* modified the structure of positions and ranks. The most important is that the ranking system with its 15 different grades is no longer explicated. Table 2.6 shows the corresponding changes in the position name after 2006. Prior to the change, dividing all the leading positions and non-leading positions into 15 grades did not adequately reflect the considerable size of the Chinese civil service and the wide-ranging nature and requirements of its various positions. To facilitate the management and wage payment, civil service positions are now divided into 27 grades determined by the 'level of responsibility and degree of difficulty of the task and the civil servant's capability, political integrity, practical success, and work performance' ('2006 *gongwuyuan gongzi gaige ziliao daquan*' (Collection of materials on 2006 civil service wage reform)).The current structure of the Chinese civil service in terms of positions and grades is shown in Table 2.6.

Now, five positions are included in the 'state-level head position' (*guojiaji zhengzhi*) category: (1) the President of the PRC; (2) the general secretary of the CCP; (3) the Premier; (4) the Chairman of the standing committee of National People's Congress; and (5) the Chairman of National Committee of Chinese Peoples' Political Consultative Conference. Ten positions are included in the 'state-level deputy position' (*guojiaji fuzhi*) category: (1) Vice President of the PRC; (2) members of the standing committee of the Politburo; (3) members and

Table 2.6 Position and grade structure change

| Position name before 2006 | Grade before 2006 | Grade after 2006 | Position name after 2006 |
|---|---|---|---|
| Premier | 1 | 1 | State-level head positions |
| Vice Premier, State Councilor | 2–3 | 2–4 | State-level deputy positions |
| Minister, Governor | 3–4 | 4–8 | Provincial-level head positions |
| Vice Minister, Vice Governor | 4–5 | 6–10 | Provincial-level deputy positions |
| Bureau Chief | 5–7 | 8–13 | Bureau/department-level head positions |
| Deputy Bureau Chief | 6–8 | 10–15 | Bureau/department-level deputy positions |
| Division Chief | 7–10 | 12–18 | Division/county-level head positions |
| Deputy Division Chief | 8–11 | 14–20 | Division/county-level deputy positions |
| Section Chief | 9–12 | 16–23 | Section/township-level head positions |
| Deputy Section Chief | 9–13 | 17–24 | Section/township-level deputy positions |
| Section member | 9–14 | 18–26 | Section member |
| Office clerk | 10–15 | 19–27 | Office clerk |

Source: Wu (2009: 69).

alternate members of the Politburo; (4) secretariats of the Communist Party Secretariat; (5) Vice Premiers; (6) state councillors; (7) Vice Chairman of the standing committee of National People's Congress; (8) Vice Chairman of National Committee of Chinese Peoples' Political Consultative Conference; (9) the President of the Supreme People's Court; and (10) the Procurator General of the Supreme People's Procuratorate. I found that unlike the practice in many other countries, no distinction is made between politicians and civil servants in China. State leaders such as the President and cabinet members such as the Premier and Vice Premiers, who normally would be considered as politicians in political systems with competing political parties and elections, also come under the civil service in China.

## Political and organizational context for managing civil servants

Before examining the implementation of civil service reforms in China, I will delineate the context within which the reforms were carried out. In particular, we should pay attention to the role of the Party, the authority of the *nomenklatura* and several important organizations that were involved in civil service personnel decision and management at both the central and local levels.

### The role of the Party

Civil service management in China is embedded in a system of one-party rule where the CCP plays the leading role. Authorities have enshrined the long-standing principle that the Party manages and controls the cadres (*dang guan ganbu*) in the law. According to the *Civil Service Law*, China's civil service system

> shall conform to the guidance of Marxism-Leninism, Mao Zedong Thought, Deng Xiaoping Theory and the important thought of Three Represents as well as to follow the basic line of the primary stage of socialism, observe the line and policies of the CCP on cadre matters and adhere to the principle that the Party exercised leadership over cadre matters.
>
> (Article 4)

As discussed above, China has an extremely large pool of state cadres. The power to manage the cadres, including civil servants, has always been concentrated in the Party, specifically, the Politburo, Central Committee and its Organization Department (OD) at the center and party committees and their organization departments at various local levels.

The highest organ of political power in China, the Central Committee of the CCP, and the Politburo inside it are responsible for long-term policy planning and setting out the principles for public sector personnel management. There is a small leading group within the Politburo to oversee 'the organization and personnel work', which includes the management of the civil service. One of the nine standing members of the Politburo is the chair of this small group. Civil service management policy is made by the CCP's OD under the supervision of the Politburo and at the center is implemented by the Ministry of Human Resources and Social Security (HRSS, formerly the Ministry of Personnel) and in particular, by the Ministry's Civil Service Bureau.[3] Personnel decisions for the non-leading positions in the civil service, including selection and appraisal, are managed and approved by the party core group within the relevant bureau under the supervision of the organization department at the same level. Leading positions are managed according to the *nomenklatura* authority. Civil service discipline work (anticorruption) is handled by the Party's Central Discipline Inspection Commission and the government's Ministry of Supervision.

## *Authority of* nomenklatura

The term '*nomenklatura*' comes from the Soviet political terminology, meaning 'a list of positions'. Communist parties have elaborate *nomenklatura* systems that enable them to exercise political and personnel control over almost the entire state apparatus. The *nomenklatura* system is a leadership selection system that gives territorial party committees at each administrative level monopoly power to select officials for positions within their jurisdiction (Burns 2006: 34). Each Party committee at various administrative levels has its own list that describes the positions over which it has personnel authority. The appointment, promotion, transfer or removal of any these position-holders in the list requires the approval of the party committee. The CCP has also established an elaborate *nomenklatura* system (Burns 1994a, 1989c, 1987c; Chan 2004; Manion 1985). Each party committee from below the Central Committee has a list of positions over which it has final authority over selection. Generally, the lists are divided into two parts: a list of positions over which the party committee must first give its approval before an appointment may be made and a list of positions the filling of which must be reported to the OD. The OD may veto appointment on the second list (Burns 2006: 34). The system also includes lists of reserve candidates for each position that are also managed by the territorial party committees and sets of principles and procedures for matching candidates to positions. Through the *nomenklatura* system, the CCP exercises control over the selection and appointment of leading cadres in the entire public sector. The system also works as an instrument for the upper-level Party-government to control the lower levels. In the 1980s, the central leadership in China decentralized certain personnel management to local governments through administrative reforms, but kept the principle of *nomenklatura* control untouched. On the contrary, the OD issued a revised *nomenklatura* in May 1990 to take back some of the power delegated to the State Council in 1988. This move also recentralized some of the power previously delegated to the provincial-level party committees in 1984 (Burns 1994a). Every time the OD issues a revised *nomenklatura*, the direct consequence is that the Party center takes back some of the personnel powers from the government or from the lower levels of the Party-government (Burns 1994a; Chan 2004).

## Organizational context

On behalf of the State Council, the Ministry of HRSS is responsible for the formulation and interpretation of regulations regarding civil servants as well as the coordination of the implementation of these regulations. The Ministry of HRSS directly manages civil servants appointed by the State Council. It provides guidance and supervision for the management of civil servants for various functional departments under the State Council and for various local government bureaux. As for the relationship between OD and HRSS, the Ministry of HRSS implements the policy under the supervision of the OD. The OD tightly controls the Ministry through an 11-member party core group (*dangzu*) by requiring that civil servants in the Ministry be party members and through a system of concurrent appointments at the leadership level that leaves the same individual holding leadership positions in both the Ministry and the OD.[4] The Minister of HRSS is concurrently Ministry party core group secretary, chief of the Ministry's Civil Service Bureau and a Deputy Head of the OD. The 11 members of the Ministry's party core group include another OD Deputy Head (concurrently a Vice Minister of HRSS), a Vice Minister who is concurrently deputy chief of the Civil Service Bureau and deputy secretary of that Bureau's party core group and a member of the Central Discipline Inspection Commission stationed in the Ministry. Other party core group members are the Vice Ministers of HRSS. Although they are supposedly separate organizations, the Party and the government for the most part operate in lockstep on the management of the civil service. Evidence of their close relationship is the practice of seconding Ministry personnel to the OD to work on special personnel projects. For all practical purposes, the Ministry is an extension of the OD and is focused mostly on policy implementation. Alternatively, we can say that government personnel agencies are administratively subordinate to organization departments at various levels.

Organization departments of the local party committees at the province, prefecture/city and county level are responsible for supervising the implementation of the party line in civil service management and related personnel regulations. They also hold veto power over the candidates for government positions on behalf of the relevant party committees (under *nomenklatura* authority). The personnel bureaux in various functional departments under the State Council are responsible for the management of the civil servants of their departments and the management of civil servants who are affiliated with the functional departments. The personnel bureaux in the local governments at and above the county level are responsible for the comprehensive management of the civil servants in their own jurisdictions and, on behalf of local governments at the same level, directly manage the civil servants appointed by them. Similar interlocking arrangements link the organization departments and personnel bureaux at the local level.

As for the discipline of civil servants, civil service management authorities share the responsibility for monitoring and supervising the civil servants with the CCP's discipline inspection commission system, audit, public security, the judiciary and the procuratorate. On the government side, the Ministry of

Supervision is responsible for the discipline of the civil service. The Ministry of Supervision was established in 1949, abolished in 1959 and restored in 1987 (Huang 1995). To some extent, the Ministry works as the administrative subordinate to the Party's Central Discipline Inspection Commission (CDIC). The Minister of Supervision is concurrently a deputy secretary of the CDIC. In terms of their task description, the two organizations overlap considerably. Before the Ministry was re-established in 1987, there was no distinction between violations of administrative discipline and those of the Party discipline. Currently, the CDIC disciplines party members who are working in party organizations whereas both the Ministry of Supervision and the CDIC, with the CDIC taking the lead, are in charge of the disciplinary duties for the civil servants and administrative cadres (whether they are party members or not). Local supervision bureaux are subject to dual leadership by the upper-level supervision bureaux and the corresponding local governments.

In order to keep up with the leadership's directive to reduce bureaucratic redundancies, the CDIC and the Ministry of Supervision were merged in 1993 while the latter still exists under the State Council bureaucratically. The merger exemplifies the Chinese bureaucratic tradition of 'one organization, two signs'. After the merger, the organization was reduced in size (Shambaugh 2008a). The merged organization has 23 functional departments with 1,400 personnel in the headquarters plus several thousands more throughout the country. The Ministry of Supervision has a staff of 800, divided into 21 functional departments in the headquarters in Beijing (Shambaugh 2008a). At the local level, discipline (anti-corruption) work is handled by the discipline inspection commissions of various party committees and the supervision bureaux of local governments.

As for the civil service training infrastructure, there are three extensive national network of institutions, namely the party schools (*dangxiao*), administration schools (*xingzheng xueyuan*) and socialism colleges (*shehui zhuyi xueyuan*). At the apex of these institutions is the Central Party School in Beijing. On appointment, all those promoted to the rank of Vice Minister and equivalent must undergo a three-month residential course of training in the Central Party School. The Central Party School presides over about 2,700 provincial and local party schools nationwide (Shambaugh 2008b: 831). Party schools are responsible for training the country's most senior leaders at each administrative level. The Central Party School is headed by a leading member of the Politburo Standing Committee. This underscores the importance that the CCP puts on the training programs and party school system. Hu Jintao was head from 1992 to 2002 and Zeng Qinghong from 2002 to 2007. Hu's successor-in-waiting Xi Jinping is the current head. The curriculum of party schools includes Marxist-Leninist ideology and the latest party policy documents, methods of party organizational control and administration, management and leadership skills as well as knowledge and information in broader fields such as economics, accounting, history, international relations and philosophy.

The National School of Administration (*guojia xingzheng xueyuan*) was formally established under the State Council in 1994. It now presides over about

2,000 provincial and local administration schools across the country. The administration schools are in charge of training senior and middle ranking civil servants from the State Council, provincial and local governments. There is some overlap in the students trained in the National School of Administration and the Central Party School, but there is a substantial difference in the curriculum between the two. The Central Party School has a much more political and ideological content whereas the National School of Administration is focused almost exclusively on management, economics and applied skills.

The CCP United Front Work Department maintains a nationwide system of approximately 1,000 socialism colleges that train ethnic minorities and other classes targeted for united front work (Shambaugh 2008b: 828). At the provincial and sub-provincial level, party schools are often co-located on a joint campus with either the provincial administration schools or the socialism colleges. The vast majority of civil service training takes place in the vast network of provincial and sub-provincial party schools and administration schools throughout the country.

## Legal context for civil service reforms

The promulgation of the *1993 Provisional Regulations* marked the official creation of the Chinese civil service. The *Civil Service Law*, approved in 2005, soon became the blueprint for civil service management and reforms in China and, accordingly, the *1993 Provisional Regulations* expired. In the meantime, the authority also promulgated many supplementary and trial regulations, implementation methods as well as policy directives. These documents formed the legal context for the civil service reforms. On 27 April 2005, the new *Civil Service Law* was approved by the National People's Congress to upgrade the status of the *1993 Provisional Regulations*. As for the reasons why the *Civil Service Law* was enacted, one of the policy-makers said that 'the *1993 Provisional Regulations* are transitional in nature and in fact a lower-level law; they are only administrative regulations promulgated by the State Council' (Hou 2007). The *Civil Service Law* consisted of 18 chapters with 107 articles. The new law is comprehensive in its scope, covering all the major areas of personnel management. The long-standing principle of 'the Party controls cadres' is enshrined by this law.

CCP is not interested in losing its control over the leading civil servants who are also the Party cadres. The *Civil Service Law* stipulated that in cases where there are Party regulations that concern the appointment, dismissal and supervision of leading cadres, these regulations should apply to the civil service. By this formulation, it indicated that the Party's regulations should take priority over the *Civil Service Law* in managing the leading cadres (who are also civil servants). In July 2002, the Central Committee issued the *Regulations on Selection and Appointment of Party and Government Leading Cadres* (the *2002 Regulations* hereafter).[5] The leading cadres, as will be discussed in Chapter 5, are leadership members of the following organs at the central, provincial, prefecture/city and county levels: party committees, people's congresses, political consultative

*Scope, structure and context for reforms* 37

conferences, governments, courts and the procuratorates. Civil servants who hold leading positions are classified as leading cadres too. Therefore, this document formed part of the legal context for the civil service reforms. Concerning the management of civil servants above division (*chu*) level, the *2002 Regulations* apply. This document indicated the central leadership's intention to strengthen the control over leading cadre management and its emphasis on candidates' work performance and ability. The *2002 Regulations* specified the general policy principles, basic requirements, basic procedures and disciplines guidelines regarding the leading cadres' appointment, promotion, demotion, resignation, rotation, exchange and avoidance. In particular, the document emphasized that when selecting and appointing leading cadres in China, it is important to follow a number of basic principles. These principles include meritocracy, openness, competition and selecting the best. More importantly, they stress that the Party should control and manage the cadres. For example, the first three of the six general principles are: (1) The Party controls the cadres; (2) cadres must have both political integrity and professional competence and be appointed on merits; (3) the selection and appointment of officials should emphasize the candidate's achievements as confirmed by some form of mass approbation (Article 2). The principle of the Party controlling cadres is listed as the first and overarching principle in selecting and appointing party and government leading cadres. It is true that the CCP still tightly controls the huge cadre corps in China.

## Problems of the old cadre system

To properly understand the problems of the cadre system, let us consider a principal–agent scenario within a hierarchy. The superior-subordinate relationship parallels a typical principal–agent relationship where the superior acts as the principal and subordinates as the agent. It is necessary to explain that the definition of the superior-subordinate relationship depends on the level of the government organization. The superior in a lower-level organization may simultaneously serve as the subordinate to a higher-level official. Promotion can serve as a major source of motivation for individuals in a hierarchy, since it brings about many positive outcomes such as an increase in power, influence and status. In a typical superior-subordinate relationship, promotion serves as a major motivator for both parties.

The principal–agent relationship characterizes superior-subordinate relationships at multiple levels in the Chinese government. For the rank-and-file civil servants, the multiple principals they may serve include the immediate superior, local government, central government and the public. It is true that civil servants in China seek promotion in order to obtain more power, more influence, higher status and (sometimes) more rent-seeking opportunities. One unique point of China's circumstance is that the special institutional arrangement of the Chinese government undermines the strength of promotion as a job motivation for the subordinates. As Table 2.1 and Table 2.2 showed, about 94 percent of the civil servants are at the section-chief level or below and about 60 percent work in county- and township-level governments. Promotion opportunities are limited for these rank-and-file civil servants. In their view, promotion opportunities are rare and the benefits that are associated with promotions, such as power, influence and status are beyond their reach. Therefore, they prefer the status quo and attach more importance to obtaining more welfare, more spare time and more leisure.

On the contrary, the superiors seek promotion ambitiously. The Chinese government practices the leading cadre responsibility system under which the work performance of the leading cadres is evaluated based on the performance of the organization under their charge. In other words, the performance of the organization under their charge determines the likelihood of promotion (see detailed discussion in Chapter 5). The superiors want to improve organizational performance by a qualified personnel and scientific personnel management. Their specific requirements may be to select qualified agents and put proper performance appraisal and compensation methods to shape the agents' incentives to perform. The fact that promotion only serves as motivator for superiors but not subordinates causes conflicts.

The principle-agent model highlights the problem of the conflict of interests that undermines the overall achievement for both parties. The principal requires the agents to work hard to improve the performance of their unit. While this will lead to the principal's own promotion, the agent will have a tendency to minimize the amount of work they need to do. Apart from the conflict of interests, information asymmetry also affects the performance of a principal–agent relationship. Given that administrative work cannot be easily observed and measured, the agents have an information advantage over their principals regarding their input. The old cadre system in China was not equipped with measures to deal with the problems of the conflict of interests or the information asymmetry. Adverse selection, moral hazard and shirking occurred in almost all personnel procedures. In general, the system was characterized by central planning, allocation of graduates to jobs through government-determined manpower plans, non-institutionalized performance appraisal and position-based pay (Barnett 1967; Burns and Wang 2010; Cooke 2003; Harding 1981; Lee 1991; Schurmann 1968; Tsao and Worthley 1995).

First, recruitment practices under the cadre system nurtured adverse selection. Running a central planning economy, governments at various levels were responsible for estimating the demand for human resources, making manpower plans and allocating jobs to new graduates, demobilized soldiers and other cadres. Government agencies were staffed from several sources: university students were assigned to some government jobs upon graduation, demobilized soldiers from the People's Liberation Army filled other government jobs and cadres from factories or public service units, such as hospitals and schools, were transferred to fill the remaining positions (Burns 2001). This approach was over-centralized and irrational. The cadres in charge of work allocation could not get all the necessary information regarding the work unit's staffing needs or the candidates' professional ability. In addition, once assigned to a unit, candidates would have little chance to select their job or transfer to another job. Therefore, there were frequent mismatches between the candidates and the job. For example, employees were assigned to agencies that required professional skills that they did not have. Consequently, agents were often not capable of performing the principal's tasks. On the other hand, some candidates were assigned to jobs where they were not able to utilize their professional talent. Furthermore, without open competitive examinations, recruitment exercises were conducted in a secretive manner through political channels. Rather than focusing on candidates' problem-solving ability, criteria of selection were generally based on the political loyalty to the CCP and social class background. This secretive, non-competitive process increased the possibility of corruption. The cadres charged with job allocation wielded great staffing power and could hire their protégés or relatives as they liked. Finally, there was no institutional mechanism to check for the corrupt use of power by the recruitment officials. For example, entry-level openings were filled in such a way that professors could choose which candidate could go to a job interview and, ultimately, decide which student got the job. The professors and party secretaries at the universities played key roles in these decisions (Bian 1994). Therefore, personal rapport (*guanxi*) between the personnel cadres and the candidates rather than the candidates' merit was often the main factor in staffing decisions.

Second, under the cadre system, poor performance was tolerated and the practice of performance appraisal failed to motivate the agents or deter them from shirking. Due to a lack of clear position specification, there was no adequate description of the performance indicators and, hence, performance appraisal was not strictly enforced (Chan 2001; Chow 1993, 1988, 1987; Li 1990). The emphasis of the performance appraisal focused on the employee's political loyalty rather than his work performance. Instead of working conscientiously, the agents achieved better performance appraisal results by cultivating personal rapport with their superiors. As a result, the appraisal system failed to make a real impact on staff performance due to its inability to identify poor performers and to translate appraisal results into effective staffing measures such as a non-discriminatory system for punishment and reward. The fact that the performance appraisal was not linked with a proportional pay reward left the agents with little motivation to put any effort into their work and even less motivation to participate in training and updating their knowledge and skills (Chew 1990a, 1990b).

Third, the cadre system used a system of flat rates to compensate state employees. Within the public sector, different professions requiring different skills all shared a universal pay structure. Staff wages for state-owned enterprises underwent independent review until 1985. And until 1993, independent wage reviews were extended to public service units such as hospitals, schools and other research institutes (Cheung and Poon 2001; Chew 1990a, 1990b). In 1977, bonus payments were reinstituted to employees of state-owned enterprises with the purpose of improving their work incentives. By linking rewards with performance, the wages of state-owned enterprises quickly outpaced the wages for the civil service. Before 1985, the cadre salaries were not as attractive in comparison to what the state-owned enterprises were able to offer to their staff.

Moreover, before 1993, there were no regular wage reviews against the general price index (Chou 2009). Poor pay demoralized government workers, triggering an exodus from the civil service. Before 1985, officials of the same rank received the same pay regardless of the complexity of their duties or actual work performance. There was no mechanism that enabled salary adjustment to reflect the growth of working experience, seniority and length of time spent in a position. Although the 1985 wage reform intended to solve these problems, the impacts of the reform on the rank-and-file civil servants were limited (see detailed discussion in Chapter 3).

As discussed above, promotion was considered as a formal instrument to motivate individuals to put a conscious effort into their work. The old cadre system failed in this regard. Political loyalty to the Party, connections to powerful superiors and appropriate social class background (family origin) were the main criteria for promotion for cadres before the civil service reforms (Chow 1993, 1991, 1988, 1987; Li 1990; Liu 2001). The purpose of training is supposed to reduce the gap between the cadres' current qualifications and the requirements of their designated positions. In order to close this gap, formal education and practical work experience at a lower level is sometimes required. Training programs before the reforms put too much emphasis on literacy and political training while attention to job-oriented skills training was insufficient (Chou 2003). Moreover, given that the problem-solving ability and work performance were not the main considerations during performance appraisals and promotion, employees did not have an incentive to voluntarily participate in training programs to update their work-related knowledge and skills.

Lastly, the cadre system was almost a life-tenure system as there were no strict rules specifying when cadres should retire. In practice, cadres postponed their retirement to gain more retirement benefits. A life-tenure system and the reluctance to retire contributed to an aging bureaucracy (Chew 1990a, 1990b; Manion 1993, 1985). The regulations of establishment stipulated the staff size of government bureaux, but not the number of deputy chiefs or the proportion of non-leading officials in government bureaux. In some government bureaux, there were more high-ranking officials than low-ranking ones with many high-ranking officials as deputy bureau chiefs or non-leading officials at the same level.[6] The grade inflation and an over-staffed bureaucracy made it impossible to control the administrative expenditure.

In summary, the cadre system had serious defects. It was a highly centralized and undifferentiated approach to personnel management. The power of cadre management was over-concentrated and the people who handled personnel affairs lacked professional knowledge. The management methods were outdated and overly simplistic. The recruitment and promotion of the public employees were not based on competition, but on political loyalty to the Communist Party and social class background. Not only were there vague guidelines for promotion, performance appraisal and training, different positions that required wildly different skills all shared a similar pay structure. As a result, poor performance was tolerated while incentives for performance were insufficient to motivate cadres.

# 3 Civil service reform policy and implementation

According to the principal–agent theory, agency problems include information asymmetry and conflicts of interests. This chapter is organized around these two problems. I argue that China's civil service reform policy included mechanisms designed to address the agency problems that were associated with the cadre personnel management system. The reform initiatives included measures to foster competition, reduce information asymmetries and align the incentive structure. The evaluation and analysis of the effectiveness of these measures presented in this book will give due recognition to the fact that civil servants serve multiple principals including their immediate superiors, the local government, the central government and the public.

The effectiveness of these measures was mixed. In general, I found that the civil service reforms in China successfully addressed some adverse selection problems while failing to adequately address the incentive alignment issues. On one hand, some new measures to obtain additional information were effective. For example, open, competitive selection and promotion led to positive outcomes as critical information about the job candidates was made available through standardized test procedures. On the other hand, other measures to improve information availability were unsuccessful. For example, performance appraisal for individual civil servants was ineffective and the monitoring system was weak. As for the incentive alignment measures, formal policy instruments such as pay and promotion did not serve as motivators for the rank-and-file civil servants. Ironically, the real motivation came from the informal incentive alignment measures: superiors and their subordinates collaborated in illicit activities such as the buying and selling of government posts. In other words, the official policy to align the incentives of the principals and agents in China's civil service reforms failed while the informal or illegal motivators successfully aligned the incentives of corrupt superiors and their subordinates. This shows that discipline is now emerging as an urgent issue for the civil service in reform.

This chapter is divided into four sections. The first section reviews the reform programs that aimed to address the problem of information asymmetry. The second section focuses on the reform programs related to the incentive alignment issues. The third section discusses the wage reforms. Specifically, the authorities increased the civil servants' salaries, subsidies and pensions remarkably in recent years with the assumption that high salaries would foster a clean government. As such, civil service pay levels became reasonably competitive with the private sector, which made a career in the civil service appear very attractive. However, considering other important objectives of wage reforms such as motivating performance, eliminating financial mismanagement of local governments and tackling regional gaps of civil service welfare, the implementation of wage reforms fell short of their promise. The last section elaborates on the enforcement of discipline.

## To discover more information

Reform policies focused on finding out more information about civil servants' abilities and work behavior. The principal–agent paradigm suggested that prospective job candidates might hide such information from their prospective superiors. In China, the reform policy required more open and competitive selection to elicit relevant information about the candidates' ability. Additional monitoring and a new set of performance appraisals were also adopted in order to find out the true qualification of the existing civil servants. I will turn to each of these strategies below and discuss several types of reform policies on selection, including a one-off transitional selection through which cadres were transferred to the new civil service, entry-level selection and selection on promotion.

### *One-off transition*

In the second half of the 1990s, a one-off exercise was carried out throughout the country to filter out poor performers. Government functionaries were required to take examinations within the first three years of the introduction of the new civil service arrangements to determine whether they were qualified to retain their position under the new system. This initiative was rooted in the expectation that the transition exercise could filter out unqualified officials and encourage current position holders to voluntarily update their knowledge and skills. By September 1997, the expected completion date of the new system, all provincial-level governments reportedly completed the transitional process. However, only 85.4 percent of prefecture-level governments, 55.4 percent of county-level governments and 'some' town and township governments had actually completed the task (Hou 2007: 131).

Data from the field sites indicated that many localities probably failed to screen out the poor performers. For example, only 0.3 percent of the officials in the Haidian district of Beijing failed to transfer to the new civil service. In Ningbo, where standards were somewhat more stringent, 97.6 percent of the 19,029 officials of the city government were accepted into the new service (see detailed discussion in Chapter 4). Therefore, although the authorities provided a one-time-only filtering process, the system was very undiscriminating and failed to effectively identify the poor performers. One reason was that the bureaucratic norm that supervisors should take care of their co-workers' welfare was in conflict with the goal of filtering out the poor performers. Another reason was that since local governments were left with the discretion to design and administer their own transitional process (Li and Zeng 1994: 163; Ministry of Personnel 1994b), supervisors were allowed to adopt filtering methods that maintained social harmony at the expense of workplace efficiency.

*Entry-level selection*

Under the reforms, entry into the civil service is determined to a significant extent by individual performance in competitions such as written entry examinations and interviews. Officials set up an annual nationwide civil service *entry-level* selection system for persons with a college or graduate school education as well as for 'members of society' from 1993. The process generally required candidates to apply for a specific post (openings that were listed online). The employing agency would check whether the prospective candidates met the minimum requirements (e.g., age, educational level, gender in some cases and party or youth league membership) and invite those who qualified to the examination. Following the examination, candidates would undergo a more in-depth interview process or another round of specialized examinations. The entire process was managed by the party core group of the employing agency and was implemented by the employing agency's personnel unit and overseen by the CCP organization department at that level. In 2009, more than 775,000 people were competing for some 13,500 centrally managed jobs, an indication of the competitive nature of the formal civil service selection process (see Table 3.1). The government further increased the level of competition by removing barriers to competition such as the requirement for an urban residency permit (*hukou*) for some posts.

These changes were accompanied by a dramatic improvement in the educational level of the senior civil service during the 1980s and the 1990s. In 1998, the share of leading cadres with college education and above increased 64.1 percent compared to 1979. By 1998, 80–90 percent of the top civil servants at ministry, bureau and division level were university or community college graduates (Organization Department of CCP 1999).[1] In the first ten years of the competitive recruitment, civil servants on average became more educated and younger. In 2002, staff with a college degree and above formed 69 percent of the whole service, an increase of 37 percent compared with 1993. Moreover, civil servants under the age of 35 made up 38.8 percent of the whole service, those between the age of 36 and 50 made up 51.5 percent and those who were 55 and older made up only 5.5 percent (Yin 2003).

However, the competitive selection of entry-level civil servants was delayed in many places by the 1998 downsizing campaign launched by the former Premier Zhu Rongji in March 1998. According to the downsizing requirements, 15 government ministries would be axed or merged by the end of the year and three million civil servants would be dismissed over the course of three years. The 1998 downsizing campaign was considered to be the most radical plan to

44  *Reform policy and implementation*

*Table 3.1* Number of vacancies and applicants for centrally managed civil service positions, 1994–2009

| Year | No. of applicants (A) | No. of vacancies (B) | (B)/(A) (%) |
|---|---|---|---|
| 1994 | 4,306 | 440 | 9.80 |
| 1995 | 6,726 | 490 | 13.70 |
| 1996 | 7,160 | 737 | 9.70 |
| 1997 | 8,850 | NA | NA |
| 2001 | 32,904 | 4,500 | 7.20 |
| 2002 | 62,268 | 4,800 | 13.00 |
| 2003 | 87,772 | 5,400 | 16.30 |
| 2004 | 140,184 | 8,000 | 17.50 |
| 2005 | 406,000 | 8,622 | 46.90 |
| 2006 | 535,574 | 12,724 | 42.10 |
| 2007 | 356,300 | 12,725 | 28.00 |
| 2008 | 637,344 | 13,278 | 48.00 |
| 2009 | 775,000 | 13,500 | 57.40 |

Sources: Interviews, Ministry of Personnel 22 July 1996, 12 August 1999 and 19 March 2004; Posts advertised in 2005 for 2006 recruitment www.china.com.cn/chinese/MATERIAL/1014867.htm (accessed 31 October 2005); *Xinhua*, 'Half a Million Chinese Compete to Become Civil Servants', 21 November 2006; Zhongguowang, 'National Civil Servants Exam Question and Answer', http://big5.china.com.cn/education/zhuanti/pta/txt/2008–10/13/content_16604619.htm (accessed 23 February 2009); Sohu, 'Number of Applicants for National Civil Servants Exam Reaches Historical High', http://learning.sohu.com/20081119/n260721601.shtml (accessed 23 February 2009).

Note
Centrally managed posts include posts in the central government and posts managed by central institutions (e.g., Customs, People's Bank of China, etc.). The number of applicants includes both undergraduates/postgraduates and those openly recruited from society.

downsize and restructure the government because it was launched at a time when millions of state-owned enterprises workers were laid off and when thousands of Chinese citizens were complaining about the bureaucracy and corruption of government officials (Cooke 2005). In my data, the education bureaux in all three cities were affected by this campaign, which precluded them from recruiting new staff for much of the period reviewed in this study. For a variety of reasons, however, local governments continued to fill positions through means other than competitive selection. For example, it was found that the central government would compel local governments to find civil service positions for large numbers of demobilized soldiers during the nationwide downsizing campaigns. In these cases, neither examinations nor other competitive selection systems were used to screen the demobilized soldiers; thus, it contributed to adverse selection problems. As will be discussed in Chapter 4, from 1998 to 2001, the Haidian district government only recruited 24 new civil servants through the competitive system, but absorbed at least 215 demobilized soldiers into various bureaux. The case of Ningbo was similar. Without any competitive screening, Ningbo absorbed 1,273 demobilized soldiers into its three levels of government (city, county and township) from 1997 to 1999, who then made up about 6.9 percent of the total civil service there (Ningbo Personnel Bureau 1999).

The recruitment examination of civil service was further divided into the national examination and regional examinations. The national examination selected employees for the central government in Beijing as well as many centrally managed civil service positions while various provinces designed their own recruitment examinations to select employees for local governments. The regional recruitment examinations were also open to both university graduates and the general public. Although recruitment was no longer restricted to individuals with urban residency, in reality, only residents of the locality where the recruitment took place were actually considered. For example, in recruiting civil servants for the Ningbo city government, only residents of Zhejiang province were considered as qualified applicants. Such measures suggested the intention of various local governments to protect employment opportunities for their residents.

A new trend observed in the civil service recruitment was the increasing demand for applicants with working experience in the grassroot-level positions. Applicants for a certain position were expected to have served in at least one of the lower positions (Civil Service Bureau 2009). The logic of this requirement was consistent with the current policy for promotion, which required a minimum service period in the current rank as a prerequisite to be promoted to the next rank. The rationale was to provide relief for the pressure in the job market for university graduates. The job market for university graduates was more and more competitive as higher education expanded. To prevent university graduates from seeking high-level positions in government as their first jobs, this requirement encouraged them to start with the lower-level positions first. Moreover, recruiting from the grassroots helped to prevent corruption through increasing social mobility. Official reports suggested that the country recruited 120,000 new civil servants altogether in 2009. Among them, 70 percent of recruits for central-level organs had working experience at the lower levels and 60 percent of the recruits for provincial organs had working experience at the lower levels ('Gongwuyuanfa' 2010).

Not surprisingly, given the competition involved in the civil service recruitment and selection process, authorities uncovered cases of abuse. In nationwide competitions for central government positions, cases of abuse were reported frequently. There were 1,605 cases of cheating in civil service examinations from 2006 to 2009 and 935 cases were reported in 2009 alone. The number of local cases also increased (Civil Service Bureau 2010a).

## *Selection for promotion*

Civil service reforms also included the introduction of more competitive promotion exercises to encourage hard work and to provide more information to employers about a candidate's aptitude for higher-level responsibilities. The process of promoting civil servants in China today is undoubtedly more open, transparent, competitive and merit-based than it was under the cadre personnel management system. The formal process included democratic recommendation (*mingzhu tuijian*), open recruitment (*gonkai xuanba*), internal competition for posting (*jingzheng shanggang*), public notification (*gongshi zhidu*) and mass evaluations (*minzhu pingyi*). Before the reforms, leading cadres' promotion was secretive and the process was dominated by a small circle of leaders of local party committees. As discussed in Chapter 2, the Central Committee of CCP promulgated the *Regulations on Selection and Appointment of Party and Government Leading Cadres* in 2002 (the *2002 Regulations*). This document required that the principles of openness, competition and meritocracy be institutionalized into the formal procedures of promoting leading cadres. Chapter 3 of the *2002 Regulations* stipulated that democratic recommendation should be used in the selection of candidates considered for the leading positions. It required the local party committees to consult the retired local leaders and leaders of local state organs before they nominated candidates to the local leadership groups (*lingdao banzi*). Article 12 stipulated that if the candidates were nominated to leadership positions in the governments, people's congresses or political consultative conferences, the democratic recommendation should include representatives from democratic parties, local branches of the All-China Federation of Industry and Commerce and significant persons without party affiliations. If consensus on the list of nominees could not be reached, local party committees could produce the final list of nominees by voting, provided that there were more standing candidates than the number of vacancies. The wide consultation and competition involved may help to reduce the possibility of local party secretaries manipulating appointment decisions.

The principles of transparency, competition and meritocracy were also illustrated by two types of open competitions for leading positions introduced by the authorities since the late 1990s. The first type was open recruitment, which suggested that both insiders and outsiders of the state organs were qualified to apply for the positions. The second type was internal competition for posting. In contrast with open recruitment, internal competition for posting was restricted to the candidates from particular departments or groupings of the functional bureaucracy (*xitong*) (Article 49, the 2002 Regulations). At the experimental stage, the method of internal competition for posting was applied only to the personnel staff of the Party-government. The Organization Department and the former Ministry of Personnel started to implement it nationwide in 1998 and 28 provinces implemented it in that same year. From 1999 to 2001, altogether 170,000 civil service positions were open to internal competition (Yin 2003). From 2003 to 2007, more than 200,000 civil servants were recruited into the leading positions through internal competition. Among them, more than 600 got bureau-level positions and more than 330,000 got division-level positions (Civil Service Bureau 2010b). Internal competition for posting helped to improve the quality of civil servants. For example, the State Industry and Commerce Bureau implemented this method in 2008. When fully implemented, the average age of the bureau-level leaders was 48.1, a reduction of 3.3 from previous levels. The average age of division-level leaders also dropped to 42.3, after a corresponding decrease of 3.6 years (Civil Service Bureau 2010b). The aim of the open recruitment process was to address the inadequacy of the internal competition for posting. Bribery and corruption were common when only insiders were qualified to apply for the positions. Thus, open recruitment was to increase competition and combat corruption by allowing outsiders to apply. However, the practice was limited in scope compared to the internal competition for posting. Internal resistance to outsiders taking up senior middle management positions could explain this phenomenon (Chan 2003: 409).

The public notification system required the release of information when an appointment was made in order to increase the openness and transparency of the appointment process. Article 38 of the *2002 Regulations* stipulated that after candidates for any leading positions up to the prefectural level were selected, the results should be posted for public consultation for a period of time. The public notification system was designed to ensure that the selected candidates were truly qualified. There were cases that the public protested against the selected candidates, which resulted in the nullification of the appointment (Burns 2004b: 38).

Through the use of competitive examinations, the government was able to gather more information about the prospective employees, which helped to reduce adverse selection problems. Likewise, the use of competitive promotions enabled the government to gauge a candidate's aptitude for higher-level responsibilities. As will be discussed in Chapter 4, data from the Haidian district indicated that government personnel quality improved in terms of the educational level of civil servants. During the period of 1991–2000, the number of civil servants with higher education (a postgraduate or university degree) increased dramatically from 11.4 percent of all staff to 29.2 percent. The personnel quality of the Ningbo Education Commission also improved. The number of staff with higher education (university degree) increased from 38 to 66, that is, from 50.7 percent to 83.5 percent of all staff. This led to the conclusion that the new competitive entry and promotion reforms were accompanied by improvement in the quality of officials in the cases. More competitive entry and promotion selection processes leading to quality improvements for the civil service clearly served the interests of the public.

Authorities also carried out mass evaluations and performance audits to limit the number of promotions. I would speculate that use of mass evaluations undermined the use of punishments, including dismissals, to control subordinate behavior. From 1996 to 2003, only about 2,000 civil servants were dismissed nationwide each year (Zhang 2006). Because supervisors must go through the mass evaluation process for promotion considerations, their subordinates then became their stakeholders. As a result, supervisors avoided using punishments for fear that their subordinates would retaliate during the mass evaluation and give them a poor review. This would explain why institutionalized punishment practices were not an effective deterrent for suboptimal performance of the subordinates after the implementation of the mass evaluations.

## Monitoring and performance appraisal

Monitoring refers to putting into place various monitoring devices such as reporting routines, supervision and inspection processes. These devices allow supervisors to observe their subordinates' behavior. One of the aims of monitoring is to overcome information asymmetry. Constant monitoring may be effective in reducing agency losses, but it is too costly to implement in reality and it carries the possibility of collusion between subordinates and their monitors (Tirole 1994). Moreover, administrative work is sometimes difficult to monitor. Considering that the mission of a government bureau is often abstract and non-measurable, the task of implementing or enforcing rules for individual bureaucrats is far from simple and easy. Reformers in China sought to improve civil servants' performance through strengthening monitoring mechanisms. Such mechanisms included system-wide surveillance and monitoring systems such as the 'leading cadre responsibility system' and progress reports that outlined the extent to which policy targets set for local governments are fulfilled (Edin 2003; Whiting 2000). Monitoring systems also focused on checking and evaluating individual performance. Civil servants were required to undergo periodic appraisals so that their performance would be monitored.

Unlike the cadre personnel management system that preceded it, the competitive civil service system required annual appraisals of civil servants to evaluate their performance during the reporting period. Under the cadre system, individual performance was formally assessed using politically oriented criteria, not work performance, which resulted in moral hazard. For example, instead of improving the quality of their work, subordinates invested considerable effort in cultivating personal rapport with their superiors in order to gain better performance appraisal results. To counter such problems, the reforms sought to refocus the evaluation on work performance with a stated limit that no more than 15 percent of the members in any work unit could receive the highest ratings. Moreover, the good performers were entitled to a bonus and pay rise. Although the regulations seemed rational, the performance appraisals were conducted in a highly pro forma manner. Almost all employees got similarly high scores in the performance evaluation. Indeed, given the limited opportunities for rewarding good performers, this was rational supervisory behavior. The classification of individual performance was turned from a four-grade system into a de facto two-grade classification: 'outstanding' and 'competent'; thus, over 99 percent of all civil servants were entitled to a bonus and pay rise. Many appraisers refrained from giving an 'incompetent' grade and less than 0.3 percent of the civil servants were rated as 'incompetent'.[2] In addition, linking 'incompetent' grades with demotion decisions were rare and far from institutionalized. In theory, two consecutive 'incompetent' ratings should lead to dismissal. However, since the consequences were so severe, few civil servants actually received unfavorable performance ratings. From 1994 to 2003, approximately only 4,000 civil servants got demotions due to poor performance ratings nationwide (Yin 2003). In my data, most of the civil servants who were assigned incompetent grades were not demoted, but were usually transferred to other positions at the same rank.

Data from the field sites revealed a similar story. In Haidian, if a civil servant was judged to be 'basically competent' at an annual performance appraisal, he received 50 percent of the original annual bonus. Those ranked as 'incompetent' went through a probation period of about six to 12 months and received no bonus. From 1994 to 1998, 34 people in the Haidian district government were ranked as 'basically competent' and 24 as 'incompetent' in annual performance appraisals. Only one person was dismissed because of failing the appraisal. Up to October 1998, no individual lodged an appeal regarding the performance appraisal results (Haidian Personnel Bureau 1998). In Ningbo, only about 0.1 percent of civil servants (numbering 28 and 39 individuals in 1997 and 1998 respectively) were assessed as 'incompetent' in various city government bureaux (Ningbo Personnel Bureau 1999). In Changchun, slightly more civil servants were evaluated as 'incompetent' (0.4 percent in 1995). The Party in Changchun issued special regulations to punish poor performers that resulted in the dismissal of several dozens of officials in subsequent years (1998 and 1999) (Changchun Local History Editorial Committee 2000). In 2000, 14.67 percent of civil servants were assessed as 'outstanding' in the annual performance appraisal and 0.14 percent as 'incompetent'. In 2001, the figures were 14.99 percent 'outstanding' and 0.14 percent 'incompetent' (Changchun Local History Editorial Committee 2001). On the whole, the appraisal system remained largely undiscriminating and ineffective.

## To align the incentives

To reduce the conflict of interests, the incentives between the principal and the agent should be aligned. This may be done through performance-based reward and promotion systems (Milgrom and Roberts 1992). There are successful cases where the incentives of superiors and subordinates are aligned. Civil service training could serve as a motivator for civil servants in China. It is suggested here that promotions in the Chinese hierarchy have been constrained by structural factors and, therefore, could not serve as an instrument for incentive alignment. Reformers sought to improve civil servants' performance by trying to align the incentive systems of the superiors and subordinates in pursuit of official policies. To try to establish a performance-based reward system was one such reform. I would argue that the formal system of performance-based rewards introduced in the reforms was relatively ineffective in aligning the incentives for a variety of reasons. The complicated process of wage reforms will be discussed in the subsequent section.

### *Successful alignment case*

Changchun was a success case where it achieved incentive alignment through the use of performance contracts. In 2001, the city government of Changchun launched an annual exercise to rank all government bureaux according to various performance criteria. Bureau leaders understood that being ranked a 'good' performer was beneficial to the bureau as a whole and to their own career. Bureau leaders of the Changchun Education Commission signed performance contracts with each administrative staff within the bureau. In the contracts, the bureau leadership promised an extra bonus to each staff member if the bureau was able to rank within the top five in the city-wide competition. The bureau chief signed performance contracts with his immediate subordinate division chiefs, who in turned signed contracts with section chiefs.

Targets were specified in the contracts and the contracting parties were held personally responsible for achieving the targets. For example, in his performance contract signed with the bureau chief, the division chief of basic education pledged to increase the number of primary schools that could provide English courses to students. The target in 2003 required 90 percent of the primary schools under the Changchun Education Commission to provide English courses. Over time, the performance targets were adjusted in response to changing circumstances. The 2004 performance contract set the new target at 95 percent. In 2003, the Education Commission ranked third in the city-wide competition and a bonus of RMB1,800 was issued to every employee. The bonus was not financed out of the bureau's budget, but came from the bureau's collective funds, namely, the income of the partially for-profit service units set up by the bureau such as teachers' training schools and publishing houses affiliated to the bureau.[3]

The practice of the Changchun Education Commission provided a good example of credible commitment. The principal first committed herself to a promise of bonuses to induce desirable behavior among agents. The signing of the performance contracts made the agents believe that the commitment from the principal was credible. During interviews, officials revealed that they believed that the rewards would follow their conscious efforts to work. Credible leadership led to hard work in this case. Whether the system I found in Changchun could continue to be effective would depend on the commitment of the local officials to provide bonuses. Budget deficits and the removal of 'extra-budgetary' income were significant risks to the operation of such a system.

## *Promotion is constrained*

Performance-based reward and promotion systems can provide key incentives for employees to work hard (Milgrom and Roberts 1992). China's civil service reforms attempted to align the incentives between the superiors and subordinates, but faced several structural problems. First, nearly 60 percent of civil servants were employed at the county and the township level where promotion opportunities were rare (see Table 2.1). The typical career ladder in a county, for example, where most officials would expect to spend their entire career, included only five ranks (section member, deputy section head, section head, deputy county head and county head), which were far too few to sustain motivation. Second, although there were six to 14 pay steps for each rank, the difference in base pay between each rank was very minimal, usually around a few tens of *yuan* per month (see Table 3.4). That is, the formal career ladder in the local civil service where most government officials were employed was extremely compressed and with minimal base pay differences. Within such a system, supervisors found it difficult to encourage compliance from their employees. Given the structural problems and a weak evaluation system, it should come as no surprise that implementing a performance-based reward or promotion system was especially difficult in China. I found that although pay levels had increased overall in line with the official policy, civil servants did not perceive that their pay was linked to performance. As will be discussed in Chapter 4, most officials (65 percent) in the environmental protection domain and officials in Changchun (73 percent) thought that their pay was not properly linked with their work performance.

## *Training as a motivator*

Civil service training programs included pre-service training for new recruits, pre-promotional qualification training, knowledge update training and other types of professional continuous education. According to Article 61 of the *Civil Service Law*, all newly recruited civil servants must go through pre-post training during their probation. The induction training would last for a minimum of ten days. Passing the induction training was mandatory. Once on the job, civil servants were required to take regular training courses. Course content ranged from dissemination of government documents, new information technology and management skills to new procedures relating to the profession. All civil servants were supposed to receive a three-month refresher training program every five years to update their knowledge and skills related to administrative work. Training was also an important part of the cadre system. However, the emphases of the two systems were different. The training programs of the cadre system focused mostly on teaching Marxist political ideology and fostering loyalty to the Party. Party Schools at the national and local levels provided education and training for both party and government cadres. The government recognized that updating the skills and knowledge of the civil service was an essential task in modernizing the service. To implement the new civil service system, the authority established the National School of Administration in 1994, a key education and training institution for senior civil servants. Provincial and local administration schools were also established or converted from party schools to train and educate middle-level civil servants in their respective jurisdictions. While these schools continued to teach political ideology, they also sought to provide civil servants with the knowledge and training they would need to manage the government (Tong *et al.* 1999). The training programs of various administration schools emphasized professional and technical courses on economy, political and legal systems of other countries, finance and trade regulation and general development of science and technology.[4]

Civil service training served as a motivator for civil servants in China. In general, it was considered an honor and prestige to be selected for a training program from all members of a government organization. This was particularly

52  *Reform policy and implementation*

the case for students of the Central Party School. Civil servants, who were about to take a course at the Central Party School, were probably in line for a promotion. Therefore, training was considered as a professional net plus, rather than a bureaucratic burden. Civil servants in China took the training seriously and regarded the training institutions and programs as good places to develop work connections (Shambaugh 2008b: 839). In other words, the training experience not only helped civil servants to update their knowledge, but also provided ample opportunities for them to enlarge their social networks. The provision of civil service training was comprehensive and to some extent effective. From 1998 to 2002, about 10,810,000 places of these training programs were filled nationwide with some civil servants enrolling into multiple programs. From 1999 to 2002, 356,000 civil servants took the induction training; 189,000 civil servants took the pre-promotion training; 2,860,000 civil servants received continuous professional training and 3,240,000 civil servants took the knowledge update training (Yin 2003). In recent times, China also began to send more and more senior civil servants and other leading cadres for overseas training in renowned universities. However, researchers found that many civil service training programs involved overseas excursions and lavish spending, thus raising public concern over the efficiency and effectiveness of these training programs (Chou 2009, 2008).

## Wage reform

Wage reforms are an important component of the civil service reform in China. These reforms were policy responses to several major problems such as government budget deficits, large share of the wage bills in government expenditure and an overstaffed and disincentivized bureaucracy (Cheung and Poon 2001; Chew 1990a, 1990b). This section will first examine the reform patterns since the 1950s. The basic features of the current wage system, which was adopted in 2006, will then be outlined. The section concludes by evaluating the policy outcomes of the wage reform.

### *The 1956 system*

A 'grade (*jibie*) wage system' was established in 1956 after the Soviet model. For the first time, the CCP adopted a policy of rewarding cadres with monetary benefits (Chew 1990a). In the context of a centrally planned economy, the system was universally applied to the entire public sector, which encompassed the huge cadre corps in the government, the CCP, the military, state-owned enterprises, public service units and other mass and social organizations. Under the system, the state assigned manpower to work units at various levels. Wages, pensions, medical insurance and other benefits were determined by the state according to a single standard. Housing, transportation and even children's education were taken care of by the unit to which the cadre was affiliated. The 1956 system resembled a rank-in-person classification system, which meant that employees did not lose their rank even if they switched to a less important position, unless the switch was the result of disciplinary action (Chew 1990a). Wages, pensions and other benefits were all based on rank. Take the monthly salary as an example. It was determined by one's grade or rank. Each office holder was assigned to one of the 30 grades in the administrative hierarchy. At that time, the Chinese bureaucracy was run by many veteran revolutionaries who got promoted to their rank based on their contribution to the revolution, but not on how they performed as administrators after the revolution. One's monthly salary was separated from the nature of job responsibilities and actual work performance.

The fact that staff members who worked in jobs with different levels of difficulty and responsibility received similar rewards was inconsistent with the principle of distribution according to work (*anlao fenpei*). When individuals working at significantly different levels of difficulty and responsibility are paid the same, it is only natural that those in the more demanding posts would resent the inequality and adjust their effort downwards. Besides impairing the incentive structure, the 1956 wage system also led to grade inflation and an oversized cadre bureaucracy, which translated into serious budget deficits. Because salaries and pensions were based on rank, many cadres postponed retirement to improve their retirement benefits. A life-tenure system and the reluctance to retire contributed to an aging bureaucracy.

## *The 1985 system*

To follow the principle that people should be remunerated according to their work, China reformed the wage system and established the 'structural wage system' in 1985. The system only applied to cadres in the government and party organs and public service units; thus separating the wage system for the state-owned enterprises from the cadre corps. The 'structural wages' included post pay, basic salary, seniority pay and bonus. The post pay was based upon the responsibilities of a position and skills that the position required. Each post, along the promotion ladder for cadres, had its own range of salary points (six to ten). On top of his post pay, an employee in a given position would advance to a higher point with seniority and satisfactory performance. In the government's perspective, the post pay was meant to reflect the nature of the work and responsibility associated with the specific assignment. The post-pay component of the structural pay system embodied the principle of work-based remuneration and accounted for the largest portion of the total pay (Chew 1990b). The basic salary ensured a basic living standard for all cadres while the seniority pay reflected a cadre's length of service. Bonus was to be allocated on the basis of job achievement. This additional income was issued once every year upon satisfactory completion of the annual appraisal and by convention, equivalent to what one received for his or her monthly salary in December.

Compared with the 1956 system, the 'structural wage system' downgraded the role of the 'grade' and focused more on one's position in determining the

54  *Reform policy and implementation*

monthly salary. This time, the wage system was comparable to a rank-in-position classification system. The post pay became the major component in the total pay. Because the basic salary and seniority pay tended to be equally distributed between colleagues and what one would receive for bonus tended to be hard to predict, wage differentials thus were mainly derived from differences in the post pay.

Official reports acknowledged that the 1985 system's emphasis on skills, job positions and achievements were not taken into account by the previous wage system (Cheung and Poon 2001). The introduction of the post pay was a good addition for leading position holders while for the rank-and-file cadres (on or below section chief levels), their post pay did not differ significantly. Under the system, employees received their pay increase through promotions. However, given the considerable size of the rank-and-file cadres and the limited opportunities for promotion up the career ladder, this system actually demoralized them. In addition, while bonuses were distributed, they were distributed equally so that the same amount was granted to all the staff of the same government organization. Such an egalitarian wage distribution inevitably bred disincentives to work.

## *The 1993 system*

The promulgation of the *1993 Provisional Regulations* marked a new round of wage reforms. A 'post and grade wage system' was established. The wage reform of 1993 sought to rationalize the wage system by three measures. First, it separated the wage system for public service unit staff from that for the cadres in government bureaux, party organs and mass organizations. Public service units were encouraged or even ordered in some cases to become financially independent through marketizing their services and products since the economic reforms in 1980s.[5]

Second, the government adopted several new principles for civil service pay to accommodate the transition to a market economy. Determined to a large extent by the market, the pay and rewards for the staff of state-owned enterprises increased in the 1980s and 1990s when the economic reform yielded positive results. This signaled a relative decline in the status and income for the civil service. Remedial measures were adopted to not only balance the pay for civil servants and the employees of state-owned enterprises, but also link wages with consumption costs and ensure regular wage rises.

Third, 1993 reform reincorporated the grade pay in order to provide additional motivation for civil servants. The wage system comprised of five elements: basic salary, post pay, grade pay, seniority pay and bonus. Civil servants were ranked on a 12-position, 15-grade scale from 1993 (see Table 2.6). The post pay in 2004 was determined on a scale of six to 14 salary points. There were 15 levels under the grade pay with the amount for each grade held fixed. The rest of the wage component was inherited from the 1985 structural wage system with some modifications. Under this system, civil servants could enjoy a one-point wage rise under the post-pay component every two years as long as they passed an annual evaluation test. Those who were rated 'outstanding' for three consecutive years or 'competent' for five consecutive years were entitled to move up one level in grade pay.

As the official documents claimed, the reformers paid particular attention to the rank-and-file cadres. Positions at the bottom of the career ladder could enjoy a larger wage increase according to grade level and post-pay scales than the top positions. Scholars found that wage differentials for top positions were smaller than those of the lower-level positions (Cheung and Poon 2001). In designing this, the reformers had hoped that lower-level administrative staff would become more motivated to work hard and compete for the pay rise even without a job/post promotion. In practice, the grade pay did not provide adequate motivation for the civil servants. On one hand, there were only 15 grades. On the other hand, promotion from one grade to the next grade up represented a raise of less than one hundred *yuan* and this amount was not enough to serve as a real motivator.

The wage system evolved from a universal system for the entire cadre corps to a diversified structure of management by category. As discussed in Chapter 2, the huge cadre corps included cadres in the government, the CCP, the military, state-owned enterprises, public service units and mass and social organizations. Staff wages for state-owned enterprises underwent independent review in 1985. Independent wage reviews were extended to public service units such as hospitals, schools and research institutes in 1993. In retrospect, the wage system of the government was moving away from a purely rank-in-person system in the 1950s towards a mixed design with characteristics of both the rank-in-person system and the rank-in-position system. This trend towards a combined design was increasingly discernible throughout the subsequent decades and was further confirmed by the 2006 reforms.

## *The 2006 system*

In the middle of 2006, another round of wage system reforms was launched after the *Civil Service Law* came into effect at the beginning of the same year. Under this system, a typical compensation package for civil servants included both a visible and an invisible component. The visible part was mainly the base income, which constituted a small part of the whole remuneration while the invisible part included allowances, subsidies and bonuses. Specifically, the visible part was the part of the salary that was determined by a standard wage system applied to the entire civil service of the country while the invisible part referred to the remainder of the salary that was made up of subsidies, allowances and other staff benefits, which were separately determined by locally maintained and arbitrary wage systems and, hence, remained 'invisible' to outsiders.[6] For example, among the interviewees of this study, an environmental official of Changchun did not know how many kinds of fringe benefits an environmental official in Ningbo would enjoy. As for the base income, the 2006 reforms dropped the components of the basic salary and seniority pay, which existed in the prior systems since they constituted a very small part of the whole remuneration. Therefore, the base income of the 2006 system was comprised of two main elements: the post pay and the grade pay. The official policy also claimed that the seniority element was to be carried by the grade pay in the 2006 system ('*2006 gongwuyuan gongzi gaige ziliao daquan*' (Collection of materials on 2006 civil service wage reform)).

The new wage system operated under a new post and grade structure (see Table 3.2). Under a new classification of government posts, the post pay only had a single salary point for each post level while previous systems included several salary points for posts at the same level (see Table 3.3, which illustrates the post pay for both leading and non-leading positions). A degree of variation across government employees of the same post level was maintained through the grade pay of the base income. The aim of the 2006 wage reform was to strengthen the motivating factor of the grade pay. The new system not only expanded the number of grade levels from 15 to 27, but also introduced six to 14 sub-steps (*dangci*) into each grade level (see Table 3.4). Under the 2006 wage system, each post corresponded with a specific range of wage grades that served as increments added to the overall base income for any civil servants achieving satisfactory performance in year-end appraisals. In terms of the post and grade structure, each administrative position corresponded to a number of grades. For example, a division head would belong to grades 12 to 18 in a scale of 27 grades. Each grade would be further broken into six to 14 sub-steps. A salary increase (besides promotion), could be achieved either through moving to a higher grade that corresponded to a given position or through moving upward a sub-step within a given grade.

A civil servant could advance along the grade pay scale with seniority and satisfactory performance. On average, a civil servant could enjoy a one-level grade pay rise every five years as long as she passed an annual evaluation test. Every two years, a civil servant could get a one sub-step grade pay rise within her grade level if she were rated 'outstanding' or 'competent' in the annual performance appraisal. Bonus allocation also depended on the results of the annual performance appraisals. This new arrangement introduced greater variation in income across individual civil servants, which translated to an expanded pay scale with real, though small, wage differences for civil servants occupying different positions on the career track.

As for the invisible pay (an unreported hidden part of the remuneration), the PRC, beginning in the 1950s, established a system to provide allowances and subsidies to government officials (Burns 2003b). Depending on the job nature and where the civil servant was based, the civil servant was eligible for regional allowances, hardship allowances and position allowances. Regional allowances were issued to those who worked in areas of higher living costs, typically in the metropolitan areas along the coast. Because the cost of living varied substantially throughout the country, regional subsidies varied accordingly as well. Regional subsidies were paid equally to all civil servants regardless of the rank. Hardship allowances were created for government officials who worked in

Table 3.2 Chinese civil service position and grade structure

| Rank (zhiwu) | Grade range | Grades |
|---|---|---|
|  |  | 1 2 3 4 5 6 7 8 9 10 11 12 13 14 15 16 17 18 19 20 21 22 23 24 25 26 27 |
| State-level head positions | 1 | ✓ |
| State-level deputy positions | 2–4 | ✓ ✓ ✓ |
| Provincial-level head positions | 4–8 | ✓ ✓ ✓ ✓ ✓ |
| Provincial-level deputy positions | 6–10 | ✓ ✓ ✓ ✓ ✓ |
| Bureau/department-level head positions | 8–13 | ✓ ✓ ✓ ✓ ✓ ✓ |
| Bureau/department-level deputy positions | 10–15 | ✓ ✓ ✓ ✓ ✓ ✓ |
| Division/county-level head positions | 12–18 | ✓ ✓ ✓ ✓ ✓ ✓ ✓ |
| Division/county-level deputy positions | 14–20 | ✓ ✓ ✓ ✓ ✓ ✓ ✓ |
| Section/township-level head positions | 16–23 | ✓ ✓ ✓ ✓ ✓ ✓ ✓ ✓ |
| Section/township-level deputy positions | 17–24 | ✓ ✓ ✓ ✓ ✓ ✓ ✓ ✓ |
| Section member | 18–26 | ✓ ✓ ✓ ✓ ✓ ✓ ✓ ✓ ✓ |
| Office clerk | 19–27 | ✓ ✓ ✓ ✓ ✓ ✓ ✓ ✓ ✓ |

Source: '*2006 gongwuyuan gongzi gaige ziliao daquan*' (Collection of materials on 2006 civil service wage reform).

*Table 3.3* Composition of 2006 wage system (responsibility wages) (*zhiwu gongzi*)

| Rank (*zhiwu*) | Grade | Wage of leading position (*lingdao zhiwu* (yuan)) | Wage of non-leading positions (*fei lingdao zhiwu* (yuan)) |
|---|---|---|---|
| State-level head positions | 1 | 4,000 | – |
| State-level deputy positions | 2–4 | 3,200 | – |
| Provincial-level head positions | 4–8 | 2,510 | – |
| Provincial-level deputy positions | 6–10 | 1,900 | – |
| Bureau/department-level head positions | 8–13 | 1,410 | 1,290 |
| Bureau/department-level deputy positions | 10–15 | 1,080 | 990 |
| Division/county-level head positions | 12–18 | 830 | 760 |
| Division/county-level deputy positions | 14–20 | 640 | 590 |
| Section/township-level head positions | 16–23 | 510 | 480 |
| Section/township-level deputy positions | 17–24 | 430 | 410 |
| Section member | 18–26 | – | 380 |
| Office clerk | 19–27 | – | 340 |

Source: '*2006 gongwuyuan gongzi gaige ziliao daquan*' (Collection of materials on 2006 civil service wage reform).

Table 3.4 Composition of 2006 wage system (grade wages (yuan))

| Grade (Jibie) | Sub-grade (Dangci) | | | | | | | | | | | | | |
|---|---|---|---|---|---|---|---|---|---|---|---|---|---|---|
| | 1 | 2 | 3 | 4 | 5 | 6 | 7 | 8 | 9 | 10 | 11 | 12 | 13 | 14 |
| 1 | 3,020 | 3,180 | 3,340 | 3,500 | 3,660 | 3,820 | – | – | – | – | – | – | – | – |
| 2 | 2,770 | 2,915 | 3,060 | 3,205 | 3,350 | 3,495 | 3,640 | – | – | – | – | – | – | – |
| 3 | 2,530 | 2,670 | 2,810 | 2,950 | 3,090 | 3,230 | 3,370 | – | – | – | – | – | – | – |
| 4 | 2,290 | 2,426 | 2,562 | 2,698 | 2,834 | 2,970 | 3,106 | 3,510 | – | – | – | – | – | – |
| 5 | 2,070 | 2,202 | 2,334 | 2,466 | 2,598 | 2,730 | 2,862 | 3,242 | 3,378 | – | – | – | – | – |
| 6 | 1,870 | 1,996 | 2,122 | 2,248 | 2,374 | 2,500 | 2,626 | 2,994 | 3,126 | 3,258 | – | – | – | – |
| 7 | 1,700 | 1,818 | 1,936 | 2,054 | 2,172 | 2,290 | 2,408 | 2,752 | 2,878 | 3,004 | 3,130 | – | – | – |
| 8 | 1,560 | 1,669 | 1,778 | 1,887 | 1,996 | 2,105 | 2,214 | 2,526 | 2,644 | 2,762 | 2,880 | – | – | – |
| 9 | 1,438 | 1,538 | 1,638 | 1,738 | 1,838 | 1,938 | 2,038 | 2,323 | 2,432 | 2,541 | 2,650 | – | – | – |
| 10 | 1,324 | 1,416 | 1,508 | 1,600 | 1,692 | 1,784 | 1,876 | 2,138 | 2,238 | 2,338 | 2,438 | – | – | – |
| 11 | 1,217 | 1,302 | 1,387 | 1,472 | 1,557 | 1,642 | 1,727 | 1,968 | 2,060 | 2,152 | 2,244 | 2,152 | – | – |
| 12 | 1,117 | 1,196 | 1,275 | 1,354 | 1,433 | 1,512 | 1,591 | 1,812 | 1,897 | 1,982 | 2,067 | 1,986 | 2,065 | – |
| 13 | 1,024 | 1,098 | 1,172 | 1,246 | 1,320 | 1,394 | 1,468 | 1,670 | 1,749 | 1,828 | 1,907 | 1,838 | 1,912 | 1,986 |
| 14 | 938 | 1,007 | 1,076 | 1,145 | 1,214 | 1,283 | 1,352 | 1,542 | 1,616 | 1,690 | 1,764 | 1,697 | 1,766 | 1,835 |
| 15 | 859 | 924 | 989 | 1,054 | 1,119 | 1,184 | 1,249 | 1,421 | 1,490 | 1,559 | 1,628 | 1,574 | 1,639 | 1,704 |
| 16 | 786 | 847 | 908 | 969 | 1,030 | 1,091 | 1,152 | 1,314 | 1,379 | 1,444 | 1,509 | 1,457 | 1,518 | 1,579 |
| 17 | 719 | 776 | 833 | 890 | 947 | 1,004 | 1,061 | 1,213 | 1,274 | 1,335 | 1,396 | 1,346 | 1,403 | – |
| 18 | 658 | 711 | 764 | 817 | 870 | 923 | 976 | 1,118 | 1,175 | 1,232 | 1,289 | 1,241 | 1,294 | – |
| 19 | 502 | 651 | 700 | 749 | 798 | 847 | 896 | 1,029 | 1,082 | 1,135 | 1,188 | 1,141 | – | – |
| 20 | 551 | 596 | 641 | 686 | 731 | 776 | 821 | 945 | 994 | 1,043 | 1,092 | – | – | – |
| 21 | 504 | 545 | 586 | 627 | 668 | 709 | 750 | 866 | 911 | 956 | 1,001 | – | – | – |
| 22 | 461 | 498 | 535 | 572 | 609 | 646 | 683 | 791 | 832 | 873 | – | – | – | – |
| 23 | 422 | 455 | 488 | 521 | 554 | 587 | 620 | 720 | 757 | – | – | – | – | – |
| 24 | 386 | 416 | 446 | 476 | 506 | 536 | 566 | 653 | – | – | – | – | – | – |
| 25 | 352 | 380 | 408 | 436 | 464 | 492 | 520 | 596 | – | – | – | – | – | – |
| 26 | 320 | 347 | 374 | 401 | 428 | 455 | – | – | – | – | – | – | – | – |
| 27 | 290 | 316 | 342 | 368 | 34 | 420 | – | – | – | – | – | – | – | – |

Source: '2006 gongwuyuan gongzi gaige ziliao daquan' (Collection of materials on 2006 civil service wage reform).

remote and poor provinces and locations. Position allowances were targeted for assignments that involved special skills or danger. For example, government employees who worked in public security (the police, courts and the procuratorate), auditing and customs were eligible for position allowance. There were also subsidies for medical and housing expenses. Besides all the monetary remuneration on the payroll, most civil servants today continued to enjoy these privileges such as buying discounted apartments, almost-free medical care and office cars for personal purposes (Zhu 1998: 148).

There were cases of financial mismanagement where public funds were used to provide additional/illegal subsidies for civil servants (Chou 2009: 101). The situation was particularly serious in economically developed areas. Given the relatively high cost of living in these areas, the standard levels of pay were insufficient to afford the kind of comfortable, middle-class lifestyle that most civil servants expected to lead. Civil servants looked for additional sources of income as a result. The ability of some civil servants to supplement income this way depended in large part on the availability of local revenue, mostly from fees and charges levied for routine transactions and services (Wedeman 2000). To attract and maintain the talented, local governments with large tax revenues chose to set aside public monies in order to provide further remuneration for their employees. The financial discretion was therefore exploited by these local governments. One of the objectives of 2006 wage reform was to eliminate the malpractices of local governments of providing additional subsidies for their employees by public funds. The 2006 wage reforms policy stipulated that departments responsible for staff discipline inspection, organization, supervision, personnel management, auditing and financial affairs should take the initiative to eliminate malpractices in the implementation of the wage reforms ('*2006 gongwuyuan gongzi gaige ziliao daquan*' (Collection of materials on 2006 civil service wage reform)).

## *The evaluation*

There were discrepancies between the policy objectives and the real outcomes of the wage reforms. First, increasing job motivation was one of the reform objectives. Before 1985, cadres of the same rank received the same salary irrespective of their responsibilities and work performance. The 1985 wage reform introduced the post pay under the principle of distribution according to work. It also introduced a merit bonus. The 1993 wage reform reincorporated the grade pay in order to provide additional motivation for the rank-and-file civil servants whose opportunities to get promoted were limited. The 2006 wage reform not only expanded the number of grade levels from 15 to 27, but also introduced six to 14 sub-steps into each grade level. Though the reform policies tried to inject more motivating factors into the wage system, the actual monthly salary differentials were too small to motivate the civil servants. The reform created a structure for promotion along the grade-pay scale and post-pay scale based on performance. As the discussion on performance appraisal suggested, the absence of an effective scheme to meaningfully distinguish civil servants according to job performance undermined the impact of the wage reforms in this regard.

Scholars concluded that the wage reforms failed to increase job motivation for the civil servants because the wage differentials between the top and bottom ranks were insignificant (Cheung and Poon 2001). My findings were in general agreement with this conclusion. However, I would argue that by just comparing changes in the base income is not enough. Before examining the extent of the success of the wage reforms in this regard, we have to make it clear whether the base income itself could serve as an effective job motivator. Among the many job motivators for a civil servant in China, the base income was not the most effective one. It is safe to say that for top and middle rank civil servants, income was only a relatively small part of the actual overall benefits that their official positions provided. The fringe benefits, which came in the form of various allowances and subsidies as well as the use of official residences, transport services and many other privileges that were provided by the government were the more significant and hidden part of the overall pay that served as the real motivator for most middle rank civil servants.[7] For the rank-and-file civil servants, the introduction of post and grade pay differentials had a positive, if limited, impact on their job motivation.

Second, the wage system reforms aimed to (1) make the civil service salaries comparable to the private sector, (2) link government salaries with inflation and (3) institutionalize regular pay rises. The *Civil Service Law* stipulated 'that the state shall systematically raise the salary scales of civil servants in accordance with the nation's economic development and increases in the cost of living and price indexes, so that a civil servant's real salary level continually rises' (Article 75). Besides ensuring that official salaries would keep up with the inflation, Article 75 also stated that the salary levels for civil servants 'shall be commensurate with an employee of a state-owned enterprise holding an equivalent position'. This part of the reforms was relatively successful. A mechanism of regular pay increase was installed. After the 1993 wage reforms, civil service pay rose across the country in July 1997, July 1999, January and October of 2001 and July 2003. Only in 2001, civil service pay was raised twice by a total of 30 percent while the economy was in deflation and unemployment was on the rise (Hou 2007: 232). The wage reforms in part made a career in the civil service more attractive. Given the status and income for civil servants in contemporary China, government recruitment was highly competitive.

Third, besides the monthly salary, Chinese civil servants enjoyed a large range of allowances, subsidies and other benefits. To catch up with the wage increase in the state-owned enterprises and the rising living cost, the informal wage elements (various subsidies and allowances) were enlarged by drastic measure in the 1980s, thus reducing the share of the base income within the total pay received by a civil servant. The informal wage elements were distributed in equal shares to all workers in the same government unit. One of the objectives of the wage reforms was to eliminate this egalitarian approach in the distribution of fringe benefits (bonuses, subsidies and allowances) within one government unit. However, this part of the reforms was not successful.

62  *Reform policy and implementation*

Fourth, the amount of subsidies varied substantially within the same local government. Civil servants in 'administrative agencies' (where no product was either sold on the market or delivered to the public) were paid poorly. Some bureaux with excellent revenue-generating ability dispensed subsidies multiple times more than these 'administrative agencies'. As a result, there was a high degree of disparity between the take-home incomes for civil servants of the same rank, or who performed similar duties, in the different functional departments of local governments (Gong 2006; Wedeman 2000). The formal authority to increase civil servants' salary rested with the central government according to Article 78 of the *Civil Service Law*. In practice, the authority to allocate hidden subsidies was decentralized to local governments and its subordinate departments. Effective system-wide oversight was absent. Much of the subsidies were paid out of departments' secret bank accounts (*xiao jinku*) used for hiding any illicit income away from the finance and audit bureaux. Though the 2006 wage reform aimed to stop the abuse of public funds for civil servants' subsidies, this part of the reform was not successful.

Fifth, the central government permitted local governments to adjust subsidies according to regional variations in economic development since 1993. These subsidies were decided by the local authorities and financed out of the local coffers. This generated regional inequalities among different localities, exacerbating the disparity between coastal and inland provinces and between rural and urban areas. The regional inequalities in the implementation of the wage reforms became an issue about local governments' financial autonomy and capability. It was found that unofficial revenues of various kinds tended to be disproportionately devoted to administrative expenditures such as salary supplements in local governments (Wedeman 2000: 501–3). All these salary supplements were financed by the local extra-budgetary funds, which were officially sanctioned sources of revenue (such as various fees and charges) that were not recorded in the consolidated state budget, but accounted for in special budgets and accounts. Scholars reported that extra-budgetary funds in China comprised a very significant proportion of the local government revenue. In particular, in 1995 extra-budgetary funds were estimated to be equivalent to 26 percent of total local government spending (Wedeman 2000: 500–3). Substantial pay rises were largely limited to affluent regions. Many lower-level governments in less developed regions were not financially secure enough to follow suit. These regions faced a long-standing brain drain problem owing to low salaries and poor working conditions. The central policy was to abate the regional inequalities. However, given that the availability of a local subsidy was contingent on the economic conditions of the respective local government, it contributed to unevenness in civil servant income across regions. The wage reforms failed to put an end to the income inequality. Table 3.5 suggests the total wage bill of various provinces and the average year salary of officials in 2007. As for the yearly salary, the average level for the whole country was 28,171 *yuan*. Officials in Beijing received the highest yearly salary, followed by Tibet, Zhejiang and Shanghai. It is well known that civil servants in metropolises like Shanghai and

*Reform policy and implementation* 63

*Table 3.5* Wage bill and average year wage in various provinces, 2007

| Province | Officials | Total wage bill for officials (1,000 yuan) | Average year wage (yuan) |
| --- | --- | --- | --- |
| China | 12,496,572 | 352,043,847 | 28,171 |
| Beijing | 295,564 | 16,614,328 | 56,212 |
| Tibet | 65,761 | 3,499,985 | 53,223 |
| Zhejiang | 481,563 | 25,601,561 | 53,163 |
| Shanghai | 166,347 | 8,447,442 | 50,782 |
| Jiangxi | 368,177 | 7,301,595 | 19,832 |
| Shanxi | 447,129 | 8,900,478 | 19,906 |
| Shaanxi | 408,933 | 8,229,962 | 20,125 |
| Hebei | 719,000 | 14,549,379 | 20,236 |

Source: National Bureau of Statistics (2009: 167–70).

Beijing and coastal provinces like Guangdong received much more subsidies. The official reason given to justify the high level of subsidies was the high standard of living in these places. Civil servants working in Tibet and Xinjiang were also given hardship allowances for the harsh natural environment and geographic remoteness. Poor regions where officials received the lowest yearly salary included Jiangxi, Shanxi, Shaanxi and Hebei. The highest yearly salary (56,212 *yuan*) was almost three times the lowest one (19,832 *yuan*). These statistics illustrated the wage inequality of officials among various provinces. Important issues such as local GDP performance, fiscal revenues, price levels and geographic conditions all served as influencing factors for the wage inequality.

## Discipline policy

As for the incentive alignment measures, formal policy instruments such as pay and promotion did not serve as the motivators for the rank-and-file civil servants. Ironically, real motivation came from the informal incentive alignment measures: superiors and their subordinates collaborate in illicit activities such as the buying and selling of government posts. In other words, the official policy to match the incentives of principal and agents in China's civil service reform failed while the informal or illegal motivators successfully aligned the incentives of corrupt superiors and their subordinates. This indicated a failed implementation of the disciplinary policy in the civil service reforms.

When the incentives were aligned between the supervisors and subordinates in pursuit of official policy goals, less monitoring and sanctioning mechanisms were needed. As the discussion of wage reforms suggested, the formal system of performance-based rewards introduced in the reforms was relatively ineffective for a variety of reasons. Paradoxically, corruption opportunities encouraged a perverse incentive alignment that allowed networks of superiors and subordinates to pursue their own private goals at the expense of the public. Relatively large numbers of official positions, mostly at district and county levels, were filled through corrupt practices. In particular, many superiors and their subordinates were involved in the buying and selling of government posts (Gong 2009, 2008, 2006, 1994; Lu 2000; Manion 2004; Sun 2009, 2004). In the late 1990s, officials sold scores of government jobs in Wenzhou city (Zhejiang), Pizhou county (Jiangsu), Beihai city (Guangxi), Huaibei city (Anhui), Tieling city (Liaoning), Guanfeng county (Jiangxi) and in Heilongjiang province.[8] Even central and provincial-level leaders sold government posts. They included former National People's Congress Vice Chairman Cheng Kejie, executed in 2000 for corruption, who was convicted of selling government posts.[9] In June 2004, the former head of the Jiangsu provincial CCP Organization Department was dismissed for soliciting 100 million *yuan* in bribes from lower-ranking officials seeking promotion.[10] Given the centralized nature of personnel decision-making in China and that the evidence that senior officials in such sensitive positions were able to sell government posts, the practice was likely to be widespread throughout the Jiangsu province. The former governor of Hubei province, Zhang Guoguang, was convicted in December 2004 of accepting more than 300,000 *yuan* for helping individuals to get promoted when he was party secretary of Shenyang. Zhang was caught when the corruption of 62 senior officials in Liaoning province was made public. Those caught in Shenyang also included the mayor, the top judge, the senior prosecutor and the tax bureau chief. In November 2004, a district head in Sichuan's Nanchong city was dismissed for selling 61 departmental posts between 1999 and 2003. In March 2005, the former party secretary of Heilongjiang's Suihua city went on trial for accepting bribes from 18 people between 1992 and 2002 in securing their promotions. In this particular case, 260 officials were caught. In May 2005, the party secretary in charge of the personnel in Guangdong's Heyuan city was convicted of selling posts from 1992 to 2003.[11] In these cases, corrupted superiors sought not only to enrich themselves through collecting bribes, but also to gain additional information in the selection process about a candidate's intentions: were they willing to collude with corruption?

Sun (2004: 146) suggested that the sale of government posts was particularly prevalent in poor areas where alternative income sources were scarce. This might be the characterization of the 1990s, but more recent data indicated that opportunity to do so might also play a significant role (Guo 2008). I identified certain functions which, when they are carried out, could provide civil servants with opportunities to collect rents from the public and, thus, enable the civil servants to pay for their positions. These functions could be classified as 'wet' functions (see Table 3.6). Civil servants know that in these positions they will be able to obtain a return on their investment in purchasing an office, the price of which I speculate varies depending on the income-earning power of the position, bid up perhaps by the increasing competition of the civil service reforms. Press reports indicated that a junior position in a city-level planning and resource bureau in Liaoning in 2005 would cost from 30,000 to 50,000 *yuan*.[12] As Sun (2004) pointed out, if top leaders were to engage in these activities, they would

*Table 3.6* 'Wet' functions

| 'Wet' function | Channels to make extra money |
| --- | --- |
| Administration | Procurement |
| Banks | Loans |
| Communications/transport | Licenses |
| Construction | Approvals |
| Customs | Import tariffs |
| Drugs | Approvals |
| Education | Inspections; textbook approvals |
| Environmental protection | Inspections; levying fines |
| Forestry | Forestry sales |
| Industry and commerce | Inspections; licensing |
| Labor safety (mines) | Inspections; levying fines |
| Land and natural resources | Zoning approvals |
| Personnel/organization | Promotions |
| Planning | Land use; investment approvals |
| Population control | Birth certificate |
| Press and publications | Licensing; approvals |
| Public security/judiciary/people's armed police/courts | Fines; investigation |
| Securities regulation | Listings; discipline |
| Social security/pensions | Investments |
| Tax | Fines |

Source: Author's database.

use more rigorous selection policies in order to obtain information about the candidate's willingness to engage in corrupt practices. In this kind of environment, a more competitive civil service might actually be used to drive up the price of each post, making corruption even worse.

I would argue that the efforts to impose tighter monitoring and discipline on civil servants were relatively ineffective. The official performance-based reward system did little to properly align the incentive systems of the superiors and subordinates in pursuit of official policy goals while corrupt practices encouraged a kind of perverse incentive alignment at the expense of the public. As the above analysis suggested, effective institutions to control the sale of government posts were apparently weak. The widespread and endemic nature of corruption in China indicated the weakness of the civil service reforms as a monitoring and supervisory system. As will be discussed in Chapter 4, officials in the field sites of this study were also corrupt. In this regard, the experience of officials in the field sites was apparently not atypical.

The possibility of prosecuting the offender in China was very low. From 1993 to 1998, fewer than half of the corruption cases investigated led to criminal charges and only 6.6 percent of these led to the sentencing of the corrupt officials (Hu 2001). Given the low probability of prosecution, engaging in corrupt practices appeared to be a relatively low risk activity. Rational actors, witnessing that their peers were enriching themselves with relative impunity, would be encouraged to do the same. In agencies where 'wet' functions predominated such as those issuing licenses (to trade, for land development, and so forth) or regulatory agencies (such as customs, securities, drugs approval and personnel), I would speculate that new inductees learned through imitation that corruption was acceptable behavior. Informal norms that condoned corrupt behavior perpetuated these behaviors. Implementation of China's civil service reforms, paradoxically, had gone hand in hand with the mushrooming of official corruption. The reforms clearly failed to put in place effective monitoring and sanctioning mechanisms to curb this kind of behavior.

While supervisors sought to maintain a good working relationship with their subordinates, they could also abuse this relationship and collude with their subordinates to carry out corrupt activities. I identified various 'wet' functions that, because of institutional failures, enabled candidates to reap certain monetary benefits after they bought their way into their position. Therefore, the informal perverse system of aligning incentives in the pursuit of private goals succeeded, rendering the formal civil service reforms regrettably ineffective.

# 4 Local implementation of civil service reforms

Decentralization is a common characteristic of many policy areas in China including the public personnel management. The Chinese leadership is responsible for setting out the general personnel management reform framework through the CCP Central Committee and its Organization Department, State Council, the Ministry of Personnel and other relevant ministries. Provincial and subprovincial governments are not only charged with the responsibility to adapt the framework to local realities, but also to design and implement the concrete programs. In other words, the central government only provides general policy guidelines and leaves the local governments a great deal of autonomy during the implementation process. This autonomy allows local governments to implement policies using their own interpretation of the general guidelines in order to address local, rather than national, needs. Such practices increase the possibility of regional deviation from the policy design as originally conceived by the central government. It is necessary, therefore, to examine how various local governments implement civil service reforms in China. Chapter 4 provides three case studies of the local implementation of these reforms. Given the size of the country and the uneven development among its regions, conditions for implementing policies in China varied significantly. Balancing the requirement for uniformity in the civil service reforms with the diverse regional circumstances and the different levels of government proved to be extremely challenging. In the discussion section, I will point out a number of experiences that were common to all three local governments in the implementation of the reforms as well as the differences between them. A preliminary assessment on the extent to which the intended goals of the reforms were achieved will be also provided. Findings showed that each local government's ability to bear the financial and administrative costs of implementing the reforms was different from one another. In addition, without the necessary political support from local leaders, the implementation process was slow and arduous.

## Civil service reforms in Haidian

Haidian was chosen by the Beijing municipal party committee and government as a pilot district to test out the new civil service system in June 1992. An ad hoc leading committee (*lingdao xiaozu*) was formed soon after and took charge of the experimental implementation. The deputy secretary of the Haidian District Party Committee in charge of the organizational and personnel work was the chair of this committee. Other members included the deputy head and senior officials from the personnel bureau, the supervision bureau, the finance bureau of district government and senior officials from the organization department of the district party committee. The pilots were first carried out in the Family Planning Committee, the Civil Affairs Bureau and the Audit Bureau (Haidian Personnel Bureau 1998).

The Haidian Personnel Bureau published a book detailing the experimental implementation of the civil service system in 1994 (Chen 1994). The book reported in detail the implementation of the 'three fixes' programs, position classification, performance appraisal, training, promotion and avoidance. By specifying the function, structure and size of each agency, the 'three fixes' programs were geared towards restructuring the government agencies. The 'three fixes' referred to the specification of the functions of each bureau, the organization of the bureau and the number of employees that each bureau should employ. This was a program that aimed to restructure the local government bureau before cadres were converted into civil servants. The logic was that once the number of positions in the civil service was controlled through establishment planning, then the size of the civil service could also be controlled. Based on the experiences and lessons drawn from the pilot project, the leading committee developed and proposed a *Haidian District Plan for the Implementation of the Civil Service System*, which was approved by the Beijing Personnel Bureau at the end of 1994. Haidian then began to implement its plan in all district government bureaux. The leading committee issued the *Method of Implementing State Civil Service System of Haidian District* in 1995.

## *Transition*

After the 'three fixes' programs in 1995, Haidian government consisted of 38 district-level bureaux. There were 14 urban street offices and eight townships under the Haidian government.[1] Specifically, there were 3,434 positions in 52 administrative organs in the Haidian government (including 38 district-level bureaux and 14 urban street offices). Among them, 1,762 positions belonged to the district government while the other 1,672 positions belonged to the urban street offices. Together, 2,906 position specifications were made including 1,539 for the district government bureaux. In October 1996, Haidian finished the position classification work, which received a very positive assessment from the Beijing Personnel Bureau in December. The leading committee then formulated a plan for civil servants' transition for the whole district. A general mobilization meeting was held on 15 November 1996. The transition training programs for government staff were also arranged, with 3,910 employees participating in the programs at the time.

The transition program was completed in December 1996. As summarized in Table 4.1 below, 2,432 people, or 81.2 percent of government employees, were

*Table 4.1* Transfer method in Haidian, 1997

| Action | Number | Percent |
| --- | --- | --- |
| Direct transfer (no exam) | 2,432 | 81.20 |
| Transferred through exam | 395 | 13.20 |
| Delayed transfer | 92 | 3.10 |
| Transferred through administrative investigation (*shenpi*) | 68 | 2.10 |
| Failed to transfer | 9 | 0.30 |
| Total | 2,996 | 100.00 |

Source: Haidian Personnel Bureau (1998).

directly transferred to the civil service, 68 people were transferred through administrative investigation (*shenpi*), 395 people were transferred through examinations, 92 people postponed their transfer and nine people failed to transfer as civil servants.

However, the fact that 81.2 percent of Haidian government employees were directly transferred without examinations was problematic. As it was originally conceived, the central government suggested local governments hold examinations for current position holders to determine whether they were qualified to serve under the new system. In Haidian, only 13.2 percent (or 395) of government employees were transferred through the examination process. Among these 395 employees, 377 came from urban street offices. In other words, only 18 district officials were transferred into the new civil service via the examination route. Interviews with personnel bureau officials indicated that the central government left the screening method to the discretion of local governments. The interviewee explained that while the central government did suggest examination was a good method to conduct the transition program, 'it costs too much'. The interviewee further explained that those who were transferred through the examination route were the ones who received only a high school education. Given the high number of employees who were transferred successfully, Haidian might have failed to identify the underperformers since only 0.3 percent of officials failed to transfer to the new competitive service. Those who delayed their transfer, 92 of them in total, came from the Haidian Education Commission, which finished the transition as late as 2000. Among these 92 officials, some were given longer preparation time for the examination while others were to retire soon or transferred outside the Commission.

## *Recruitment and selection*

Since Haidian was chosen as the testing ground for the civil service system, it began its open recruitment of college graduates as early as May 1993, several years before the existing staff completed the transition to the new civil service. Competitive examinations were used by eight district bureaux to recruit 35 people with 20 people selected as a result. By October 1998, 243 people were

Table 4.2 Haidian civil servants selection, 1995–2002

| Year | Number | Recruitment type | | | Education level of newcomers | | |
|---|---|---|---|---|---|---|---|
| | | From society | University graduates | Post-graduate | University | Community college | High school |
| 1995 | 25 | 0 | 25 | 3 | 18 | 3 | 1 |
| 1996 | 53 | 33 | 20 | 6 | 25 | 21 | 1 |
| 1997 | 64 | 27 | 37 | 7 | 39 | 16 | 2 |
| 1998 | 0 | | | | | | |
| 1999 | 0 | | | | | | |
| 2000 | 24 | 0 | 24 | 4 | 15 | 0 | 5 |
| 2001 | 0 | | | | | | |
| 2002 | 200 | 60 | 140 | NA | NA | NA | NA |

Source: Haidian Personnel Bureau (2002).

selected for more than 60 party and government organs through open and competitive examinations (as summarized in Table 4.2). Haidian opened the recruitment process to the whole residential population of Beijing, not just the permanent residents of the district. It also claimed that every civil servant ranked below the section chiefs would enter the government through examinations.

Interestingly, local governments in China were required to implement other policies that had the effect of working against the purpose of the civil service reforms. Beginning in 1998, the personnel authorities of the central government carried out a nationwide downsizing campaign that effectively prevented many local governments from using competitive recruitment. Table 4.2 showed that Haidian only recruited 24 new civil servants through the competitive system from 1998 to 2001. The Chinese government was required to absorb demobilized soldiers into the civil service after they were discharged from active service. As a result, the demobilized soldiers entered into government without going through a competitive selection process. In particular, the district government as a whole was assigned a certain quota of demobilized soldiers every year and was expected to offer them employment. Table 4.3 summarizes the absorption of demobilized soldiers in Haidian. As mentioned above, from 1998 to 2001, Haidian only recruited 24 new civil servants; it employed at least 215 demobilized soldiers who entered into government without competitive examinations.

*Performance appraisal*

The performance appraisal for individual civil servant in Haidian was quantitative in nature. The quantitative evaluation contained three parts: evaluation by the management of the organization to which the person under review belonged, evaluation by the upper-level organization and peer evaluation. These three parts were assigned different weights. In general, evaluation by the management

*Table 4.3* Demobilized soldiers transferred into Haidian, 1995–2001

| Year | Total number | Female | Type of employer ||||
|---|---|---|---|---|---|---|
| | | | Party-state organs | Service units | Enterprises | New developing area (shiyanqu) |
| 1995 | 66 | 25 | 26 | 21 | 3 | 16 |
| 1996 | 96 | 37 | 48 | 20 | 8 | 20 |
| 1997 | 111 | 48 | 69 | 22 | 3 | 17 |
| 1998 | 137 | 58 | 69 | 37 | 12 | 25 |
| 1999 | 187 | 80 | 45 | 95 | 16 | 31 |
| 2000 | 178 | 64 | 61 | 78 | 3 | 36 |
| 2001 | 97 | NA | 40 | 48 | 9 | 0 |

Source: Haidian Personnel Bureau (2002).

constituted 30–50 percent of the overall score while the corresponding figures for the upper-level organization evaluation and the peer evaluation were 20–30 percent and 20–50 percent respectively (Haidian Personnel Bureau 2002).

According to the *Provisional Method of Performance Appraisal for Haidian Civil Servants* issued by the district government of Haidian in 1996, as the result of an annual performance appraisal, the assessment ranked a reviewee into one of four performance grades: 'outstanding' (*yiuxiu*), 'competent' (*chengzhi*), 'basically competent' (*jiben chengzhi*) and 'incompetent' (*bu chengzhi*). Among these ranks, 'basically competent' served as a kind of warning to those under review. If an employee was judged to be 'basically competent', he received 50 percent of the original annual bonus. Those judged to be 'incompetent' would go through a probation period of about six to 12 months and would not receive the bonus. From 1994 to 1998, 34 people were ranked as 'basically competent' and 24 as 'incompetent' in the annual performance appraisals. One person was dismissed after failing the appraisals. By October 1998, no appeal was lodged regarding the performance appraisal results (Haidian Personnel Bureau 1998).

Based on the results of the performance appraisals for the period 1994–1998, if civil servants were assessed as 'outstanding' for two consecutive years or 'competent' for three consecutive years, they would get a pay rise by one-level increment for their post wage. Some people were rewarded a rise of two increments for their post wage during this period. If civil servants were assessed as 'outstanding' for three consecutive years, their grade wage would go up by one increment. A total of 102 civil servants were rewarded a grade wage increment increase based on their appraisal results.

### *Training*

There were four types of civil servant training: induction training, training for civil servants who were promoted to leading positions, training to update knowledge and skills and professional continuous education. Training for civil servants who were promoted to section-chief level began in October 1993 in Haidian. By the end of 1998, there were six rounds of this kind of training, which involved 341 section-chief-level civil servants. Professional training in Haidian focused on training civil servants who were in charge of personnel and general office work. Haidian initiated special training to update government employees' knowledge and skills with different programs intended for different purposes. For example, Haidian Personnel Bureau provided a basic computer course for civil servants aged between 45 and 50. In total, 1,017 civil servants passed this course. A more advanced computer application program was provided for civil servants at section-chief or more senior levels and who were under 40 years old. A total of 195 civil servants passed this course and some of them felt satisfied with the quality of the program.[2]

As mentioned above, governments were responsible for absorbing demobilized soldiers into the civil service after they completed their military duty. The district government as a whole was assigned a certain quota of demobilized soldiers every year and was expected to provide them with employment. Some of these demobilized soldiers were considered poorly educated; hence, special training programs were specifically put in place to cater for their needs. The training courses covered the legal system, public administration, the economy and some work-related skills. By October 1998, 404 demobilized soldiers finished such training. Compared with the total number of demobilized soldiers transferred into Haidian from 1995 to 1998 (410 at the end of 1998), the participation rate was as high as 98.5 percent. Again, the shortcoming of this practice was that the demobilized soldiers did not need to pass any examinations upon the completion of their training. Interviews with the officials from the personnel bureau indicated that they were under pressure to provide training courses for the demobilized soldiers and did not ask them to sit for examination upon completion. Both the upper-level government personnel bureau and the various employers (district government organs) requested this kind of training because they realized that some of the demobilized soldiers were poorly educated. However, there was no examination by the end of the course because the personnel bureau was concerned that the potential employer would reject veterans who failed the examination.

### *Rotation and avoidance*

Haidian issued the *Method on Civil Servant Rotation* in July 1997. From 1997 to October 1998, 109 employees from 17 organs rotated to various posts, but all reported to (*bei'an*) the personnel bureau. Among these people, 71 were civil servants at or above the level of section chief and 38 were section members. Haidian Industrial and Commercial Bureau began the rotation system in 1994. By October 1998, 96 percent (79) of section members and 72.7 percent (402) of ordinary cadres rotated their posts. These ordinary cadres were not civil servants, but were market-regulators working on a contract basis, so-called *Shiye Bianzhi* (*bianzhi* means the number of officially approved positions). The practice of contract-based regulation enforcement manpower appeared in Haidian as early as the 1990s.

Avoidance (*huibi*) is the transfer of officials to other related positions because they have either relatives working in the departments or working relationships with other officials. Avoidance was put in place to prevent nepotism and corruption. In a survey in 1998, 160 government employees were in a situation that required avoidance. Haidian reassigned positions for 158 people by the end of 1998. Among these people, one of them was a division chief, three were deputy division chiefs, 18 were at section-chief level, 30 were at deputy section-chief level and the rest were section members.

## *Compensation, reward and discipline*

From 1994 to 1997, 1,396 civil servants were given a one-level grade wage increase as required by the national policy for regular pay rises. At the end of 1996, Haidian employed 2,996 civil servants and more than half of them received a pay increase indicating Haidian's strong financial ability to implement wage reform (compared with Changchun). Based on the results of the performance appraisals for the period 1994–1998, if civil servants were assessed as 'outstanding' for two consecutive years or 'competent' for three consecutive years, they would receive a pay rise by one-level increment for their post wage. Some people were rewarded a rise of two increments for their post wage during this period. If civil servants were assessed as 'outstanding' for three consecutive years, their grade wage would go up by one increment. A total of 102 civil servants were rewarded a grade wage increment increase based on their appraisal results (Haidian Personnel Bureau 1998).

Haidian issued regulations on the penalties for poor performers in 2001 (Haidian Personnel Bureau 2002). As discussed above, if a person was judged to be 'basically competent' in an annual performance appraisal, he would receive 50 percent of the original annual bonus. Those ranked as 'incompetent' would go through a probation period of about six to 12 months and would not get the bonus. Furthermore, the reviewee who received the worst evaluation of his or her organization would face one of the following punitive measures: warning, demotion, a reassigned post or training before allocation to a new post. The methods used to identify those who were ranked the lowest were quite quantitative in nature. The evaluation contained three parts: evaluation by the management of the organization to which the person under review belonged; evaluation by the upper-level organization and peer evaluation. These three parts were assigned different weights. In general, evaluation by the management constituted 30–50 percent of the overall score while the corresponding figures for the upper-level organization evaluation and the peer evaluation were 20–30 percent and 20–50 percent respectively (Haidian Personnel Bureau 2002). From 1994 to 1998, 34 people were ranked as 'basically competent' and 24 as 'incompetent' in annual performance appraisals. One person was dismissed after failing the appraisal (Haidian Personnel Bureau 1998).

## Summary of Haidian's case

High-capacity civil service systems are characterized by open and competitive selection processes and mechanisms that appropriately utilize talent, ensure that all employees are adequately trained, set and communicate the performance standard, evaluate performance and report the results of the evaluation back to employees and link performance to rewards (Burns 2005). To a large extent, Haidian's experience of implementing the civil service system was an approximation of this ideal model. First, the recruitment of new civil servants was open and competitive (see Table 4.2). From 1995 to 2002, a total of 366 people became civil servants through open and competitive examinations. Of these, 246 were graduates of higher education and 120 were from the general public. These newcomers were also well educated: 20 received postgraduate education while 97 received a university education. More than 70 percent of these newcomers were educated at the university level or above.[3] Another improvement was that the training programs for Haidian's civil servants were not only comprehensive and effective, but the trainees themselves were satisfied with the training. Furthermore, in order to motivate the officials to improve performance, Haidian initiated strict performance appraisal measures and linked the results with rewards. Before each performance evaluation, the performance standards were set and made public. From 1996 to 2001, Haidian issued 21 rules and regulations on civil service management (Haidian Personnel Bureau 2002). Several interviewees reported satisfaction with Haidian's implementation of the civil service system.[4]

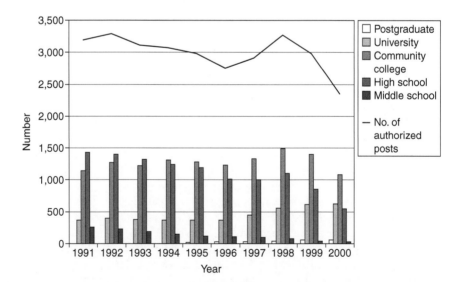

*Figure 4.1* Number of civil servants and their educational level in Haidian, 1991–2000 (source: Interviews, Haidian district, 2002).

Table 4.4 Number of civil servants, their education level and age in Haidian Personnel Bureau, 1991–2000

| Year | Bianzhi | Education level | | | | Age | | | |
|---|---|---|---|---|---|---|---|---|---|
| | | Post-graduate | University | Community college | High school | 30 and below | 31–9 | 40–9 | 50 and above |
| 1991 | 28 | | 6 | 19 | 3 | 9 | 13 | 6 | |
| 1992 | 34 | | 7 | 24 | 3 | 11 | 14 | 9 | |
| 1993 | 32 | | 6 | 23 | 3 | 6 | 17 | 9 | |
| 1994 | 32 | | 5 | 24 | 3 | 8 | 17 | 7 | |
| 1995 | 32 | | 11 | 18 | 3 | 7 | 19 | 6 | |
| 1996 | 33 | | 11 | 20 | 2 | 7 | 17 | 9 | |
| 1997 | 35 | | 13 | 20 | 2 | 7 | 15 | 13 | |
| 1998 | 34 | 3 | 16 | 15 | 0 | 7 | 14 | 12 | 1 |
| 1999 | 31 | 3 | 19 | 9 | 0 | 4 | 13 | 13 | 1 |
| 2000 | 31 | 5 | 17 | 9 | 0 | 5 | 12 | 13 | 1 |

Source: Haidian Personnel Bureau (2002).

76  *Local implementation of reforms*

More importantly, officials of the personnel bureau thought that the personnel quality of the Haidian government had improved since the reform and believed that the improvement was brought about by the reform.[5] One interviewee explained that as old government employees with poor education retired, this provided vacant positions to newcomers who entered the government via the intensive competition process. Hence, the number of civil servants with higher education rocketed. Figure 4.1 shows clearly that the educational level of employees of the Haidian government increased. During the period of 1991–2000, the government of Haidian was downsized and the number of staff was reduced from 3,193 to 2,351 (26 percent reduction). The number of highly educated staff (with postgraduate or university degree) increased drastically from 11.4 percent to 29.2 percent of the entire staff (from 365 to 687 employees). Meanwhile, the number of civil servants with high school qualifications declined. During the same period, the number of community college graduates pulled ahead of those with only high school credentials. The improvement in the quality of the staff of the Haidian Personnel Bureau followed a similar pattern (see Table 4.4). The number of staff with a higher education degree drastically increased while the average age of all staff also experienced a slight increase. In particular, the number of staff aged below 30 decreased, those aged between 30 and 40 remained almost the same and those aged above 40 increased.

## Civil service reforms in Ningbo

A small ad hoc leading group was formed on 26 July 1995 to be in charge of the implementation of the civil service system in Ningbo (Ningbo Personnel Bureau 1999). The former mayor, Xu Yunhong,[6] chaired the group and its membership included the leading cadres of the Ningbo Party Committee, the Organization Department of the Ningbo Party Committee and the leading officials of the personnel bureau, the supervision bureau and the finance bureau of Ningbo government. Its executive arm, the Office of Implementation, was also established under the personnel bureau.

### *Transition*

Ningbo issued the *Method of Implementing State Civil Service System* for city government bureaux in October 1995. By November, a mobilization meeting was held to mobilize the whole staff corps and assigned the tasks to various bureaux. The emphasis was put on the training program for transition, position classification and the transition of cadres into civil servants. Six rounds of training programs for the transition were provided for the cadres working in the party and government organs. A total of 20,750 cadres received this training. Every bureau under the city government was required to draft up a plan for the transition process. If a bureau's 'three fixes' plan was approved by the city government, it would begin the transition work. By the end of 1997, 44 out of 51 city government organs had their 'three fixes' plan approved by the city government and finished position classification for 2,045 posts (Ningbo Personnel Bureau 1999).

All of the cadres underwent the examination process in order to be transferred to the civil service in 1996, 1997 and 1998. By December 1998, all of the government bureaux at or above township level in Ningbo completed this transition. Previously, the total workforce in city, county and township level bureaux was 19,029. Among these, 18,564 (or 97.56 percent) were transferred to the civil service according to the results of examinations and other performance appraisals. Only 37 persons failed to transfer due to their failing grades in the examinations. Of these 37 persons, eight worked in the city government and 29 worked in the county- and township-level governments. Another 428 persons who failed this transition came from three groups: those who were either approaching retirement age or whose education was limited to middle school education, those who were under disciplinary procedure (*chufen*) during the transition period and those who quit their job to work in the business sector (Ningbo Personnel Bureau 1999).

## *Recruitment and selection*

In keeping with the spirit of the reform policy of the Organization Department of the Chinese Communist Party (CCP) and the former Ministry of Personnel, Ningbo began to recruit government employees through examinations in 1989. In 1996, the city government opened the recruitment process of civil servants to the general public. This was the first time an open recruitment process took place in the Zhejiang province. In April 1996, 43 city-level organs and five district-level organs planned to recruit 192 newcomers. As a result, 1,658 applicants registered for the examinations and 152 people were selected. Among them, 106 went to positions in the city-level organs and 46 in the district-level organs (Ningbo Local History Editorial Committee 1998: 316).

County-level government organs opened their recruitment process to the general public in 1997. For the Zhejiang province, this was the first time that applications were not restricted to Ningbo permanent residents or to cadre status. All peasants and workers were eligible to apply and could register for the civil service examinations. Under this new arrangement, 1,904 people, including 65 peasants and 576 workers, registered for the examination. Through competitive examinations, interviews and physical test (*tijian*), 178 people, including five peasants and 37 workers, were selected and appointed as civil servants by various county governments. In 1996 and 1997, the city and county governments in Ningbo selected 356 new recruits from the general public. From 1998, however, a centrally imposed downsizing campaign stopped further attempts to recruit new civil servants.

Another important pool from which new civil servants were selected was the university and college graduates. In 1997, various local government bureaux selected 618 new civil servants (or new cadres, since some of them are not civil servants, but cadres whose management referred to the civil service system) who came from the university and college graduate pool. Of these 618 recruits, 146 were hired at the city level, 336 at the county level and 38 at the town and township level. Others were assigned to organs that managed their employees using the civil service system as a reference (*canzhao guanli*). Taken together, the newcomers of 1996 and 1997, 356 and 618 new recruits respectively, made up about 5.2 percent of Ningbo's 18,564 civil servants. The 146 newcomers who entered the city government were appointed to different bureaux. The general office, the education commission and the civil affairs bureau took five recruits each. The agriculture bureau, the audit bureau and the technology inspection bureau were each assigned four newcomers. The petition office, the construction committee, the environmental protection bureau, the planning bureau, the medicine management bureau, the forest bureau, the labor bureau and some other organs were each assigned three newcomers (Ningbo Personnel Bureau 1999).

Because of the 1998 downsizing campaign, Ningbo stopped recruiting new civil servants from the pool of higher education graduates and the general public; however, the absorption of demobilized soldiers continued. From 1997 to 1999, Ningbo took in 1,273 demobilized soldiers at three levels (city, county and township) of the government bureaux. Given that most demobilized soldiers were poorly educated, it was likely that their influx lowered the quality of Ningbo's civil service (see Table 4.5).

## *Performance appraisal and training*

In 1997, 28 civil servants were assessed as 'incompetent' in various city government bureaux where they constituted 1 percent of all civil servants who participated in the performance appraisal. In 1998, 39 civil servants were assessed as 'incompetent' in various city government bureaux and they constituted 1.4 percent of all those who underwent review (Ningbo Personnel Bureau 1999).

The Organization Department of the Ningbo Party Committee and the Personnel Bureau issued the *Implementation Method for Civil Servants' Training* in January 1997. The Personnel Bureau was responsible for designing the training programs for civil servants. They conducted a questionnaire survey of 1,700 civil servants and received 1,331 responses in return. Based on the survey results, 31 different rounds of training programs were arranged. The programs included language training, computer application and knowledge training of the

*Table 4.5* Ningbo absorption of demobilized soldiers, 1997–1999

| Year | No. of demobilized soldiers | Dependent people |
| --- | --- | --- |
| 1997 | 358 | 37 |
| 1998 | 369 | 40 |
| 1999 | 546 | 67 |

Source: Ningbo Local History Editorial Committee (2002).

legal system and the economy. In total, 8,410 places of these training programs were filled with some individuals enrolling into multiple programs (Ningbo Personnel Bureau 1999). In May 2000, the National School of Administration arranged a special training program for Ningbo's personnel officials where 40 personnel officials (personnel bureau chiefs at or above county level) took part. This was the first time the National School of Administration provided a special training program for local personnel officials,[7] which had the effect of motivating the personnel officials of the Ningbo government.

## Summary of Ningbo's case

To some extent, the implementation of the reform had a positive impact on the quality of the civil service in Ningbo. First, the transition program helped to filter out incapable cadres. Of the 465 cadres who failed to transfer to the civil service, more than 50 percent belonged to the old or the poorly educated. Second, the educational level of Ningbo government personnel improved. This was evident in the environmental protection bureau (see Table 4.6). In 1996, the bureau did not employ any postgraduate degree holders, but by 2000, the bureau employed three such degree holders. The number of poorly educated people decreased from three to one during the period 1996 to 2000. The staff quality of the education commission showed a similar trend (see Figure 4.2). The number of staff with higher education (university degree) in the Ningbo Education Commission drastically increased from 38 to 66, that is, from 50.7 percent of all staff to 83.5 percent from 1991 to 2000. The largest increase in

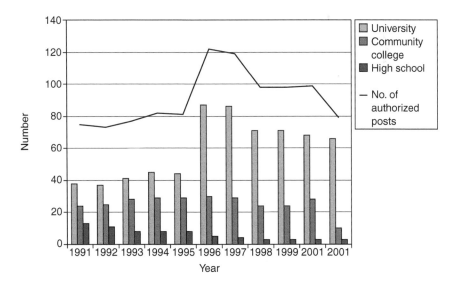

*Figure 4.2* Number of civil servants and their educational level in Ningbo Education Commission, 1991–2001 (source: Interviews, Ningbo, 2002).

*Table 4.6* Number of civil servants, their education level and age in Ningbo Environmental Protection Bureau, 1996–2000

| Year | Bianzhi | Education level | | | | Age | | | |
|---|---|---|---|---|---|---|---|---|---|
| | | Post-graduate | University | Community college | High school | 30 and below | 30–40 | 40–50 | 50 and above |
| 1996 | 21 | 0 | 9 | 8 | 4 | 1 | 6 | 3 | 11 |
| 1997 | 25 | 2 | 11 | 7 | 4 | 4 | 7 | 4 | 10 |
| 1998 | 22 | 3 | 9 | 8 | 2 | 4 | 8 | 3 | 7 |
| 1999 | 23 | 3 | 9 | 9 | 2 | | | | |
| 2000 | 22 | 3 | 8 | 9 | 2 | | | | |

Source: Ningbo Personnel Bureau (2002).

the number of university graduates employed occurred from 1995 to 1996, before the implementation of the more competitive hiring policies of the civil service system in Ningbo. Despite the downsizing of the civil service that began in 1998, the share of university graduates in the entire government workforce continued to grow.

## Civil service reforms in Changchun

An ad hoc leading committee was established to oversee Changchun's implementation of the reforms in November 1994. The former Mayor, Mi Fengjun, was the chair of the committee.[8] The leading committee formulated a plan to implement the civil service system, which was approved by the Personnel Department of Jilin province in 1995 (Changchun Personnel Bureau 1997).

### *Transition*

After the 'three fixes' programs in 1995, there were 60 party and government organs at city level in Changchun with eight party organs and 52 government bureaux. The leading committee distributed study materials to various organs in September 1995. Training courses were arranged for personnel officials of these organs as a way to inform them of the new civil service system. Party and government organs were required to design their own plan in terms of transferring their cadres to civil servants. By the end of 1995, the plans submitted by 21 organs were approved by the leading committee. A mobilization meeting was held and the questions and concerns raised by various organs were addressed on 14 December 1995. Most of the concerns focused on the question of how to reallocate redundant personnel. Subsequently, the work of transferring cadres to the civil service began and, by the end of 1996, 55 organs finished their position classification and transition work (see Table 4.7). The transition work of the Public Security Bureau (*gong'an ju*) was delayed and carried out in 1997.

*Table 4.7* Position classification in Changchun, 1996

| Level of position | No. of position |
|---|---|
| Bureau chief and deputy | 228 |
| Non-leading position at bureau level | 67 |
| Division chief and deputy | 949 |
| Non-leading position at division level | 514 |
| Section chief and deputy | 934 |
| Section member | 487 |
| Total | 3,179 |

Source: Changchun Personnel Bureau (1997).

## Recruitment and selection

All 52 city-level government bureaux opened their recruitment process to the general public in 1996 and planned to recruit 544 people in total. The recruitment drive attracted 5,727 applicants and, by the end of the process, 489 people were offered employment including 39 peasants, 36 workers and 22 unemployed job-seekers. Changchun claimed that its open recruitment of civil servants was not limited to applicants with permanent residence or cadre status. In 1997, 57 party and government organs planned to recruit 339 new civil servants. Employment was offered to 336 of the 6,233 applicants on a competitive basis. The open recruitment of civil servants ceased in 1998 due to the downsizing campaign of 1998. While the government suspended open recruitment of higher education graduates and the general public, it continued to absorb the demobilized soldiers. In the four years from 1996 to 1999, Changchun government absorbed 147, 108, 151 and 376 demobilized soldiers respectively, amounting to a total of 782 soldiers (Changchun Local History Editorial Committee 2001). In 2002, Changchun resumed the recruitment of new civil servants from higher education graduates and the general public through competitive examinations. This round of recruitment yielded 397 successful applicants who were appointed as civil servants by the city government.

## Performance appraisal

Civil servants were assessed according to the three levels of competence after the annual performance appraisal. In 1995, the proportion of civil servants who ranked as 'outstanding', 'competent' and 'incompetent' were 15.1 percent, 81.4 percent and 0.4 percent respectively. It should be noted that considerably more civil servants were evaluated as 'incompetent' in Changchun in 1995 than in either Haidian or Ningbo (0.4 percent compared with 0.14 percent). As a result, Changchun had initiated some special measures in its performance appraisal practices. In 1997, the Organization Department of the Changchun Party Committee together with the Personnel Bureau and the Supervision Bureau issued regulations on the punitive measures for poor performing officials. The regulations required every organization to report to its superior organization the civil servant with the lowest ranking in the annual performance appraisal. In 1997, 38 civil servants were given a warning after failing the annual performance appraisal. In 1998, 44 civil servants were dismissed as a result of failing the appraisal. In 1999, 272 civil servants who ranked last in their organizations were reported to the Organization Department of the Changchun Party Committee by various party and government organs. Follow-up investigations were carried out on these cases with 91 of them receiving an administrative warning (Changchun Local History Editorial Committee 2000). In 2000, 14.67 percent of civil servants were assessed as 'outstanding' and 0.14 percent as 'incompetent' in the annual performance appraisal. The corresponding figures for 2001 were 14.99 percent and 0.14 percent respectively (Changchun Local History Editorial Committee 2001).

## Training and rotation

Training programs were attended by a total of 3,767 civil servants in 1996 with 140 of them coming from the division-chief level and above. In 1997, 4,327 people received such training. The Changchun Administration School (*Changchun xingzheng xueyuan*) was established in August 1997, making training for civil servants more systematic. In 2000, 2,827 civil servants received professional training. 900 personnel officials of various organs were asked to sit in for examinations that assessed their knowledge of personnel policy and regulations. In 2002, 3,000 civil servants received professional training and 2,000 civil servants received knowledge-update training. In 1996, 391 civil servants of various party and government organs rotated their positions.

## Discussion

While the implementation of the civil service reforms by these three local governments revealed a number of common shared experiences, they also presented differences. In this section, I will provide some preliminary assessment on the extent to which the intended goals of the reforms were achieved. First, the transition of all (or part of) the cadres to the new civil service included three sub-programs in all the local cases. The first one was the creation of special institutions by local authorities to lead and organize the implementation of the new civil service system. These special institutions included an ad hoc leading committee and an executive arm—the office of implementation. Since implementing the new system was an important task, the leading committee members usually included leaders of the important local party and government organs such as the organization department of local party committee, the personnel bureau, supervision bureau and finance bureau of local government. The executive arm office was usually attached to the personnel bureau. The second sub-program was the 'three fixes' program, which served the purpose of clarifying and specifying the functions, the organization and the size of the staff establishment of each bureau. This program restructured the local bureaux before transferring the cadres into civil servants, thus enabling the local governments to first control the number of positions in the civil service through establishment planning and then to further control the size of the civil service.

The third sub-program was transferring the cadres to the civil service. To maintain and improve the capacity of the civil service, government officials were asked to sit in for examinations to determine whether they were qualified to be transferred. The leading committee and the implementation office designed examinations or other evaluation methods to allow only the qualified cadres to be transferred to the new civil service system. The transition examination required an understanding of the rules and regulations of the new civil service system. Successful transition depended not only on the transition examination but also the results of performance appraisal. As demonstrated in the three cases, the transition programs led to some positive consequences. First, they filtered out old or poorly educated government workers. For example, of the 465 cadres in Ningbo who failed the transition examination, more than 50 percent were either the old or the poorly educated. Second, after the transition, the proportion of employees with college or university education increased as evident in the educational level of the staff of the Haidian district government, Haidian Personnel Bureau, Ningbo Environmental Protection Bureau and Ningbo Education Commission. Third, during the transition, the possibility of rejection and unsuccessful transfer served as an effective motivation for officials to prepare for examinations and update their work-related knowledge.

However, the transition program had weaknesses. The *Implementation Plan of China's Civil Service Reform* and *Handbook for Civil Service Transition* issued by the former Ministry of Personnel did not specify the method of transition, thus leaving the transition method to the discretion of the local governments, namely, the leading committee and the implementation office. As the analysis above showed, most of government employees in Haidian were transferred to the new civil service without taking any examinations. Some interviewees reported that the examinations were too easy and this could very well be the case given that the rate of successful transition was very high: 97.56 percent in Ningbo and 96.6 percent in Haidian. Some interviewees had the impression that most of their colleagues got transferred. Indeed, only 0.3 percent of the officials failed to be transferred to the new civil service in Haidian. In Ningbo, despite appearing to be more stringent, 97.6 percent of the 19,029 city officials were accepted into the new civil service. The high passing rate of transition tests suggested that the civil service transition was probably not that effective in weeding out the underperformers.

Second, in the recruitment and selection process, all these three local governments had opened recruitments and claimed that the recruitment exercise did not target only those holding permanent residence or cadre status. As well, all three local governments selected high-quality newcomers from a pool of university or college graduates and the recruitment process was highly competitive. The ratio of applicants to recruits increased year after year, which helped to increase the quality of the newcomers in the long run. The interview with a personnel official suggested that officials believed the introduction of competition had led the staffing practices in the right direction.[9] One additional benefit of the competition was that it put pressure on the current government employees as they became motivated to update their knowledge and work-related skills. For example, during my fieldwork in Haidian Education Commission, four of 15 interviewees mentioned that people there had sought to improve their professional knowledge and skills through training programs and self-study. All these four interviewees were enrolled in part-time master's programs at the time the fieldwork was conducted.[10]

Moreover, various bureaux in all three local governments had the autonomy to select their potential employees. This autonomy was manifested in the membership of the selection committee where at least one member from the employment bureau was included into the selection committee. Of course, the employment bureau could only select from qualified candidates who had already passed the common entrance exam. More importantly, interviews with candidates were organized by the employment bureau. To a large extent, the open and competitive recruitment and selection was a success. Capable people were selected into local governments, which led to the improvement of quality within the local government personnel.

Third, all three local governments practiced annual performance appraisal. Civil servants in Ningbo were evaluated according to the three grades of competence. The three-grade classification was too limited to discriminate employees' performance. Usually, more than 80 percent of the personnel were rated as 'competent'.[11] In order to get a more discriminatory classification system, Haidian and Changchun introduced the grade of 'basically competent' between the grades of 'competent' and 'incompetent'. Therefore, civil servants in Haidian and Changchun were evaluated using the four grades classification system. Being rated as 'basically competent' served as a warning to the civil servant under review. The former Ministry of Personnel approved these innovations and introduced them to other parts of the country.[12] Both Haidian and Changchun implemented special measures to make full use of the appraisal results. Based on the appraisal results, they both issued punitive measures to poor performers. These punitive measures deterred against laziness or other undesirable behaviors. Trying not to be identified as poor performers within their own organization became the goal of most of the staff. Government workers began to take performance evaluation seriously and have since then become more performance-oriented.

Fourth, all three local governments managed to increase their civil servants' pay to fulfill the national policy requirement. However, the pay system was the target of most complaints during my interviews with the local officials. Interviewees did agree that their pay had increased compared with the pay they received before reforms.[13] However, most thought that their pay was not linked to their performance. As Table 4.8 shows, when I asked the interviewees whether their pay was somewhat linked to their work performance, most of them did not think so. For instance, most officials (65 percent) in the environmental protection

*Table 4.8* Perception that pay and performance are linked, Haidian and Changchun (number of interviewees)

|  | *Yes* | *No* |
| --- | --- | --- |
| Total education | 12 (46%) | 12 (46%) |
| Total environmental | 5 (19%) | 17 (65%) |
| Haidian education | 6 (55%) | 4 (36%) |
| Haidian environmental | 4 (36%) | 6 (55%) |
| Changchun education | 6 (40%) | 8 (53%) |
| Changchun environmental | 1 (7%) | 11 (73%) |

Source: Fieldwork survey, March–April 2004.

domain and officials in Changchun (73 percent) thought their pay was not properly linked to their work performance.

Based on this part of the data, I concluded that the wage reform included in the civil service reforms failed to provide the degree of motivation for the civil servants as originally anticipated. However, I cannot conclude that the wage reform failed completely since other objectives of the reforms were achieved. For example, one of the objectives of wage reform was to increase the civil service pay compared with inflation, rising living cost and salary of enterprises employees. This part of the reforms was, in fact, relatively successful. A mechanism of regular pay increase was installed. After the 1993 wage reforms, civil service pay rose across the country in July 1997, July 1999, January and October of 2001 and July 2003. We found that only in 2001, civil service pay was raised twice by a total of 30 percent while the economy was in deflation and unemployment was on the rise that year (Hou 2007: 232). Civil service pay became more competitive and a civil service career became quite attractive for graduates of higher education. Moreover, not only did the pay serve as a motivator for those working in the government, there were also considerations for higher social status and the so-called 'grey income'. Working in a governmental organization as a civil servant was considered to be prestigious as the job often came with authoritative power and material rewards. Many of these rewards, often classified as 'grey income' and unapproved by the state, were difficult to capture.

Competition was the focus for the processes of selection, promotion and reward. The positive consequences of this competition included improvement in the quality of the civil service and the renewed enthusiasm for and interest in training. In the recruitment and selection process, the qualifications and experience required of the recruited were increased. Only graduates of college and university were selected by the government since the reforms. The improvement of the education level of the newcomers undoubtedly increased the quality of the civil service and put pressure on the current civil servants. Given that the competition for promotion and reward became intense with education as a major indicator of the qualification of candidates, the current civil servants were put under pressure to improve their education by enrolling into training programs or through self-study. In my fieldwork, 88 percent (46 of 52) of the interviewees had participated in training programs. Of the 46, 35 had been given the opportunity for training by the organization they belonged to while the remaining 11 participated in self-funded training programs. Some interviewees reported that the training programs had helped them significantly. For example, civil servants in the planning division of the Ningbo Environmental Protection Bureau thought that the computer training increased their work efficiency. With the newly acquired computer skills, they were able to provide environment quality reports in an efficient way and with greater accuracy. As well, they were able to compile statistics reports for the upper-level government in a much speedier manner.[14] All these measures, such as participating in training courses and intentionally raising the education level, had positively influenced the quality of the civil servants and their work efficiency.

The civil service reforms not only motivated officials to work hard but also pushed them to adjust the way they exercised discretion. Since the adoption of the civil service system, clients and the general public played a role in the process of evaluating the civil servants. That is, in conjunction with the evaluation by their superiors, a democratic appraisal meeting (*mingzhu pingyi*) would take place where colleagues and 'the masses' gathered to evaluate a particular civil servant. The term 'masses' (*qunzong*) refers to the representatives of the level immediately below the unit that was undergoing the said evaluation. In the case of the Ningbo Environmental Protection Bureau, the masses included the staff of district environmental protection bureaux and managers of city-regulated enterprises. All six of the bureaux in my study solicited clients' opinions during the staff performance appraisal. Typically, the clients were asked to fill out a questionnaire rating the work performance of the appraisee on a scale from 'outstanding' to 'incompetent' along the four criteria of political integrity, competence, attitude and work achievements. The rating was conducted anonymously. Although some scholars dismissed the democratic appraisal meetings as having little practical effect (O'Brien and Li 1999), in my study, interviewees argued the ratings sent important signals to the superiors/principals and influenced civil servants' behaviors. If a majority of the people expressed dissatisfaction with the performance of a civil servant under appraisal, the superiors or the personnel office would begin an investigation.[15] Such an investigation would issue a warning to the civil servant, which would have a negative impact on his career. Thus, as clients' opinions became relevant to performance evaluations, civil servants adjusted their attitude in serving their clients and the general public.

The above analysis is about the common shared experiences of the three local governments in implementing the reforms. Some of these shared experiences shed light on the positive impacts of China's civil service reforms such as more open and competitive selection, more formalized performance evaluation, improved quality of civil service and better attitude towards citizens. However, I also found that the impact of the reforms in all three places was undermined by other policies that were being implemented simultaneously to the reform policies, for example, the downsizing campaign as well as the welfare and patronage policies that required local governments to employ demobilized soldiers.

The implementation of civil service reforms in the three places was also undermined by the widespread informal practices such as corruption. For instance, officials in the field sites were corrupted. In 2000, the former Mayor and Party Secretary of Ningbo, Xu Yunhong, was convicted of colluding with criminals and diverting public money for personal use.[16] In 2008, the former Mayor and Party Secretary of Changchun, Mi Fengjun was found guilty of corruption by the Central Discipline Inspection Commission. His last position was the Chair of Jilin People's Congress, which made him the highest official who was found guilty of corruption in Jilin province. He had stayed at the vice-provincial positions for 17 years before his crime was made public. Ironically, both the corrupted leaders of Ningbo and Changchun (Xu Yunhong and Mi Fengjun) were chairs of the ad hoc leading committee that was responsible for the implementation of the new civil service system. This was a sign of the failed discipline of the civil service system if not a total failure of the civil service reforms in Ningbo and Changchun. In 2004, Changchun authorities punished 1,250 officials for corruption. Of these, one was a bureau-level official, five were at deputy bureau level and 46 at division level. 54 of the 1,250 received prison sentences and others had their administrative rank and party membership removed.[17] In 2007, the Haidian District Head, Zhou Liangluo, was arrested for participating in illegal real estate deals.[18] All this suggested that officials in the field sites were corrupt.

Now I turn to the differences experienced by the three places. Existing literature found that the implementation of civil service reforms in China was conducted across the country at an uneven pace. This uneven progress was also evident in the multiple programs included in the reforms (Burns 2005; Chou 2003). I expected that, given its proximity to power, Haidian would implement the reforms earlier and would deviate less from the stated goals of the civil service reform than the other two areas. Given Ningbo's wealth, I expected that the city would implement those parts of the reforms that required additional spending (such as pay increases and performance-based pay) relatively earlier than the other cases. Finally, I also expected that the differences in population size and the structure of economy might also have an impact on the relative size and composition of various civil service agencies. Generally I found considerable variation among the three places as they implemented the reforms.

First, the timing of the one-off transition exercise varied. Haidian, which was a pilot in the civil service reform in 1992, completed all transition work by December 1996. The other two cities, which started the reforms later (Changchun in November 1994 and Ningbo in July 1995), not surprisingly completed them later (Changchun in 1996, except for the police, and Ningbo in December 1998). Given Haidian's proximity to power, I expected earlier compliance even though Haidian's rank (prefecture level) was below the rank of the other field sites. Implementation of civil service reform was usually a top-down exercise. Haidian began recruiting openly (from among undergraduates and from society) in May 1993, several years before the existing staff in the Haidian government completed the transition to the new system. Ningbo and Changchun both began recruiting openly in 1996. Again, Haidian's proximity to power might explain the early start.

Second, different local governments' abilities to bear the administrative costs of implementing the new system were different. Local governments in impoverished regions were more likely to fail in implementing some programs. As scholars found that in poorer counties where personnel costs could amount to 70 percent or more of the total expenditure, paying bonus and increments (which were required by the wage reform policy) was very difficult (Burns 2005). In this study, I found Changchun to have experienced difficulty in implementing some reform programs due to a shortage of resources. Among the three cities, Changchun was relatively poor. In terms of incomes, the per capita GDP of Haidian and Ningbo in 2006 (RMB64,988 and RMB74,458 respectively) was

*Local implementation of reforms* 89

almost double that of Changchun (RMB39,341). The poorer Changchun failed to implement the training programs due to the lack of the necessary financial resources. The limited resources also led to Changchun's poor performance in providing one public service—environmental protection.

Interviews with officials revealed that Changchun failed to implement training programs.[19] In particular, I found that neither the environmental bureau nor the education commission of Changchun had enough resources to provide training for their staff. Table 4.9 identifies the average hours of training the staff of four bureaux received in year 2003. I found that on average, staff at the Changchun Environmental Protection Bureau received only 24.5 hours of training to update their work-related knowledge and skills, which was far less than the 86.5 hours of training given to staff at the Haidian Environmental Protection Bureau. The staff at the Haidian Education Commission also received more training than the staff in Changchun.

Scholars argued that training was helpful for the government employees to fulfill their missions since the lack of training would lead to poor policy implementation. For example, according to one survey, 65 percent of the officials in the environmental protection bureaux in Guangzhou, Nanjing and Zhengzhou said that a lack of technical knowledge was the major problem while 56 percent of them cited a shortage of technical staff as the major problem in implementing environmental protection policy (Chan *et al.* 1995). The evaluation of environmental performance in Changchun in this study was consistent with the above survey. The lack of financial resources and the subsequent lack of training were perceived to be the important constraints on bureau performance. Respondents in Changchun identified this as 'a key bottleneck'. They argued that government had committed too few financial resources to environmental protection. According to them, many new environmental problems had emerged with economic development, which the resource-starved Environmental Protection Bureau had difficulty handling. Accordingly, they asked for more financial resources to renew equipment and to provide more technical training.[20]

The poor performance of Changchun in environmental protection might also be due to the limited human resources. According to another study, limited

*Table 4.9* Training hours

| Policy domain | | Bureaux | | | |
| --- | --- | --- | --- | --- | --- |
| Education | Environment | Changchun education | Haidian education | Changchun environment | Haidian environment |
| 61 | 65 | 5 | 69 | 25 | 87 |

Source: Fieldwork survey, March–April 2004.

Note
The interviewees were asked to point out hours of refresher training (training to update work-related knowledge and skills) they received in year 2003. Data in table are the average level.

human resources was an important constraint for environmental protection work. 'They [environmental protection bureaux] need more staff, more skill, and more expertise to implement environmental policies' (Swanson *et al.* 2001: 487). The limited human resources of the Changchun government were manifested in the bureaucratic infrastructure. The city appeared to have been under-resourced in both environmental protection and education. In my study, environmental protection bureaux ranged from 28 to 30 employees. In spite of variation in population, the environmental protection bureau in Changchun with twice as many people was the same size as the bureau in Ningbo. The education bureaux/commissions, by contrast, varied in size from 64 employees in the more populous Changchun to 90 or more in the less populous Ningbo and Haidian districts.[21]

At the outset of the reform in Changchun, considerably more civil servants were evaluated as 'incompetent' (0.4 percent in 1995) than in either Haidian or Ningbo. Unusually, the Party in Changchun issued special regulations to punish poor performers that resulted in several dozens of officials being dismissed in subsequent years (1998 and 1999). I speculated that Changchun, faced with very real downsizing targets and the inability to transfer officials to other posts, used the appraisals to identify underperformers for dismissal and achieved a more efficient outcome that was more in line with the civil service reform objectives than Haidian or Ningbo. Subsequently, the percentage of employees that was rated as 'incompetent' in Changchun fell to 0.14 percent in both 2000 and 2001, which was closer to the norm. In practice, the individual performance evaluation system introduced by the reforms, as it has come to be practiced, was relatively undiscriminating.

As discussed above, local governments conducted annual performance appraisal and evaluated individual civil servants according to one of the four grades classifications. Within a local bureau, only 15 percent of the staff could be graded as 'outstanding'. These 'outstanding' employees would be entitled to rewards. The aim of the reward program was to instill a sense of competition and, hence, to motivate civil servants. However, the reward program could fail if the subordinates of a bureau colluded with one another and went behind their superiors. From the principal–agent perspective, the horizontal (subordinate-subordinate) trust of an organization is likely to cause harm to organizational productivity. This is because when horizontal trust of an organization increases, new principal–agent problems will emerge. These new principal–agent problems usually take the form of collusion among agents. The agency lost to the collusion problem can be illustrated in the following reward practices. To improve the organizational productivity, the principal of the organization may launch a competitive reward program. The principal hopes that the competition for the rewards may induce more effort from the agents and, accordingly, the collective performance (organizational productivity) will improve. However, ordinal measures of performance rather than cardinal measures are used in competition and reward practices. That is, the principal just compares the agents with one another because he does not know every agent's absolute performance. In other words, these practices evaluate and then compensate one agent's performance relative to that of other agents. Such schemes will fail when the agents collude with one another against the principal. How do the agents collude? They do not put in the extra effort by merely continuing their work routine. Sometimes, they may even shirk. Under such circumstances, when the principal wrongly identifies the 'good' performer and distributes the reward, the agents will find it in their interest to collude with one another since it appears to them that reward is not related to performance. As such, the principal pays extra costs (the rewards), but the organizational productivity does not improve.

Evidence showed that in the Ningbo Education Commission and the Haidian Education Commission, serious collusion problems emerged during their implementation of reward programs. When asked about the implementation of the program, one official from the Ningbo Education Commission stated that he and his colleagues had a kind of common understanding. They would simply continue their work routine and claim the rewards in the yearly rotation.[22] In the interviewee's opinion, it was in the interests of the bureau superiors to maintain the harmony within the bureau and, thus, the superiors would not reward one subordinate twice while giving none to the others. If this was the common understanding shared among the staff of the Ningbo Education Commission, I would conclude that quite a serious collusion problem had emerged under the current program design. The interviewee's opinion was confirmed by another interviewee in the Ningbo Education Commission. She commented that the superior's preference for organizational harmony within the bureau was understandable since that is the preferable state in traditional Chinese culture.[23]

I also found a collusion problem among officials in the Haidian Education Commission. One interviewee revealed that 'there was no competition at all'. Upon realizing that the bureau superiors favored organizational harmony and would treat the subordinates equally, he saw there was little point in putting more effort into his work.[24] Another interviewee commented that the monetary value of the reward, generally 300–400 *yuan*, was limited. This amount was not enough to motivate the subordinates to compete. 'We do not care about it,' the interviewee said.[25] I concluded that the reward program failed in the Haidian Education Commission due to the emergence of collusion and the disappearance of competition.

## Conclusion

The impacts of reforms were shown to vary among the three fieldwork sites. These differences in reform outcomes were crucial to the understanding of the civil service reforms given that local policy implementation was constrained by many factors. It was likely that given its proximity to power, Haidian felt confident about allowing more of its cadres into the new civil service and it implemented the reforms earlier than the other two areas. Haidian started first (as a pilot within Beijing) and opened up civil service posts to competition the earliest, followed by Ningbo and then Changchun. Differences in economic development might account for the variation in the relative size and composition of the various civil service agencies. With a less developed economy, Changchun appeared to be under-resourced compared to the other two places, a condition that might have affected their capacity to implement civil service reform and the staffing levels of the education and environmental protection bureaux compared to population size. Still, Changchun used individual appraisals more effectively to weed out the underperformers, especially in the early days of the reform. One explanation could be that it had no option but to terminate their employment to meet downsizing targets.

# 5 Control of the bureaucracy and reform outcomes

This book views the civil service reform not only as a means to improve government administrative efficiency, but also as an instrument for the Chinese Communist Party (CCP) to control the government and for the central government to control the local governments.[1] This chapter focuses on the ability of the Chinese leadership to control policy implementation within a decentralized bureaucratic system. Since the late 1970s, the central government has devolved a wide range of decision-making powers to the lower levels of government with an aim to promote local incentives and effective governance. As decentralization got underway, bureaucratic non-compliance emerged as one of the most challenging problems faced by the leadership (Chang 2001; Pei 2006, 1994). The leadership realized this and reformed the civil service management and other administrative monitoring measures accordingly. Reforms within the CCP and some anticorruption measures were initiated and implemented from the 1990s. This chapter will examine whether the implementation of the civil service reforms and other related programs helped the central leadership to strengthen its control over the local governments and bureaucrats. In particular, this chapter aims to answer two questions: (1) How did the reforms affect the ability of the Chinese leadership to control the bureaucracy? and (2) what were the implications of the reforms for the relationships between the political leadership, the bureaucrats and the citizens?

Although some of the personnel power was delegated to the local governments during the reform era, the central leadership remained the only legitimate body with the authority to appoint and dismiss provincial leaders. Similarly, provincial leaders exercised tight control over their immediate subordinates through their control of appointment and dismissal decisions. This tight control extended to the very bottom of the bureaucratic hierarchy. A great deal of literature argued that the central leadership was capable of institutional adaptability and its capacity to control and monitor lower-level agents increased in China (Burns 1999a; Edin 2003; Huang 2002, 1996; Landry 2008; Yang 2004). The current principal–agent analysis reached similar conclusions. I argued that policy-makers in China improved their capacity to control the local governments and bureaucrats through the implementation of the civil service reforms and other administrative monitoring measures. The reforms were intended to strengthen the Party's ruling capacity and, to some extent, it was successful. As a result, the CCP exhibited institutional adaptability.

This chapter is structured into four sections. The first section describes the three-actor games among the central leadership, civil servants and citizens in order to explain why the leadership decentralized the personnel management system in the 1980s. The second section reviews and analyzes how the upper levels of the Party-government (*dangzheng*) have strengthened their personnel control over the lower-level bureaucrats through an array of competitive appointment and promotion, performance evaluation, rotation and avoidance. Other related initiatives such as administrative monitoring, intra-party reforms and anticorruption measures are reviewed in the third section. Section four analyzes the changing pattern observed in public service delivery and citizen satisfaction accompanied with the civil service reforms.

## Decentralization of personnel management

Exercising control over the bureaucracy is a matter that concerns not only the central leadership, but also the civil servants and citizens. Accordingly, we need to define these three actors in order to understand the games among them. In the Chinese political system, power is, in theory, concentrated in the hands of the National People's Congress (NPC). But in reality, it is monopolized by the central leadership of the Party-government.[2] A group of policy-makers, including top leaders in the CCP's Politburo, Central Committee and the central government's State Council[3] occupies all of the important positions at the top of the hierarchy of the Party-government in China and, hence, this group of policy-makers consists of the central leadership in the Chinese political system.

In between the central leadership and the citizens are the civil servants (bureaucrats). In the discussion of local bureaucrats, this book makes a distinction between leaders of the local government and officials who work in the local government agencies. Leaders of local governments—such as governors of provinces, city mayors and county magistrates—are in charge of the overall development of the regions under their jurisdiction. We may call them local leaders. The other local bureaucrats working in the various local government agencies for specific policy areas such as personnel, environment and education are responsible for the missions in their respective fields. We may call them local agents.[4] I have already discussed the incentives and behaviors of the individual local agents in Chapter 3 and Chapter 4. This chapter will discuss the motivation of the local leaders. It was found that promotion served as the strongest motivator for local leaders. They wanted to get promoted to the higher ranks of the bureaucratic hierarchy. As discussed in Chapter 2, there was a unified national bureaucratic ranking system where each official position was ranked systematically. Bureaucrats could easily compare their positions in the hierarchy even though they came from different government agencies and geographic areas. Positions high up on the hierarchical ladder were usually associated with a larger income, access to more power, more influence and resources (such as a bigger budget

*Control of the bureaucracy and reform outcomes* 95

and more manpower), more rent-seeking opportunities and higher social prestige.

Now let me put this in the context of a three-actor game among the central policy-makers, local leaders and citizens. The central leadership was the de facto principal while the citizens played the part of the symbolic principal and the local leaders were the agents. The central leadership looked for public support from the citizens while the career-oriented local leaders needed approval from the central leadership. In China, since local leaders were appointed by and responsible to their superiors, which ultimately were the central leaders, they sought to win the favor of the central leaders, especially when their prospects for promotion were heavily dependent on their rapport with the central government. Under this incentive structure, local leaders became very responsive to the management rules that the central leaders put in place for them. Moreover, the culture that the civil servants curry favor with the leadership was entrenched in the Chinese tradition. For an official, the ability to fully and correctly anticipate the superior's will was a valuable asset.

To tailor the personnel management system to the more decentralized economy and to induce more investment in human capital from local governments, the central leadership decentralized some personnel management authority. One major initiative was the replacement of the two-level-down cadre management system by the one-level-down system. Prior to 1983, the central party authorities (formally the Central Committee and the Organization Department) were responsible for cadre management at the next two lower levels. Thus, for central government posts, the Central Committee was in charge of the ministerial and bureau-level officials. For local government posts, the Central Committee was in charge of the provincial and their bureau-level officials and prefectural officials. The 1983–1984 reforms delegated bureau-level appointments to the ministries and provinces. That is, under a one-level-down system, the Central Committee managed the ministerial and provincial officials while bureau-level officials within ministries and provinces were managed by the ministerial party groups or by the provincial party committees.

As a result of this change, the party center as of 1984 was directly responsible for the appointment and removal of 7,000 cadres, a reduction of some 6,000 from the previous system (Huang 1996, 1995). Personnel power was further decentralized in the 1990s. Burns (1994a) estimated that the central *nomenklatura* positions to be numbered around 4,100 as of 1990. What was the resulted situation in the central control of the cadre management under the one-level-down system? I will examine all five levels of the administration in China: center, province, prefecture/city, county and township. Huang (1995) concluded that Beijing's political control of provincial behavior did not significantly erode. In municipalities and prefectures, the center's influence on local officials was not direct, but was still strongly felt via the center's direct oversight of the heads of municipal organization departments. That was because of the fact that the one-level-down principle did not apply to the system of party organization departments. The Central Committee maintained *nomenklatura* authority over the directors and deputy directors of both the provincial and municipal/prefectural organization departments via the Central Organization Department (Landry 2008). Unlike provinces or prefectures, the county was the first level of local government where neither cadres nor any of their leaders in party organs were controlled directly from Beijing. However, the indirect control still remained. High-level county officials (deputy county magistrate and above) were appointed by the municipal party committees and municipal organization departments were under central control.

Another critical initiative was the establishment of the former Ministry of Personnel in March 1988, which was set up to implement the civil service reforms and to manage the civil service. The Central Committee and its Organization Department delegated some personnel management authority to the former Ministry of Personnel. Specifically, the Ministry took charge of revising the drafts of the regulations on civil service management, conducting experiments with new designs, consulting with the Organization Department, and holding conferences on the civil service system.

At first glance, it seemed that the CCP gave substantial personnel power to the government (especially from the Organization Department to the former Ministry of Personnel) and that the upper-level Party-government (particularly the central leadership) delegated certain personnel power to the lower levels. However, the central leadership's delegation of power in the area of personnel management was a tactic to create incentives for the local governments and bureaucrats to perform tasks that the central leadership could not handle alone. First, the two-level-down system turned into a heavy burden for the central leadership. Too much power was concentrated at the top and the number of cadres was too large for the party center to conduct effective monitoring. The leadership claimed that the central party officials were too involved in detailed personnel decisions, leaving limited time for long-term policy planning and the formulation of broad policy principles (Huang 1996: 92–3; 1995). Second, under the two-level-down management system, two legal superiors could be in charge of its personnel matters for the same hierarchical level. This overlap not only created conflict of interests, but also conflict of instructions as subordinates found themselves reporting to two superiors. For example, for a bureau in a prefecture, both the provincial and the prefecture leaders were given control over personnel matters. It was possible for the leaders to issue conflicting instructions or to pursue incompatible personnel decisions. In some circumstances, a bureau that received conflicting instructions might go directly to its upper-level superior instead of the immediate one. This kind of behavior would have damaging effects on administrative efficiency. Third, due to the over-centralization of personnel power, local governments lacked the incentives and autonomy to invest in their own human capital (for example, provide training for their staff).

As such, devolution of power relieved the central leadership from a heavy personnel management burden. Moreover, it motivated the local governments to not only manage their immediate subordinates, but invest in human capital to a certain extent. The rationale of the decentralization of personnel management

*Control of the bureaucracy and reform outcomes* 97

was that by gaining more authority, the local party committees and local governments would take the initiatives to recruit younger and more capable employees who could best promote local economic development.

## Programs of the civil service reforms to reassert control

While decentralizing some personnel management authority improved local incentives and effective governance, the central leadership initiated, almost simultaneously, a series of reform programs to reassert its control over the local governments and bureaucrats. I will first analyze the programs of the civil service reforms and then extend the analysis to related measures such as administrative monitoring and anticorruption efforts.

There is a distinction between ordinary cadres and leading cadres (*lingdao ganbu*) in the Chinese political terminology. The leading cadres, defined as cadres at the county/division level and above, form the backbone of the political system. Specifically, they are the leading members of the Central Committee of the CCP, the Standing Committee of the NPC, the State Council, the Chinese People's Political Consultative Conference (CPPCC), the Central Discipline Inspection Commission (CDIC), the Supreme People's Court, the Supreme People's Procuratorate as well as the leading members of the party committees, standing committees of people's congresses, governments, political consultative conferences, discipline inspection commissions, courts, procuratorates and their departments at the provincial, prefecture and county levels.[5] In 1998, the leading cadres numbered 508,025 (see Table 5.1). The most important leading cadres were those at the ministerial/provincial level and they were controlled by the Central Committee's *nomenklatura*. They numbered 2,562 in 1998 and constituted only about 0.5 percent of all leading cadres. 92 percent (or 466,355) of the leading cadres were cadres working at the county/division level. Among the leading cadres, 41,689 (8 percent) people worked for the central organs in Beijing. Given the large number of the leading cadres and the fact that they held all of the important positions within the political and administrative system, controlling the leading cadres was one of the most important tasks for the central leadership. Within the civil service reform programs, the leadership reasserted control over leading cadres mainly through competitive appointment and promotion, performance evaluation, rotation and avoidance.

### *Competitive appointment and promotion of leading cadres*

The practices of appointing and promoting leading cadres should follow several important principles and the most important and basic one was that the CCP should control and manage the leading cadres. Civil service reforms did not undermine this basic principle. Instead, it was re-emphasized by several very important documents such as the 2002 *Regulations on Selection and Appointment of Party and Government Leading Cadres* that was issued by the Central Committee in July 2002. It listed the principle that 'the Party controls cadres' as

Table 5.1 Number and distribution of leading cadres, 1979–1998

| Year | Total | Provincial/ministerial level and above | Bureau/department level | Division/county level | Total numbers worked in the central government |
|---|---|---|---|---|---|
| 1979 | 159,065 | 1,646 | 22,450 | 134,969 | 15,707 |
| 1980 | 167,650 | 1,882 | 23,483 | 142,285 | 17,498 |
| 1981 | 183,927 | 1,791 | 23,875 | 158,261 | 18,878 |
| 1982 | 198,229 | 1,849 | 25,123 | 171,257 | 21,282 |
| 1983 | 199,826 | 2,179 | 26,058 | 171,589 | 22,088 |
| 1984 | 230,776 | 2,143 | 26,294 | 202,339 | 26,982 |
| 1985 | 259,596 | 2,150 | 27,906 | 229,540 | 30,056 |
| 1986 | 287,809 | 2,197 | 28,899 | 256,713 | 31,165 |
| 1987 | 305,646 | 2,156 | 29,623 | 273,867 | 31,599 |
| 1988 | 317,123 | 2,316 | 30,322 | 284,485 | 29,557 |
| 1989 | 335,018 | 2,280 | 30,699 | 302,039 | 28,878 |
| 1990 | 344,785 | 2,261 | 30,259 | 312,265 | 29,274 |
| 1991 | 361,512 | 2,285 | 31,881 | 327,346 | 32,735 |
| 1992 | 376,773 | 2,258 | 33,148 | 341,367 | 34,766 |
| 1993 | 398,189 | 2,590 | 34,498 | 361,101 | 32,015 |
| 1994 | 406,119 | 2,465 | 33,451 | 370,203 | 37,728 |
| 1995 | 445,286 | 2,459 | 35,620 | 407,207 | 43,322 |
| 1996 | 468,274 | 2,317 | 37,011 | 428,946 | 44,950 |
| 1997 | 492,328 | 2,406 | 39,181 | 450,741 | 49,411 |
| 1998 | 508,025 | 2,562 | 39,108 | 466,355 | 41,689 |

Source: Organization Department of CCP (1999: 3).

the first and overarching principle in selecting and appointing party- and government-leading cadres. The passage of the *Civil Service Law* in 2005 suggested that the principle of absolute party control over the cadres was enshrined into law. It reinforced the idea that that the Party controlled the cadres in the Chinese political system.

Putting aside the dominate role of the Party, the practice of appointing and promoting leading cadres changed significantly with the civil service reforms. Under the old cadre system, the criteria for bureaucratic promotion were political loyalty and appropriate social class background. From the superior's perspective, people who were loyal and could faithfully follow the superior's commands should be promoted and entrusted with more responsibilities. Here, loyalty included both personal attachment to the superior and commitment to the Communist ideology. Since the reforms, the appointment and promotion of the leading cadres focused on openness, competition and meritocracy. Specifically, the promotion criteria under the new civil service system focused on work performance and problem-solving ability. Deng Xiaoping first put the reform of the cadre system on the Party's agenda in his August 1980 address to the Politburo (Deng 1984). The four criteria—revolutionary, better educated, professional and young—were formally enshrined in the CCP's Constitution as a guideline for the selection of new leading cadres in 1982. The requirement of being 'revolutionary' was the only the requirement that was somewhat related to Mao's criteria for loyalty and social class background while the other three equally important criteria (better educated, professional and young) all emphasized technical competence. The focus on work performance and problem-solving capabilities could be easily deciphered from this technical consideration.

Scholars of China study noticed this change in criteria and they argued that the overemphasis on political loyalty in the Mao era was replaced by merit-based standards of education and professional competence (Bo 2004, 2002; Edin 2003; Liu 2001). Liu (2001) demonstrated that better trained and educated applicants were gradually replacing the 'ideologically correct' when it came to recruitment and advancement in positions. Professionalism, youth, competence and a cosmopolitan outlook were in demand while party loyalty was on the decline. It was generally understood that promotions were granted to applicants who were capable of promoting economic development and boosting the new leadership's legitimacy (Bo 2004, 2002).

As competition within the selection of the leading cadres increased, important documents were issued to ensure the educational level of the candidates. For example, the 2002 Regulations required explicitly that all leading cadres in party and government organizations must meet two educational criteria: (1) they must have some university-level education and (2) they must have undergone at least three months of training in a party school or an administration school within the past five years. These requirements implied a positive correlation between rank and the level of formal education. This helped to improve the quality of the Chinese civil service.

## *The leading cadres' responsibility system*

Besides competitive appointment and promotion, the central leadership strengthened its control over local governments and bureaucrats through exercising performance evaluation. A performance evaluation system served as a powerful instrument for the upper-level Party-government to ensure control over its lower-level organizations and their leading officials. Superiors would set targets for their subordinates at the start of evaluation period, assess their performance at the end of the period and, based on the results of the evaluation, issue rewards and punishments accordingly. The origin of this system dated back to 1979 when the CCP's Organization Department established a cadre evaluation system. At first, the Organization Department only outlined a vague requirement for cadre evaluations. Thereafter, it defined the content and procedure of the process in an increasingly detailed manner. Over the years, there were efforts to institutionalize this form of performance evaluation by making it a regular and systematic operation. Gradually, the various methods of performance evaluation for the leading cadres in local party and government organs aggregated into the leading cadres' responsibility system (Huang 1996, 1995; Edin 2003; Whiting 2004, 2000).

The targets given to the local party and government leaders by the central government gradually became comprehensive and concrete. The performance criteria could be adjusted and new ones could be added in response to the changing circumstances. The Organization Department established official guidelines for the annual evaluation of the local party and government leading cadres in 1988, which contained very specific performance criteria such as industrial output, output of township-run and village-run enterprises, remittances in taxes and profits (Edin 2003; Whiting 2000: 102–3). In 1998, the Organization Department promulgated temporary regulations for the assessment of the local party and government leaders. This document stipulated explicitly the institutions to organize the evaluation as well as the method, contents, process and the application of the evaluation results.[6] Besides the emphasis on the local economic development, the central leadership was also concerned about other non-economic policy areas such as family planning, environmental protection and social order. Over time, these areas were given more weight in terms of evaluating local performance. In 2006, the Organization Department promulgated a new set of regulations to assess local leaders' work performance under the name of pursuing a scientific view of development, which is the general principle of policy-making proposed by Hu Jintao. This document listed many specific indicators in evaluating local leaders' performance in both economic and non-economic areas. The indicators included the level and growth rate of GDP per capita, the level and growth rate of fiscal revenue per capita, the level and growth rate of residents' income, energy consumption and production safety, basic education, urban employment, social security, cultural life of residents, family planning, natural resource conversation, environmental protection and scientific development and innovations.[7]

In addition to specifying performance criteria and targets, the leading cadres' responsibility system also spelt out evaluation procedures in the performance contracts (*zerenzhuang*). The performance contracts specified the rewards or penalties that came with the different levels of performance. To increase the likelihood that assigned tasks would be carried out, a higher government level would typically withhold a substantial portion (as much as 15 percent) of the compensation of its subordinate organ. Allocating these funds would be solely based on the performance of the leading cadre of the subordinate organ. Thus, local leaders who performed poorly might lose out to their more successful peers. Moreover, officials at higher levels would sometimes award generous bonuses to those who attained unusually tough targets. Nevertheless, simply meeting a target would generally bring about substantial payoff (Edin 2003; O'Brien and Li 1999).

The leading cadres' responsibility system had several advantages. First, by setting and adjusting the performance criteria, the central government could send a clear message to local agents about work priorities, its expectations and the reward system. Second, the evaluations of local cadres also provided vital information for the central leadership about local performance. Based on this information, the central leadership could reward the excellent and competent local officials and demote the incompetent ones. Third, local cadres would rationally put more effort into their work given that their personal income and political promotion were tied to their work performance (particularly in economic terms) under such a system. Among scholars who extensively studied the effectiveness of the leading cadres' responsibility system, Edin (2003) found that this system was very useful for the central government to monitor and control local agents. She suggested that the Chinese Party-government possessed the capacity to be selectively effective. That is, to implement its priority policies and control its key local leaders strategically in important areas.

## *Rotation and avoidance*

Another critical initiative in the civil service system package that strengthened the central government's control over the bureaucracy was the exchange and rotation of the civil servants, a program that was widely studied in the literature (Edin 2003; Yang 2004). Under the program, local officials were regularly rotated between equally ranked positions and across different geographical areas. These practices became institutionalized as a key component of the Chinese personnel management system since the 1990s. In 1996, the former Ministry of Personnel issued the *Provisional Regulations of the State Civil Servant Position Rotation* to regulate this part of the reform. Articles 2 and 4 stated that officials in the leading positions of the government departments were obliged to participate in position rotation every five years.[8] Chapter 11 of the *Civil Service Law* summarized the prior regulations and provided guidelines in managing position exchange and rotation for civil servants. According to the document, non-leading officials in charge of human resources, finance, discipline inspection and auditing were also required to participate in regular job rotations. The rotation and exchange programs were targeted at cadres with promotion prospects. The aims were, first, to broaden the experience and vision of cadres so as to strengthen their capacity and, second, to ameliorate organizational corruption.

In practice, the former Ministry of Personnel chose 20 civil servants (28 percent) at bureau level and 57 (42 percent) at division level to participate in the rotation exercise in 1994. In 1996, the figures rose to 32 civil servants (42.6 percent) at bureau level and 78 (58.6 percent) at division level.[9] In local governments, 52,000 civil servants participated in job rotations across the country in 1996. The number rose to 145,000 in 1999. From 1996 to 2003, more than 900,000 people nationwide rotated or exchanged their positions (Zhang 2006).

From the principal–agent perspective, rotation and exchange programs resulted in several benefits and, hence, helped the central leadership to strengthen its control over the bureaucracy. First, rotation curbed local deviations from central instructions. If an official expected *ex ante* that he would be rotated to another position, his incentive to abide by the decisions of the upper-level leaders would be strengthened. This was because he would gain little in over-aggressively pursuing the interests associated with his current position given that he was expected to be rotated to another position. By the same logic, since the rotation had a fixed term, if one official was rotated to a new position, he would know *ex ante* when this rotation would end. Thus, he would not over-aggressively pursue the interests associated with this new position in contradiction with the upper leaders' instructions. Moreover, the rotators would be motivated to cooperate with other agencies since they might work together as colleagues in the future.

Second, rotation and exchange programs made available to the central leadership certain information about local implementation that would otherwise be unavailable. To elaborate, no matter how successfully an official could hide his work records from his superior, he could not hide them from his successor because his successor would inevitably acquire all of his past work records over time and, thus, any hidden information would gradually be revealed. From the successor's perspective, it would be in his interest to be upfront about his work records and accomplishments to his leaders since his performance evaluation would be based on what he had accomplished during his work term. If he could show that he had made a contribution at work or at least identified clearly what he had accomplished in his work report, he might gain a promotion or some other rewards. In this way, rotation and exchange programs helped the central leadership to obtain valuable *ex post* information about the local implementation of central policy. Given China's comprehensive personnel dossier system, this information would help the center in singling out the real performers.

Third, scholars also found that the central government had strategically accelerated the elite turnover at the local level through the rotation programs; hence, informally reduced the length of tenure of local officials (Huang 1996; Landry 2004; Li 1998). It is generally recognized that the shorter the tenure, the greater the number of new appointments. Given that each new appointment was subjected to both review and authorization by the relevant organization department, a greater number of appointments, in effect, enabled the organization departments and party committees to have greater political control over the appointment of new employees. Landry (2004) showed that the turnover among the Chinese local cadres was extremely high and that central government was successful in reducing the length of tenure of municipal officials. Among mayors, the average length of tenure shrank from an average of 3.2 years in 1990 to a mere 2.5 years by 2001. Moreover, few mayors served a full term. In 1990, 42 served more than five years in the same city compared with only ten in 2002.

The practice of avoidance as a program of civil service reform also helped the central leadership to constrain local officials in exercising discretion. The avoidance system included the avoidance of kinship and avoidance of native place. According to Article 68 of the *Civil Service Law*, kinship avoidance was applicable to spouses, lineal blood relations and collateral relatives (blood or marriage) within three generations. If any two officials were related through the above-mentioned ties, they should not work in the same work unit if both of them directly reported to the same leaders or if one was a direct superior or subordinate of the other. If one person was a leader in an agency, any person related to him should not engage in certain work duties such as personnel management, discipline inspection, auditing or financial affairs in the same unit. According to Article 69, native place avoidance required that a person should not hold a county magistrate (town mayor) or party secretary position in his or her native place. County magistrates and party secretaries who were elected to their position in their native place should be relocated after the initial term expired. The avoidance system has been adopted in China since imperial times in order to avoid nepotism and to prevent local officials from developing a local power network. It has been implemented broadly in local China since the 1990s (Li 2004). From 1998 to 2002, about 29,832 people changed their positions in line with the avoidance regulations (Yin 2003). The avoidance system reduced the tendency of the local officials to form entrenched interests with their relatives and the native elites; therefore, it guaranteed the commitment of local officials in the faithful implementation of central policies.

## Intra-party reforms and anticorruption measures

The reform of the two-level-down cadre management system to the one-level-down system delegated certain personnel management authority from the upper-level Party-government to the lower levels. After this reform, the county was the first level of local government where neither cadres nor any of their leaders in party organs were controlled directly from Beijing. At the county level and below, the chiefs of their party committees, the party secretaries, played a dominant role in selecting, appointing and promoting cadres. This domination engendered numerous corrupt practices in personnel management such as buying and selling government posts (see discussion in Chapter 3). To combat corruption, the upper-level Party-government applied measures to control the personnel management of the lower levels. These measures included counterbalancing the local party secretaries' domination in making personnel decisions and, hence, reduced the opportunities for rent-seeking, strengthened the role of the local party committees (the entire committee but not the standing committee) and strengthened the role of the discipline inspection commissions. This section will examine them in turn.

### *Counterbalancing local party committee secretaries*

To understand why local party secretaries could dominate important personnel decisions, we need to first achieve a better grasp of the organizational structure of the local party committees. Although the post-Mao authorities tried to separate the Party from the formal structure and function of the government, the decoupling was far from complete. The Party remained an intrusive force of the government. At local levels, the Party was deeply entrenched in government organizations and work units (Zhong 2003). For example, at the county level, the county party committee (*xian dangwei*) was the power center of county governance. The committee was officially elected by the county party congress that was held every five years. The county party apparatus typically consisted of the following key organizations: standing committee (*changweihui*) of the county party committee, general office, discipline inspection commission, organization department, propaganda department, united front department and party school office. The county party committee was made up of approximately 20 members (including the standing committee members plus party secretaries of large townships/towns and chiefs of important county government bureaux). At the heart of the county party apparatus was the standing committee of the county party committee. The size of this committee varied from county to county. In theory, the members of the committee should number around 11 for larger counties and 7–9 for counties of regular sizes. The committee was headed by one party secretary and 2–3 deputy secretaries. Yet, in most places, the committee consisted of 9–15 members including one party secretary and 3–4 deputy secretaries. Each of the deputy secretaries was in charge of a specific area such as industry, agriculture or mass organization (Zhong 2003: 57).

At various levels of the local Party-government, the most powerful person was the party committee secretary. All five sets of the local authorities (the Communist Party organs, the government, the people's congress, the political consultative conference and the local party discipline inspection commission) were placed under the direct control of the local party secretary. The government officials such as the county magistrate or township mayor typically occupied the position of the first deputy party secretary, which was subordinate to the party secretary. Most importantly, the party secretary was in firm control of personnel decisions in all five sets of the local authorities. Any major appointment or promotion decision was made by the local party committee, which was chaired by the party secretary. However, the personnel power could be easily abused by the party secretaries. Numerous reports revealed that party officials were involved in corruption such as buying and selling government posts (see discussion in Chapter 3).

The CCP emphasized frequently the principle of 'collective leadership', which required that all party organs refrain from the arbitrary use of absolute power without consultation in the decision-making process. Under the principle of 'collective leadership', all important decisions (including personnel decisions) should be discussed and decided by all party committee members according to the principle of 'democratic centralism' rather than just by the party secretary. To counterbalance the local party secretary's dominant role in personnel decisions, the policy-makers in China took the initiatives to decentralize power-share among the local party elites as well as to specifically strengthen the status of other members in the local party standing committee. Measures were taken to strengthen the status of the local party committee vis-à-vis the local party standing committee since the latter possessed too much control of the personnel.

A series of new regulations and operational procedures were introduced into the decision-making practices of the local party committees from 2004 (Gong 2009, 2008; Sun 2009). The regulations required that a two-thirds quorum of the members of a given committee should be present when appointment and dismissal of cadres was being discussed.[10] When the candidates for a leading position within the local Party-government were considered, a formal vote by the standing committee of the local party committee was required. For example, at the country level, a formal vote by the standing committee of the county party committee was required for the appointment and promotion decisions concerning leading cadres at the bureau level (bureau chiefs and deputy chiefs). For appointment and promotion decisions concerning leading cadres at the township/town level (party secretaries, mayors, deputy party secretaries and deputy mayors), a formal vote by the county party committee (the entire committee) was required. Through elevating other members in the local party committee, these procedural requirements placed considerable constraint on the dominance of local party secretaries.

## *Local party committee vs. the standing committee*

The power concentration problem was serious in China. For example, while the party congresses at the local levels performed symbolic functions, the real decisions were actually made by the local party committees, particularly the standing committees. Accordingly, measures were introduced so that important decisions would be made by the full membership of local party committees rather than standing committee members alone. These procedural requirements had the effect of strengthening the status of the local party committee vis-à-vis the local party standing committee. Measures were also introduced to improve the function of the local party congress. Regulations required that party congresses at all levels convene once each year. In addition to this requirement, all the meeting regulations and operational procedures should be followed by local party congresses to ensure good practices in the discussion and decision-making process. On the occasion of selecting important leading cadres, a formal vote at a plenary session of the local party congress was required. The voting method was experimented in selected provinces and cities from 2001 (Sun 2009). By 2005, Guangdong had implemented the voting method comprehensively across its cities and counties while a few other provinces, mostly developed regions, implemented the voting method at selected ranks (Sun 2009: 50).

## *Strengthening discipline inspection*

The Chinese leadership attempted to strengthen its discipline inspection mechanisms in order to combat corruption found in the personnel management system. A new Central Discipline Inspection Commission (CDIC) of the CCP was established in 1979 to put an end to the chaos caused by the Cultural Revolution. Its local branches at various levels were created in subsequent years. The organizational structure of the discipline inspection commissions was similar to the other Party organs. The local discipline inspection commissions were under a dual leadership system. In theory, provincial and lower discipline inspection commissions were subjected to the dual leadership of their immediate superiors within the inspection system (i.e., the discipline inspection commission at the next higher level) and the local party committee of the same level, but in practice, they were managed by local party committees (Gong 2009).

The missions of the discipline inspection commissions included enforcing party discipline and investigating disciplinary violation cases that involved party members. Unfortunately, the discipline inspection commissions faced institutional constraints in maintaining the discipline among the leading cadres in the Party and government organs. As a long-standing common practice, members of any discipline inspection commission including its chief were selected by the local party committee at the same level and were subsequently endorsed by the local people's congress. Such an institutional arrangement made it difficult for the discipline inspection commissions to supervise local leading cadres since the latter actually held the personnel power over discipline inspection commissions. A mechanism aimed at enhancing the authority of the discipline inspection commissions vis-à-vis local party committees proposed the vertical appointment of the personnel of the discipline inspection commissions, thus freeing them from the influence of the local party committee.

In the late 1990s, the city of Zhangjiajie in Hunan province introduced a new method to select leaders of the local discipline inspection commissions. From 1991 to 1997, chiefs of the discipline inspection commissions in four counties were selected and appointed by the city discipline inspection commission instead of the four counties' party committees. The innovation in the case of Zhangjiajie lay in moving the authority over leadership selection from the party committee to the discipline inspection commission at the next level up in order to reduce interference with disciplinary affairs by the local officials. The case of Zhangjiajie enhanced the party's discipline inspection over the local leading cadres. For example, in one of the four counties, a county (division) level official was found to be corrupted by the chief of the county discipline inspection commission and faced Party discipline sanctions. Scholars considered this a successful case in enforcing Party discipline. They argued that the key factor that enabled the exposure of and real sanction against corruption was that the county discipline inspection commission chief in question was appointed by the city discipline inspection commission who was not personally connected with the county officials (Ren 2007). This experiment, nevertheless, did not yield much impact on other localities. Over time, the experiment was terminated as it did not receive adequate political attention and support.

Besides the changes in their leaders' selection method, the reporting structure of the local discipline inspection commissions underwent changes as well. At the 2001 plenary session, the CDIC required the chiefs of the local discipline inspection commissions to be the vice party secretaries.[11] Promulgated in 2004, the *Internal Supervision Regulation* amended the reporting structure for the local discipline inspection commissions. A discipline inspection commission might report cases it deemed important directly to its immediate supervisors within the discipline inspection system without the approval of the same level party committee (Gong 2008). This measure also helped local discipline inspection commissions to supervise the behaviors of local leading cadres.

In conducting discipline investigations, the discipline inspection commissions in recent years developed a powerful means to combat corruption. Labeled as 'double regulations' (*shuanggui*), this referred to the informal but compulsory detention of officials suspected of corruption at a stipulated time and place for investigation (Gong 2008; Sapio 2008). *The Working Regulations on Case Investigation*, issued in March 1994, was the first piece of regulation on *shuanggui*. The regulations gave discipline inspection commissions the authority to 'order those concerned to appear at a specific time and specific place to provide an explanation of the matters under investigation'. Scholars found that *shuanggui* brought on improvements to the discipline inspection commissions by enhancing their efficiency and effectiveness (Gong 2008; Sapio 2008).

In its 16th national congress in 2002, the CCP decided to make the CDIC the chief coordinator of various anticorruption efforts. Since then, the CDIC dispatched ad hoc teams to various localities to conduct discipline inspection and to investigate local officials suspected of corruption. These teams reported directly to the CDIC and their work was exempt from the monitoring and intervention of local party committees. They possessed the authority to call meetings, conduct interviews and review relevant documents for investigation purposes. The assessment of the inspection team was crucial to the fate of local officials suspected of corruption. As McCubbins and Schwartz (1984) described, these inspection teams, dispatched by the CDIC to various localities, functioned like the 'police patrol' inspection. However, it was not easy for the central work groups to uncover suspected corruption cases since local officials were in a more advantageous position with regards to information. Moreover, the extensive social networks common among local officials also increased the difficulty of investigation especially when multiple officials were involved. Therefore, the effectiveness of the police patrol system was uncertain.

In the preceding sections, I described and analyzed how the central leadership tried to reassert control over the bureaucracy over the past three decades. How was it possible that the central leadership strengthened its control of the bureaucracy after devolving personnel power to the local government and bureaucrats? This was possible because from the perspective of the principal–agent logic, the central leadership and the local governments were not locked in a zero-sum game. Neither a reduction in formal power nor central relaxation of control in certain areas represented a sign of diminishing central control. On the contrary, with more aligned interests, the redistribution of power among the central and local governments increased local incentive to comply while also increasing the central government's ability to control. By decentralizing personnel power, signing performance contracts and practicing competitive appointment and promotion, the central leadership constructed an incentive structure that induced compliance from the local agents. Moreover, periodic rotation and exchange programs in China's civil service system and other related administrative monitoring measures provided information about the local agents' behaviors that would not be attainable by the central government otherwise.

## Public service delivery and citizen satisfaction

The success of the control of the bureaucracy lay in the capacity of the central leadership to ensure that the substantive decisions and behaviors of local governments remained consistent with Beijing's broad policy principles. Of course, it

108  *Control of the bureaucracy and reform outcomes*

was impossible to monitor the daily behaviors of the thousands of local governments in China. Nevertheless, scholars agreed that the ultimate test of the control of the bureaucracy was not whether specific local decisions were explicitly cleared by the central leadership, but whether local decisions and actions conformed in significant ways to the broad requirements set by the central leadership (Landry 2008). In the following section, I will first analyze local governments' behavior and performance in delivering public services. The objective statistics and a detailed case study of one public service—environmental protection—constituted important empirical tests of the central government's ability to set policy targets and ensure their implementation at the local levels. Finally, findings of the citizen satisfaction surveys will be presented. The high levels of citizen satisfaction of local government performance in delivering two public services—environmental protection and basic education—indicated that local implementation largely conformed to the requirements of the central policy.

### *Provision pattern of environmental protection service*

According to the National Environmental Protection Bureau, the environment of two of the three cities included in this study improved from 1994 to 1999 (see Table 5.2). If, as many apparently believed, the government had a major responsibility for environmental performance, I would then expect the interviewees to perceive that bureau performance improved in Ningbo and Changchun. In Beijing, however, the environment apparently deteriorated during the said period. Accordingly, I would expect the interviewees, especially clients who tended to be more critical, to perceive that bureau performance declined during the period. Interestingly, the perception data from the officials and clients actually indicated an improvement in the performance of all three places in dealing

*Table 5.2* Environmental performance scores, 1994 and 1999

| Measures | Beijing | | Changchun | | Ningbo | |
| --- | --- | --- | --- | --- | --- | --- |
| | 1994 | 1999 | 1994 | 1999 | 1994 | 1999 |
| General evaluation | 83.62 (2) | 79.03 (17) | 70.88 (27) | 79.67 (14) | 70.17 (29) | 85.33 (3) |
| Environment quality | 22.31 (18) | 20.78 (26) | 18.36 (33) | 26.03 (10) | 20.46 (24) | 28.17 (3) |
| Pollution control | 44.01 (3) | 22.58 (9) | 35.06 (32) | 22.01 (17) | 36.89 (28) | 22.49 (11) |

Source: National Environment Protection Bureau (2000, 1996).

Note
The lower the score, the worse the performance. The scores are a composite of from 6 to 10 different indicators. The number in brackets is the cities' rankings out of 37 cities in 1994 and 38 cities in 1999.

Table 5.3 Perception that bureau performance has improved (percent)

|  | Environment |  |  | Education |  |  |
| --- | --- | --- | --- | --- | --- | --- |
|  | Officials | Clients | Total | Officials | Clients | Total |
| Beijing | 87.5 (8) | 100.0 (6) | 93.0 (14) | 80.0 (5) | 50.0 (10) | 60.0 (15) |
| Changchun | 87.5 (8) | 90.9 (11) | 89.5 (19) | 100.0 (6) | 100.0 (7) | 100.0 (13) |
| Ningbo | 100.0 (6) | 100.0 (10) | 100.0 (16) | 100.0 (7) | 66.7 (6) | 85.0 (13) |

Source: 90 In-depth Interviews database, 2001.

Note
Number in brackets is number of respondents.

with environmental issues (see Table 5.3). This could be because the national ranking was based on the entire area of Beijing city while the survey that was conducted focused only on the Haidian district. Given that Haidian was one of the districts under the jurisdiction of the city government of Beijing, I speculated that officials and clients were less ready to blame the Haidian Environmental Protection Bureau for Beijing's deteriorating environment.

However, it is not enough to rely only on the statistics as a proxy of government performance. To deepen the understanding of government efforts in delivering public service, we should learn from the perceptions of the clients and officials. To collect the perception data, our research project team conducted 90 in-depth interviews with open-ended questions (see Appendices). Given that the perception data are subjective in nature and broad in scope, only open-ended questions can to a large extent reveal interviewees' subjective feeling and, thus, draw out as much information as possible. Given that the perception data were diversified, I tried to array the patterns based on the common points generalized from the interviews.

Better delivery of public service implies improvements in the quality, quantity, speed and reliability of the service. It also entails better service access for clients and citizens and better courtesy of the government staff (Boyne 2003). After arraying and analyzing the information and data from interviews, I found some improvements in environmental protection in all three places. I will describe and analyze the pattern one by one. First, environmental protection is a public service for the citizens and a high quality of this particular public service means clean air, less noise and the protection of citizens from harmful waste. Thus, it requires the environmental protection bureaux to strictly enforce the relevant regulations. Many interviewees pointed out that the performance of their affiliated environmental protection bureaux in enforcing the rules and regulations was improved.[12] Interviewees reported that the environmental protection bureau in Ningbo strictly enforced the regulations and, sometimes, the enforcement requirements were even more stringent than the national standards. For example, during the period of the Ninth Five-Year Plan (1996–2000), the total discharge of $SO_2$ in Ningbo was 147,100 tons. In the subsequent year during the

110    *Control of the bureaucracy and reform outcomes*

period of the Tenth Five-Year Plan (2001–2005), it was recommended that Ningbo SO$_2$ discharge should not exceed 162,000 tons. In spite of this, Ningbo took the initiative and aimed for a higher restriction by stating that its SO$_2$ emission during the period of the Tenth Five-Year Plan would not exceed the discharge level as stipulated in the previous Ninth Five-Year Plan, i.e., 147,100 tons.[13]

Second, high-quality environmental protection not only required strict enforcement from the environmental protection bureaux, but also adequate service provisions for enterprises in abating pollution. The interviewees reported that the main content of the environmental officials' work had changed. Previously, the officials only focused on enforcing the regulations, but now, they put almost as much weight on providing services to clients as on enforcing regulations. As one interviewee stated:

> Previously, they mainly focused on issuing fines to enterprises whose discharge of waste had exceeded the standard level. Now, they focused more on educating the enterprises and they always tried to give instant responses to and propose solutions for the problems faced by these enterprises.[14]

One client explained that the Ningbo Environmental Protection Bureau provided training courses for the environmental protectors of the enterprises. As an environmental protector, he would enroll in two or three courses every year.[15] One official said that 'training for the oven-operators of enterprises was one of the public services that Haidian Environmental Protection Bureau provided'. The training course provided information on how to safely operate ovens, save energy and protect the environment. Participation during the initial stage was not compulsory for oven-operators and, thus, it led to a low participation rate—just above 20 percent. However, given the importance of the training courses to the safe production and environmental protection, the Haidian Environmental Protection Bureau subsequently issued local regulations that made participation of training courses for the oven-operators compulsory. After a long period of safe operation of ovens in Haidian, this special measure received praise from citizens.[16]

Third, the quantity of environmental protection service increased. This quantity improvement was illustrated by the more frequent inspections and the increased financial input. One interviewee said that

> Previously, officials of the Haidian Environmental Protection Bureau inspected our enterprise once a month or once every two months, now they inspect more frequently, on average, three times a month. During the inspections, they answered questions and resolved problems instantly.[17]

Similarly, another client said that officers of the Ningbo Environmental Protection Bureau inspected his enterprise more than once every month.[18] Finally, an official of Ningbo Environmental Protection Bureau revealed that Ningbo's

*Control of the bureaucracy and reform outcomes* 111

expenditure on environmental protection in 1999 was 1.89 percent of its GDP. He argued that Ningbo's expenditure exceeded the national average level, i.e., 1.5 percent of the GDP.[19]

Fourth, referring to the reliability of the service, interviewees claimed that the environmental protection bureaux were able to address most of the complaints they raised. Accordingly, this would mean that the interviewees were likely to contact the environmental protection bureaux again should they confront problems in the future. In my study, complaints indicated that citizens trusted the environmental protection bureaux.[20] For example, an interviewee shared with me her personal experience in raising complaints with the Haidian Environmental Protection Bureau. The interviewee was the party secretary of an urban residential committee. While a building was being constructed near their residence, some residents found that their drinking water had a strange odor. When the interviewee complained to the Haidian Environmental Protection Bureau, the problem was resolved in one month.[21] Another interviewee raised a complaint to the Changchun Environmental Protection Bureau through the environmental protection hotline (12345 in Changchun) regarding the poor hygiene of public restrooms in his neighborhood. The problem was resolved shortly after the Changchun Environmental Protection Bureau criticized and issued a fine to the relevant urban residential committee that was in charge of this restroom's hygiene.[22]

Fifth, in terms of the speed of service provision and delivery, environmental protection bureaux addressed complaints from citizens in a timely manner. For example, officials of the Haidian Environmental Protection Bureau promised to respond to every complaint raised to them. With regards to complaints about noise problems, they promised to take action or give a response within 24 hours. One interviewee said: 'Previously I thought most of the complaints could not get any response. Now even some problems cannot be addressed immediately, they explain instantly; and give a plan about the measures that would be taken within a fixed period'.[23] Indeed, one interviewee made a complaint to the Ningbo Environmental Protection Bureau regarding the noise in the neighborhood and the officials were able to resolve the problem that very same day.[24]

Sixth, the attitude of officials to their clients and citizens was a major aspect of public service provision. Interviewees in general noticed an improvement in the attitudes of officials of the environmental protection bureaux as they became more polite and appropriate. The Haidian Environmental Protection Bureau, for instance, established special measures to prevent arbitrary enforcement of regulations. One environmental protector of an enterprise explained that 'Once they found some unusual phenomena, they would instantly inform the environmental protector of that particular enterprise to confirm the situation and make records of the situation in the presence of the environmental protector'.[25] Moreover, the interviewee said: 'The Haidian Environmental Protection Bureau transferred the data they collected regarding the waste-discharge to enterprises regularly. They asked the delegates of enterprises to confirm and sign. If some disputes arise, they would try to resolve as soon as possible'. By using these measures, the

Haidian Environmental Protection Bureau reduced the disputes arising from regulation enforcement. An interview with a vice-chief of the Haidian Environmental Protection Bureau further emphasized the importance of these measures. He said, 'When enforcing rules and regulations, such as issuing fines or recording law-breaking actions, at least two environmental protection officials must be present. The Haidian Environmental Protection Bureau uses this measure to achieve justice in regulation-enforcement'.[26] Last but not least, another client considered the officials of the Ningbo Environmental Protection Bureau as disciplined because 'They never have dinner with the entrepreneur'.[27]

Seventh, better provision of public service implied easier access for citizens. In my study, interviewees felt that nowadays, they could contact and raise complaints with the environmental protection bureaux more easily than before. As discussed above, the rising number of complaints indicated that citizens increasingly trusted the environmental protection bureaux. In addition, the environmental protection bureaux designed arrangements to elicit citizens' views, which also contributed to the growing levels of trust. The Haidian Environmental Protection Bureau conducted a survey to collect the clients' views regarding their work performance. Every year, the chief of the Haidian Environmental Protection Bureau would gather all of the staff to certain large enterprises (main clients or major regulatory targets) and would ask the enterprises to evaluate their performance of that year through the use of a very comprehensive and detailed evaluation form. As such, interviewees felt that their views were being considered.[28] The Changchun Environmental Protection Bureau also put in place certain special measures that allowed citizens to participate in the performance evaluations of the officials. Every year, ten people, who were knowledgeable about environmental protection and were willing to help improve Changchun's environment (since they are not paid for this work), would be invited to be the 'special supervisors' (*jianduyuan*) to oversee the officials' behavior. The leaders of the Changchun Environmental Protection Bureau would meet with these ten people every month and review their supervision reports. To a large extent, the views of these people played an influential role. For example, during the annual performance appraisal, officials who received criticism from the 'special supervisors' would not receive any awards for that year.[29]

## *Citizen satisfaction*

Citizen satisfaction data were considered as an external measure of service effectiveness. In this study, the research team interviewed a total of 40 officials working in the environmental and education bureaux and 50 clients of the bureaux in the 3 sites. Both officials and clients perceived that the performance of environmental protection and education bureaux improved in the recent years, that is, since the reforms of the civil service (see Table 5.3). Clients were more generous than officials in their appraisal of bureau performance in the environmental protection arena, but less generous than officials in the education arena. Generally, the survey result was consistent with the policy outcomes data presented above, except in the case of Beijing. In Beijing's Haidian district, officials and clients perceived improvement in the performance of the environmental protection bureau although in relative terms, the environment in Beijing deteriorated during the period. How can I explain this anomaly? An asymmetry in the research design might be responsible for this result. The adopted research design led to a comparison of two sub-provincial-level cities (Ningbo and Changchun) with the much smaller Haidian district in Beijing. I speculate that officials and clients were less ready to blame the Haidian Environmental Protection Bureau for Beijing's deteriorating environment.

To illustrate in detail how citizens evaluated government performance, I will present findings from the Haidian citizen satisfaction survey, which was mainly about citizens' evaluation of the Haidian government efforts to regulate basic education (see Appendices for more information on the survey). Starting in the early 1980s, China decentralized the finance and management of its basic education to the local governments. Public awareness of government activities increased in recent years largely as a result of the expanded government propaganda and enhanced coverage of government issues by the mass media in China. Before examining how people in Haidian evaluated government educational performance, I would like to first examine the extent to which the information that citizens used to make the evaluation was accurate. The survey tested how and by what channels citizens were informed about government policy and activities in Haidian. The respondents were first asked whether they knew the listed policies and regulations of the Haidian government. As Table 5.4 shows, 93 percent of the respondents knew about the regulations that prevented schools from charging

*Table 5.4* To what extent citizens are informed about government policy and activities ($N=501$)

| Do you know the following policies or regulations? | Percentage |
| --- | --- |
| Regulations to combat corruption within Haidian education system | 34.3 |
| Regulations to manage quality in basic education | 34.9 |
| Regulations to stop illegal charges by schools | 93.0 |
| Regulations on teachers' ethics and qualifications | 63.1 |
| Regulations to prevent private provision of foods to students in or near the campus | 70.7 |
| Regulations on self-evaluation and expert supervision on the implementation of comprehensive quality education | 28.9 |
| Regulations on performance measurement in the Haidian education system | 14.8 |

| Do you know of the following activities of the Haidian education system? | Percentage |
| --- | --- |
| Year of ethics building for teachers | 12.8 |
| Activity serving the tax payers | 34.9 |
| Modernization of archive management | 33.5 |
| Large-scale inspection of school facilities | 51.9 |
| Select teaching performers | 41.9 |

Source: Haidian citizen satisfaction survey database, January–March 2003.

114  *Control of the bureaucracy and reform outcomes*

*Table 5.5* Through what channels citizens know of the policies and activities (*N*=501)

| Channels | Percentage |
| --- | --- |
| Broadcasts | 41.1 |
| Work unit's activities | 16.4 |
| Newspaper and magazines | 44.9 |
| Government propaganda activities | 8.6 |
| TV | 57.3 |
| Communication with others | 23.2 |
| Internet | 5.6 |

Source: Haidian citizen satisfaction survey database, January–March 2003.

illegal fees. This shows that government propaganda enjoyed quite a high level of success. Similarly, over 70 percent of the respondents knew about the regulations that prevented private provision of foods to students in or near the campus. This illustrates that both the government and the respondents cared about children's food hygiene and health. About another 63.1 percent of the respondents knew about the regulations concerning teachers' ethics and qualifications. The respondents were then asked whether they knew the Haidian Education Commission had conducted the listed activities and half of the respondents knew about the large-scale inspection of school facilities. When asked through what channels they learnt about these policies and activities of the Haidian government, half of the people suggested TV, newspaper and magazines and broadcasts (see Table 5.5).

How did people in Haidian perceive and evaluate government performance in the area of education policy? Table 5.6 shows the respondents' evaluation of the education performance of Beijing city and the Haidian district. Overall, people were satisfied with the performance of both places. 78.8 percent of the respondents said they were satisfied or very satisfied with the Haidian district while 78.5 percent of the respondents said they were satisfied or very satisfied with Beijing city. Referring to the satisfaction with the quality of the Haidian junior middle school graduates, 61.1 percent of the respondents said they were satisfied or very satisfied.

Did different demographic and socioeconomic groups differ in their evaluation of government educational performance? In other words, did the level of evaluation persist across citizens of different gender, age, education level and income? To address this question, I used the statistical analysis of variance to detect any such differences. This analysis was designed to examine the variability in the sample in order to determine whether the population means were not equal. The results, displayed in Table 5.7, showed that gender, university education and having a child in basic education seemed to somewhat affect the respondents' evaluation of the educational performance in Haidian. In particular, I found that both women and individuals with a university degree seemed to be critical of the Haidian Education Commission. Interestingly, gender seemed to

*Control of the bureaucracy and reform outcomes* 115

*Table 5.6* General evaluation of educational performance compared with five years ago (%)

|  | Apparently improved | Improved | No change | Retrogress | Apparent retrogress | Unsure |
|---|---|---|---|---|---|---|
| Beijing city | 23.4 | 55.1 | 10.8 | 3.4 | 0.4 | 7.0 |
| Haidian district | 25.7 | 53.1 | 9.0 | 2.0 | 0.0 | 10.2 |
| Quality of Haidian junior middle school graduates | 12.2 | 48.9 | 13.6 | 6.2 | 0.6 | 18.6 |

Source: Haidian citizen satisfaction survey database, January–March 2003.

be the strongest factor related to the assessment with women being the most critical of the Haidian Education Commission. In addition, non-university educated respondents tended to give higher marks for the government's performance in the education policy than university graduates. Respondents with children receiving basic education seemed slightly more critical than those who did not have children receiving basic education. Age and income did not seem to have much impact on the respondents' evaluation since the mean of evaluations of sub-population remained constant among the three age groups and income groups.

*Table 5.7* Evaluation of Haidian education performance by gender, age, education and income (*N*=450)

|  |  | Mean | F-Ratio | Significance |
|---|---|---|---|---|
| Gender |  |  |  |  |
|  | Male | 4.24 (218) |  |  |
|  | Female | 4.05 (232) | 9.615 | 0.002 |
| Age |  |  |  |  |
|  | Young (18–29) | 4.14 (58) |  |  |
|  | Middle (30–49) | 4.12 (275) |  |  |
|  | Old (over 50) | 4.19 (117) | 0.374 | 0.688 |
| Education |  |  |  |  |
|  | Non-university | 4.2 (335) |  |  |
|  | University | 3.98 (115) | 8.774 | 0.003 |
| Income |  |  |  |  |
|  | Lower (RMB999 or below) | 4.16 (167) |  |  |
|  | Middle (RMB1,000–2,000) | 4.17 (201) |  |  |
|  | Upper (over RMB2,000) | 4.04 (82) | 1.261 | 0.284 |
| Children |  |  |  |  |
|  | Have children in basic education | 4.05 (121) |  |  |
|  | No children in basic education | 4.18 (329) | 3.126 | 0.078 |

Source: Haidian citizen satisfaction survey database, January–March 2003.

*Table 5.8* Citizens' evaluation of Haidian educational performance (*N*=501)

| Choose which one of the following is the most satisfactory job Haidian Education Commission has done (%) | Percentage |
|---|---|
| Guarantee equal access to basic education | 11.8 |
| Improve the enforcement of government regulations | 5.0 |
| Stop the illegal charges by schools | 17.6 |
| Build teachers' ethics | 4.0 |
| Improve teachers' professional qualifications | 21.0 |
| Improve school facilities | 21.0 |
| Increase financial input | 8.8 |
| Don't know | 11.0 |

Source: Haidian citizen satisfaction survey database, January–March 2003.

Overall, the respondents in Haidian thought highly of the government's educational performance. To give a more detailed picture, I tested how respondents evaluated individual government programs in the field of basic education. As Table 5.8 shows, the Haidian government efforts in improving professional qualifications of teachers and school facilities received the highest satisfaction levels. Respondents were also satisfied with the government efforts in preventing schools from charging illegal fees.

Responsiveness referred directly to the accuracy and speed of government agencies in addressing citizens' demands. The respondents were asked whether the government policy was responsive and flexible in terms of meeting their various needs. The question, rendered in the original wording, and descriptive statistics are presented in Table 5.9. Did different demographic factors play any role in the respondents' evaluation of government responsiveness? An analysis of variance presented some interesting findings. The results, as shown in Table 5.10, revealed that the evaluations of responsiveness remained constant while controlling for gender, age and income. The only possible factor that might have affected the evaluation of government responsiveness was education. It was found that university-educated respondents tended to give the government lower marks for policy responsiveness.

*Table 5.9* Evaluation of government policy responsiveness

*To what extent does Haidian educational policy meet the needs of you and your household? (%)*

| Very large extent | Large extent | Small extent | Not met | Don't know |
|---|---|---|---|---|
| 26.3 | 57.7 | 10.6 | 1.6 | 3.8 |

Source: Haidian citizen satisfaction survey database, January–March 2003.

*Table 5.10* Evaluation of government responsiveness by gender, age, education and income (*N*=482)

|  |  | Mean | F-Ratio | Significance |
|---|---|---|---|---|
| Gender | | | | |
| | Male | 3.08 (229) | | |
| | Female | 3.17 (253) | 2.299 | 0.13 |
| Age | | | | |
| | Young (18–29) | 3.11 (62) | | |
| | Middle (30–49) | 3.12 (291) | | |
| | Old (over 50) | 3.16 (129) | 0.127 | 0.881 |
| Education | | | | |
| | Non-university | 3.17 (356) | | |
| | University | 3.02 (126) | 4.526 | 0.034 |
| Income | | | | |
| | Lower (RMB999 or below) | 3.12 (184) | | |
| | Middle (RMB1,000–2,000) | 3.16 (213) | | |
| | Upper (over RMB2,000) | 3.07 (85) | 0.657 | 0.519 |
| Children | | | | |
| | Have children in basic education | 3.09 (127) | | |
| | No children in basic education | 3.15 (335) | 0.774 | 0.379 |

Source: Haidian citizen satisfaction survey database, January–March 2003.

## Conclusion

This chapter examined the ability of the central leadership to control policy implementation by a decentralized bureaucratic system. It analyzed how the upper echelons of the Party-government exercised control over the lower-level bureaucrats through competitive appointment and promotion, performance evaluation, rotation and avoidance. Other related initiatives such as administrative monitoring, intra-party reforms and anticorruption measures were also analyzed in this chapter. This chapter suggested that the implementation of the civil service reforms and other related programs helped the central leadership in China to strengthen its control over the local governments and bureaucrats. As demonstrated, the tightened control brought about improvement in public service delivery. Both the statistical data and case studies of public service delivery illustrated this improvement. The perception data of officials and citizens, especially that of the clients, revealed that the actual behavior of the local officials in delivering public service generally conformed to the directives from upper-level government. The improvement was also attested by citizens who acknowledged that the civil service is doing a better job now than before. I concluded that without its effective control over local governments and bureaucrats through the civil service reforms and other administrative monitoring measures, the central leadership's goal in terms of delivering better service to citizens would have been far more difficult to achieve.

# 6 Implications for Asian developing countries

The previous chapters have examined the implementation of civil service reforms in China. In this chapter, I will discuss the possibility of using China's reform experience as a model for other governments in Asia that face the dilemma of how to recruit, retain and motivate skilled staff at an affordable cost. To do this, I will examine four developing countries in Southeast Asia, namely Vietnam, Laos, Indonesia and the Philippines, and conduct a comparative analysis of the patterns of civil service reforms in these four countries. For each specific country, the reform policy and implementation will be analyzed and the main problems and difficulties associated with the reform will be identified. In suggesting possible solutions, I will point out particular elements of China's reform experience that might be useful for improving bureaucratic competence, performance, efficiency and effectiveness in public service delivery in these countries.

The criteria for choosing these countries include geographic location, level of economic development, political regime type, culture, and so on. All four countries are located in Southeast Asia and fall within the low (or at best middle) income range, which categorizes them as developing countries by international observers such as the World Bank, Asian Development Bank, United Nations and International Monetary Fund. As for the political regime type, two of the countries are socialist (Vietnam and Laos) while the other two are capitalist (Indonesia and the Philippines). All four countries exhibit elements of authoritarianism given that each has had a history of (or is currently under) authoritarian rule. Culturally, they share Asian values, which emphasize harmony and order as opposed to the ideas of political competition, which are driven by liberal democratic principles that are embodied in Western polities. The core of the Asian culture is the personalistic quality of the political, bureaucratic and economic organizations. The personalistic quality means that members of these organizations have strongly emphasized personal relationships both within and outside of the organization. These personal relationships are often formed around kernels of association such as kinship, mutual friendships and places of origin, schools, universities and professional associations. These relationships will involve the reciprocal exchange of favors, gifts and money and entail a deal of personal obligations. As a consequence, these organizations are rendered weak, their objectives are distorted or ignored and the informal networks continue to thrive. It is no wonder that bureaucratic organizations in these Asian countries are frequently described as distorted and corrupt and have come to be dominated by patronage and clientelism (Hodder 2010; Turner 2002). Therefore, another common issue that deserves attention is corruption. All these four governments were thought to be performing poorly with respect to corruption, which is alleged to accompany high economic growth. According to Transparency International (2009), all of the four governments are among the most corrupt in the world.

This chapter is structured as follows. First, it summarizes the experience of the Chinese government in reforming its civil service management. The extent of success in civil service reforms is a function of the kinds of initial conditions under which governments operate and the degree of resolve they bring to the task of modernizing their civil services. As such, the initial conditions of these countries are reviewed in the second section. The third section analyzes the contents and trajectories of civil service reforms in the four countries through the use of a comparative case study method. For each country, reform policy and implementation will be examined and the main problems will be identified. The chapter ends with a concluding discussion and suggests possible solutions.

## Summary of China's reform experience

The Chinese government has established a formal legislative and institutional framework for civil service management and reforms. The main objective of the reforms is to establish and maintain a competent, efficient and professional civil service bureaucracy. As such, bureaucratic streamlining and rationalization have been practiced on many occasions to make way for civil service reforms. China tries to recruit, promote and manage civil servants according to the Weberian principles of competition and merit. Specifically, civil service reforms try to establish rule-based meritocracy and reward for performance. The government also tries to install formal institutions of meritocracy and professionalize its employees through various civil service training programs. Given that the recruitment and initial placement of civil servants are crucial determinants of the enduring quality of the civil service, the Chinese civil service recruitment relies heavily on examinations and competitive selection to maintain high-quality standards. The process of selecting and promoting civil servants in China today is undoubtedly more open, transparent and competitive than it was under the cadre personnel management system.

The capacity to effectively manage the size and cost of the civil service is crucial. The Chinese government has made establishment plans and controlled the actual size of the civil service establishment. As for the civil service pay reform, the Chinese government has kept the civil service pay level reasonably competitive with the private sector, which makes a career in the civil service very attractive. The civil service wage bill should be affordable. Given the big population and large public sector, the Chinese government has seen its civil service wage bills rise over the past three decades. The civil service wage bill as a percentage of the total GDP in 2005 (as the highest over the past three decades) is less than 4 percent (see Table 2.5). This is within the lower range of OECD levels (Nunberg 2002, 1995, 1992). Therefore, scholars cannot conclude that China has performed poorly in civil service wage bill management. However, the image that civil service wage bills are still affordable largely stems from the very impressive GDP growth in China over the past three decades.

The government is trying to professionalize the civil service through human resource development initiatives, including establishing training institutions and increasing financial input for training programs. Positive elements such as openness, transparency and merit-based competition against patronage have been incorporated into the process of senior civil servants' selection and promotion. Civil service reforms in China also provide guidance to civil servants' attitude to citizens and clients through procedures such as mass evaluations. Reforms have sought to tighten the connection between civil servants and the public by taking steps to increase transparency and accountability in public administration and public service delivery.

Though performance appraisal and performance-based pay and other reform initiatives have proved difficult to design and implement in China, many flaws can be corrected when they are adapted to other Asian contexts. Important lessons that can be transferred are as follows. First, the cultivation of performance culture in the Chinese civil service has yet to be completed and the degree to which performance features as a driver of civil service behavior is hard to say. As such, establishing a performance-oriented civil service remains a critical task. Second, the process of increasing both the officials' accountability as well as public participation is still in the beginning stage. Corruption is usually thought to accompany high economic growth. Hence, establishing well-designed institutions and instruments are the most urgent tasks in combating corruption.

## Initial conditions of the five countries

It should be noted that there is not a standardized model or a set of standardized elements for developing countries in Asia that want to reform their civil services for improving government performance. Differences in political, social, economic and cultural contexts all significantly affect what is feasible in a given country. The search should be for good management practices that are suitable for that particular country. Recall that the extent of success in civil service reforms is a function of the kinds of initial conditions under which governments operate and the degree of resolve they bring to the task of modernizing their civil services. Accordingly, the initial conditions for civil service reforms in these countries are reviewed here.

Contextual factors, especially economic ones, need to be understood when assessing civil service performance and capacity. A country's economy will constrain the fiscal capacity of the government in managing and reforming its civil

*Table 6.1* Overview of economy, 2007

| Country | Population (million) | Surface area (sq. km) | GDP per capital (PPP)* | Asian rank | World rank |
|---|---|---|---|---|---|
| China | 1,325.6 | 9,590,088 | 5,325 | 17 | 100 |
| Indonesia | 228.2 | 1,904,570 | 3,728 | 23 | 120 |
| Philippines | 90.3 | 300,000 | 3,383 | 24 | 122 |
| Vietnam | 86.2 | 329,310 | 2,589 | 27 | 128 |
| Laos | 6.2 | 236,800 | 2,054 | 31 | 136 |

Source: International Monetary Fund (2008).

Note
* Purchasing Power Parity.

service. Table 6.1 provides an overview of the economy in the five countries. With the exception of China, Indonesia is the most populous country with the largest surface area. Vietnam is similar with the Philippines in terms of its population and surface area. Laos is the smallest country with the lowest population among the five countries and it is also the poorest. GDP per capita in China is more than two times that of Laos. GDP per capita in Indonesia is almost two times that of Laos. In assessing these countries' performance in reforming their civil services, we should take into consideration that the government in Laos started from a relatively lower capacity level.

As discussed above, all of these countries are among the most corrupted in the world. Table 6.2 shows the ranking of the five countries on Transparency International's Corruption Perception Index in 2009 (among 180 countries). Corruption in these countries has been attributed to the low salaries of the civil servants, erring political leadership, the ample opportunities for corruption in the public sector, and the unlikelihood of detection and punishment for corrupt offenders (Quah 2009, 2003). The rampant corruption severely constrained the capabilities of these governments in managing and reforming their civil services.

*Table 6.2* Corruption Perception Index 2009

| Country | Rank | Score |
|---|---|---|
| China | 79 | 3.6 |
| Indonesia | 111 | 2.8 |
| Vietnam | 120 | 2.7 |
| Philippines | 139 | 2.4 |
| Laos | 158 | 2.0 |

Source: Transparency International (2009).

## Patterns of civil service reforms in four countries

There are positive elements in China's experience of reforming the public personnel management system. These elements could serve as reference for other governments in Asia in their pursuit of an efficient and professional civil service. As I suggested above, the chosen elements should be modified to suit a country's particular circumstance. In other words, a range of contingent factors such as political system, public administration structure, economic condition and ethnic diversity should be taken in account before we identify what to choose and how to modify. This section will present four case studies where the basic parameters of governance will be analyzed in each case. Variables such as political regime type, party politics and public administration structure will be studied in order to analyze the political system. The scope, size, cost and quality of the civil service will be examined. Moreover, current reform efforts will be reviewed and main problems associated with the reforms will be diagnosed.

### *Civil service reforms in Vietnam*

A unified and Communist-led government took control over Vietnam in 1976. Important state organs of Vietnam include the National Assembly, the President, the executive government, the Supreme Court and local people's courts, and the Supreme Institute of Procuracy and local people's procuracy. The National Assembly, elected every five years, is the highest organ of the state with full legislative power as well as the power to alter the Constitution (by a two-thirds majority). It has more than 450 members (currently 493) and meets twice a year. The government system in Vietnam is unitary and it includes four levels, namely central, province, district and commune.

The Communist Party of Vietnam is the ruling as well as the only legal political party in Vietnam. It has a Central Committee with more than 160 members. Similar to China, there is no clear distinction between the party and the state in Vietnam's political system. Following the Soviet model, the Party firmly controls the state. While there has been a deliberate loosening of the strict requirement that all elected legislators of the National Assembly must be Communist Party members, the Party and its mass organizations continue to exert tight control over the nominations process. Many members of the National Assembly are senior officials in the civil service. For civil servants' career advancement, political training, adherence to party doctrine and loyalty to the party line are key qualifications for senior positions (Painter 2006). Scholars argue that a clear structure of roles and accountability relations between political and administrative actors is absent (Schick 1998). Officials at all levels are not immune from the influence of party and family connections and many decisions actually come about as a result of negotiations rather than standard rule applications and compliance (Ryan and Wandel 1996).

A major economic reform process known as the Doi Moi renovation was launched in 1986. In the late 1980s, Vietnam was faced with severe economic problems such as famine in the north in 1988, limited foreign trade and major deficit spending by the government that led to hyperinflation. To tackle these problems, a number of reform measures took place. Some political prisoners were released and a higher number of candidates compared to before were allowed to run for seats in the National Assembly. In 1990, 18,000 officials were dismissed or charged with corruption. The 1992 Constitution recognized private ownership and legitimized the private sector (Asian Development Bank 2001). The results of the economic liberalization and administrative reforms were impressive. The Vietnamese economy rapidly transformed from a central-planning to a market economy. A number of reasons have been found by researchers to explain this, including the timing and the gradualist approach of the policy reforms, the fact that central planning had only been partially implemented, the maintenance of political stability, the ability to benefit from being situated in a rapidly growing region in Southeast Asia and, finally, the fact that citizens perceived the reforms as being of domestic origin, which made them credible (Asian Development Bank 2001; Painter 2006, 2003a, 2003b).

A basic legal framework for civil service management was established by a 1993 ordinance stipulating the standards of positions, grades and levels and a new standardized salary system. A standard set of recruitment examinations was set out in 1994. The current legislation is the 2003 civil service ordinance. The ordinance does not attempt to differentiate employees of the state organ from employees of the Party and associated mass organizations or the judiciary. Therefore, public employees (civilian state employees) in Vietnam have five categories: (1) elected officials; (2) party officials; (3) civil servants; (4) judicial officers; and (5) civil workers in the army and police force. Civil servants are defined as being

> recruited, appointed, or assigned a regular public duty, categorized according to their training degrees and professional specialty, arranged in an administrative grade in state agencies, each grade reflecting a professional position and rank as well as title according to certain specific criteria.
> (Painter 2006: 328)

If teachers and health workers are included, the public sector in 2002 employed approximately 1.5 million people, constituting 5.5 percent of the total workforce in Vietnam, compared to 4 percent in Indonesia and 5.3 percent in the Philippines (Painter 2006: 327). Table 6.3 provides a profile of public service employment in 2002 in Vietnam.

The central personnel agency, the Ministry of Home Affairs, is responsible for civil service management and reforms. However, implementation remains faltered and decentralized. Each government agency, including the provincial and district bodies, is its own employer. Each has a personnel unit, which undertakes personnel management functions such as recruitment, promotion and performance evaluation. Even though employment and management practices should be supervised by upper-level personnel units and ultimately the Ministry

Table 6.3 Public service employment in Vietnam, 2002

| Sector | Number | Percentage |
|---|---|---|
| Public administration | 252,400 | 16.6 |
| Party and mass organizations | 66,100 | 4.3 |
| Education and training | 941,500 | 61.8 |
| Health and social work | 192,900 | 12.7 |
| Science and technology | 33,900 | 2.2 |
| Culture and spor | 36,600 | 2.4 |
| Total | 1,523,400 | 100.0 |

Source: Government of Vietnam General Statistics Office (2003); Painter (2006: 328).

of Home Affairs, system-wide monitoring, inspection and supervision are very weak. For example, there is relatively weak institutionalization of rules across all levels of government and agencies. As well, there are high levels of local discretion over personnel matters given the high level of decentralization. Accordingly, a high level of personalism and patronage was observed (Painter 2003a).

In general, a centrally managed and merit-based personnel management has not yet been established in Vietnam. The process of civil service reforms is contested, the pace of change is slow and the reach into different parts of the system is uneven. Cadres and civil servants are deficient in skills, professionalism and ethical standards while corruption remains a serious problem (Painter 2006: 325). The Vietnamese civil service has poor establishment control. The practice of estimating administrative expenditures according to the number of staff in a particular agency provides incentives for agencies to hire more staff so that the agencies can get larger budgets. In terms of recruitment, given that civil servants earn half or two-thirds of what they could earn in a comparable private sector job (including benefits and informal income), attracting and retaining qualified staff is difficult. In addition, the processes for job assignment and promotion are still not transparent and objective.

However, recruitment and selection have improved. Since 1994, every newly appointed civil servant has been expected to pass a public recruitment examination. The open entrance examinations not only help to select the best applicants, but ensure that there is social equality. However, since each government agency is responsible for its own recruitment, the process is still opaque to some extent. There has been traditionally a strong commitment to training for government employees in Vietnam, in part because of the priority given to political education. As such, administrative or managerial training are lacking. Scholars identified a number of problems of civil service training, including the lack of a clear and coordinated central strategy, confusion as a result of overlaps and competitions among institutions that run programs of varying quality (Painter 2003b). Although some results have been achieved, civil servants still lack sufficient knowledge and skills in socioeconomic management.

Despite some recent improvements, civil service salaries remain low. However, salaries only comprise one part of the civil servants' remuneration. Civil servants also receive allowances (including housing allowances) and collect various payments for services rendered in their work. Despite this, many civil servants cannot make ends meet without a second income. Decentralization in Vietnam's public administration causes negative impacts on civil service reforms. There is a high level of local discretionary power in human resource management and especially over salary determinations. There is also a high level of devolution of financial responsibilities and greater local discretion over the levying of fees and charges. Therefore, establishing centrally managed personnel and pay rules has proved to be difficult. As part of the civil service pay reforms, the central government required local governments to increase the basic pay for their public employees. Moreover, it required a portion of salary increases to be funded from locally generated sources of revenue in the form of user charges. These initiatives were very radical and caused negative consequences. Many agencies retain a degree of discretion about levying fees and charges on their own account and are able to retain some of this surplus for their own use, including supplementary salaries. The ability of some employees to supplement income in this way depends in large part on the availability of local revenues, mostly in the form of fees and charges levied on routine transactions and services. Many civil servants abuse the power of their positions by engaging in corruption and illegal profit-seeking activities.

## *Civil service reforms in Laos*

The Lao People's Democratic Republic (Lao PDR—also commonly referred to as Laos) was proclaimed in 1975 under the control of the communist Lao People's Revolutionary Party (LPRP). Laos is a landlocked, mountainous and thinly populated country with much of its population living in small and isolated villages (Asian Development Bank 2001). The LPRP had around 65,000 members in 2001 and is the country's only political party. It is governed by the Central Committee and was headed by the 11-member Politburo in 2006 (Gunn 2007). In principle, the highest authority is the Party Congress, a gathering of party cadres that meets to ratify decisions already decided by the party leadership. The congresses are held every five years. In practice, the real authority goes to the Central Committee, made up of some 55 party elites in 2006. The Central Committee members fill key political positions and lead the party between congresses. The Politburo within the Central Committee formulates policy-making in virtually every aspect of public life.

The President is the head of the state and the armed forces and is elected by the National Assembly for a five-year term. Usually the Chief of the ruling party (LPRP) is the President, also the top official of the Government. The Council of Ministers is the highest executive body and includes the Prime Minister and three Deputy Prime Ministers. The government is divided into three administrative levels. In 1995, the central government presided over 18 administrative units, including 16 provinces, the Vientiane municipality and a special zone. The provinces were organized into 133 districts in the urban area and 11,500 villages in the rural area (Klauss 2001: 185).

126  *Implications for Asian developing countries*

Any discussion of the current civil service system and reforms in Laos has to be placed in the context of a one-party communist ideological framework. In general, the civil service is seen as the implementer of party decisions (Klauss 2001). A strong party structure whose organization parallels the government administrative structure significantly influences processes within the public administration. The strong political interference renders the government to operate under an atmosphere of uncertainty and fluidity. The media and the public are strongly controlled by the state. There is an initiative to loosen the control of the state, but progress is slow. Up until 2009, Lao citizens were still not allowed to establish non-government organizations (Jonsson 2010).

Like other socialist regimes, Laos established a central-planning economy at the beginning of the republic. In this line of efforts, attempts to collectivize agriculture encountered strong opposition and, as a result, production stagnated. The LPRP took the first steps toward market-oriented reform in 1979 by easing the restrictions on private trade and encouraging joint venture between the state and the private sector. It reduced agricultural taxes and increased government procurement prices for most crops; however, it made no move to dismantle central planning in the 1970s.

A process of economic liberalization and reform had been underway in Laos since the mid-1980s. With the introduction of the New Economic Mechanism, more far-reaching reforms began in 1986. The government abandoned the collectivization of agriculture, eased many restrictions on private sector activity and gave state enterprises more decision-making power. Privatization began in 1988 and accelerated during the 1990s. With some encouraging results, the economic liberalization continued through the 1990s until the Asian financial crisis of 1997–1998. Adverse impacts of the Asian financial crisis included setting back economic development and bringing back the conservative leadership. The aging and conservative leadership of the former revolutionaries in Laos became more cautious. A major concern for them was the fear that more rapid and radical economic reforms would undermine both the legitimacy of the ruling party and the means by which it exercised its monopoly of political power.

Despite its recent record of economic growth, Laos is still very poor. The government managed to reduce poverty to 27.1 percent in 2008 from 33.3 percent in 2003 and a relatively stable growth rate of around 7 percent per year has enabled the GDP per capita to reach US$875 (Jonsson 2010). The vast majority (73 percent) of the population still live in rural areas. The economic development gap has widened, mostly along the urban-rural divide. It also reflects geographic determinants and ethnic background. Many ethnic minority groups live in remote highlands where agricultural productivity is low and poverty reduction activities are limited.

The central institutions for civil service management were created in the early 1990s. The Department of Public Administration (created in 1992) is responsible for guidelines and policy issues regarding the organization of the government at the central and local levels. Decrees addressing the basic rules that guide civil service management were approved in 1993. The National School of Administration and

Management (created in 1991) is responsible for training civil servants. There were about 70,534 civil servants in 1995 (Klauss 2001: 211). The figures for 2001 and 2002 were 82,300 and 91,330 respectively (Asian Development Bank 2001; United Nations 2005: 5). Table 6.4 provides profiles of the Lao civil service in 1995 and 2002. In general, the civil service pay level is low. Civil service wage bills amount to 4 percent of GDP, which is less than the average of 4.5 percent for other countries in the region (Asian Development Bank 2001: 26). Inflation has eroded the value of wages to the point where they are well below the minimum needed for food and basic necessities. As a result, many civil servants lack the motivation to perform their jobs effectively. Under the pressure of raising a family, civil servants are eager to make more money or seek alternative source of income. This is responsible for rampant rent-seeking and corruption across the country.

Poor pay also makes a career in the civil service unattractive. Hence, the lack of manpower in government is another problem. About 92 percent of civil servants work in provincial governments, leaving many central ministries without adequate staff to carry out critical and essential functions. The quality of the civil service in Laos is low, as illustrated by the low level of education of the civil servants. As Table 6.4 shows, civil servants with a university degree account for

*Table 6.4* Profile of the Lao civil service, 1995, 2002

|  | Number | Percentage |
| --- | --- | --- |
| *Profile of 1995* |  |  |
| *Government level* |  |  |
| Civil servants in ministerial services at central level | 7,742 | 11.0 |
| Civil servants in ministerial services at provincial and district level | 57,804 | 82.0 |
| Civil servants appointed to central party organization, mass organizations and to offices of governors and chiefs of districts | 4,988 | 7.0 |
| *Education* |  |  |
| Postgraduate level | 317 | 0.4 |
| University degree or equivalent | 10,693 | 15.2 |
| Professional level (medium level) | 23,389 | 33.2 |
| Professional level (primary level) | 28,567 | 40.5 |
| General education (primary, secondary level) | 7,568 | 10.7 |
| Total | 70,534 | 100.0 |
| *Profile of 2002* |  |  |
| *Government level* |  |  |
| Central government | 7,651 | 8.4 |
| Provincial government | 83,679 | 91.6 |
| *Gender* |  |  |
| Male | 56,095 | 61.4 |
| Female | 35,235 | 38.6 |
| Total | 91,330 | 100.0 |

Sources: Klauss (2001: 211); United Nations (2005: 5).

less than 16 percent of the whole service. Specifically, they lack the necessary management and planning skills as well as communication and administration technologies.

Furthermore, the public personnel management is not practiced under a uniformed framework. The civil service in Laos does not operate in a uniform manner across all ministries, provinces and districts. Recruitment procedures for civil servants differ significantly among ministries. National recruitment plans or schemes do not exist while the brightest students prefer to work in the private sector or for international organizations. Promotion tends to be based on seniority, clan ties and political patronage.

In routine personnel management, creativity is not rewarded. There are no grievance mechanisms if civil servants are punished for their mistakes. As a result, civil servants will pass very minor decisions upward to their superiors rather than take a risk and make the decision on their own. Civil servants are still familiar with a top-down environment, they tend to bring problems to their superior's attention; therefore they themselves do not need to take the risk of making a mistake. Job descriptions of government positions are missing and there are no clarifications on the roles and responsibilities. Therefore, conflict within the administration, lack of coordination and duplication of efforts are common occurrences. Moreover, exchanges of information between different government organizations are limited. A major structural problem is that public administration is still based on a bottom-up reporting system with no institutionalized channels for inter-ministerial communications.

## *Civil service reforms in Indonesia*

With a population of around 228.2 million people, Indonesia is ranked as the fourth most populous country in the world. People of different cultures and speaking various local languages live on more than 17,500 islands. As of 2006, Indonesia is administratively divided into 34 provinces and 440 districts (Kristiansen and Ramli 2006). The political system in Indonesia has been undergoing dramatic transformation and, as a result, the climate for civil service reforms is uncertain. The fall of Suharto in May 1998, which was in part triggered by the Asian financial crisis, led the country into a new phase of transition from authoritarian political and economic systems toward democracy and the market economy. The post-Suharto governments in Indonesia face the enormous task of building public trust and providing quality service to newly enfranchised citizens. To reform the civil service within a newly decentralized structure and to promote performance and integrity within the civil service are key tasks for the Indonesian government.

The Indonesian civil service has its roots in the Dutch colonial administration. During the first two presidencies of the new republic, under Sukarno and Suharto from 1949 to 1998, power was concentrated in the hands of the executive bodies and predominantly at the central level. Limited influence was given to elected assemblies while the civil service was developed to be a political instrument.

During the Suharto era, the civil service grew to encompass more than four million employees from central and local administrative units to the police, military, schools and health institutions (Kristiansen and Ramli 2006). Figures on the total size of the Indonesian civil service vary from source to source. A recent report suggests that there were about 3.74 million civil servants or 1.7 percent of the Indonesian population in 2005 (Tjiptoherijanto 2007: 32). Among these civil servants, approximately one million are school teachers and 300,000 are health workers. A comparative study suggests there were 1.7 civil servants per 100 people, a figure that was less than most other governments in the region, for examples the Philippines (2.1 percent) and Vietnam (3.2 percent) (Schiavo-Campo 1998). Table 6.5 provides a profile of civil service in Indonesia in 2005.

Civil service management infrastructure within the Indonesian government is fragmented and the lines of authority are not clear. Among the central government institutions, the State Ministry for Administrative Reform, the National Civil Service Board, the Ministry of Home Affairs and the Ministry of Finance all play important roles. This divided arrangement hampers civil service reform and effective allocation of human resources. For example, the practice of organizational restructure is separated from the establishment planning. Organization-related proposals such as adding or subtracting bureaux or sections must be approved by the State Ministry for Administrative Reform. While the National Civil Service Board is in charge of establishment planning, central government agencies must have their establishments approved by it. The separation of allocating personnel to organizations from organizational restructure engenders problems. First, organizations are restructured and regulated without due regard for the skills needed. Second, the manpower plans have been lax and not compatible with the new organizational structure. For decades, international funding agencies have urged the Indonesian government to establish one single central body that would set norms and standards throughout the system (Asian Development Bank 2004: 60).

The decentralization reforms in 2001 had some observable impacts on the organization and function of the civil service. The reforms had blurred the borders of responsibilities and lines of reporting in the bureaucracy and facilitated increasing rent-seeking at local levels. After reforms, regional heads at both provincial and district levels are now held accountable to regional legislative bodies rather than to higher levels of government. The devolution of power

*Table 6.5* Number of civil servants in Indonesia, 2005

| Level of government | Number | Percentage |
|---|---|---|
| Central government | 896,211 | 24.0 |
| Provincial governments | 303,724 | 8.1 |
| Regency or municipality government | 2,541,560 | 67.9 |
| Total | 3,741,495 | 100.0 |

Source: Tjiptoherijanto (2007: 33).

from central government to regional governments had facilitated regional officials to maximize their own individual gains with small risks of control and sanctions. Three quarters of the civil service, including teachers and health workers, are now assigned to local governments, predominately to the 440 districts. Since the reforms, transparency seems to have decreased and corruption escalated due to the development of new local elites at the district level. According to Transparency International (2009), Indonesia is still among the most corrupt countries in the world (rank 111 out of 180 countries).

In general, the areas that need reform include position classification, budget arrangement, recruitment and selection, incentive structures, human resource management and development. The classification of civil service positions in Indonesia is not scientific. Positions and remuneration are determined by rank. Job content and responsibilities are left undefined. There are no requirements for the position-holders to have skills that match the specific tasks. As well, the salary is not based on the complexity of the job. This is particularly noticeable in regional governments, which vary greatly in size and complexity. For example, the head of town planning in a big city with large residence has the same basic salary level and civil service conditions as the head of town planning in a small city with few residents (Film and Lindauer 2001).

Budget arrangements for civil service remuneration are divided between the recurrent and development budgets. Indonesia has kept its official personnel expenditure (i.e., those appearing in the recurrent budget) relatively low in relation to GDP growth; however, a high proportion of wage expenditures is suspected to be buried in parts of the development budget. And these parts of the budget are harder to track (Nunberg 2002). In addition, the array of opaque allowances as well as the highly decentralized personnel management with no effective system-wide oversight reduces systemic accountability and creates opportunities for undetected graft.

The recruitment process is formally made on a national basis but districts are left with a high degree of authority in the selection process. The lack of transparency and possibility of rent-seeking make the positions attractive in spite of the limited formal salaries. Selection for recruitment and promotion in the Indonesian civil service is not an open competitive process and is not based on publicly disclosed criteria of merit. While Indonesia has formal trappings of a merit system, little in the current institutional environment promotes performance or accountability in civil service management. The civil service system does not focus on professionalism and performance. Civil servants are recruited to the service when they are young on the basis of entry examination results and the level of education. Civil servants who are generalist rather than specialists are allocated to positions through manpower planning. Promotions are mainly based on seniority (experience) and formal promotional training. Civil servants are guaranteed tenure in Indonesia.

According to the law, Indonesian civil servants are prohibited from misusing government property, engaging in profit-oriented activities outside of government or holding shares in an enterprise with business related to their jobs.

However, these rules do not always apply in practice. Civil service pay is generally low and many activities are rewarded with allowances, creating an environment where civil servants are dependent on additional payments. As such, current civil service management practices actually nurture corruption, especially the practice of buying and selling positions. Positions and promotions are offered for sale and candidates invest with expectation of rewards not commensurate with formal remuneration, thus entrenching corruption. Promotions may be offered for sale and payments are required for entry into lucrative jobs. It was reported that the price of a junior position in the Ministry of Justice and Human Rights was the basic salary for the first five years (Asian Development Bank 2004: 62). These practices serve three illicit purposes. First, the person paying the bribe is assured a job with the expectation of reward that cannot be expected from basic salaries and allowances. Second, for the persons accepting the bribe, it provides some additional income. Third, it guarantees personal loyalty to the patron under whom this operation works and, thus, enforces allegiance to maintain corrupt practices and assure secrecy. Moreover, other conditions make the situation even worse. Civil servants cannot be investigated or prosecuted without approval of the higher civil service authority. And officials under investigation for corruption are allowed to remain in offices.

There are annual performance assessments for civil servants, which are prepared by their superior officers. These are descriptive and do not assess performance against targets and objectives. They are considered as part of a process for determining rewards and cannot be considered as an instrument of accountability.

## *Civil service reforms in the Philippines*

Since gaining independence from the USA in 1946, the Philippines has been a constitutional presidential democracy. However, its democratic system is frequently described by scholars as a dictatorship or clientelism that suffers from patronage and systematic corruption (Endriga 2001). The Republic of the Philippines has separation of powers, a system of checks and balance and three equal branches of government: executive, legislative and the judiciary. The President heads the executive branch. The legislative power is vested in a bicameral congress that consists of the House of Representatives and the Senate. Judicial power is vested in the Supreme Court and lower courts. The President and Vice President are elected by a direct vote of the people and may only be removed by impeachment. The heads of executive departments are comprised of members of the Cabinet. They are nominated with the consent of the Commission on Appointments and are appointed by the President, who has full control of all executive departments, bureaux and offices (Asian Development Bank 2005).

Since its creation, the Philippine civil service has gone through four kinds of regimes—American colonialism, a flawed democracy, authoritarianism and a redemocratizing regime (Carino 1989). Since President Marcos, almost every administration included civil service reform in its political agenda. However, the implementation of civil service reforms faltered. During the administration of President Marcos (1965–1986), public servants were restructured into career, non-career and technocratic officer categories. President Marcos had given the Civil Service Commission constitutional status to oversee routine civil service appointments and training. Besides these, a number of political and administrative reform initiatives were promised. For example, the Integrated Reorganization Plan of 1972 promised to decentralize and downsize the government and to standardize departmental organization. The Plan also sought to introduce structural changes and reforms to strengthen the merit system as well as professionalize the civil service system (Carino 1989). However, the implementation faltered due to lack of popular support and strong opposition from the stakeholders, who were to be affected by the program. Moreover, erring political leadership also attributed to the reform failure (Hayllar 2003). Under the guise of nation building and institutional strengthening, Marcos purged thousands of government employees and restructured the government as he deemed fit. He created many new government agencies and jobs, which almost doubled the total number of staff he could personally command. And patronage and personal loyalty were the key factors in civil service appointments and promotions.

President Aquino (1986–1992) restored democratic institutions and ratified the new Constitution. Apart from fiscal discipline, he also pursued the decentralization of the frontline services as well as improved their accountability and efficiency. To restore government integrity and public confidence, civil society organization became more visible in government decision-making and program implementation. However, the reform measures fell short of their promise. Under the name of streamlining the bureaucracy, thousands of civil servants were removed from their position during the Aquino administration. Subsequently, numerous new positions were created to accommodate political appointees. The reform measures, which aimed to downsize the bloated government, resulted in the increases of the number of public agencies, civil servants and political appointees. The proliferation of political appointees blurred the merit and career system of the civil service and hindered the continuity and stability of policies and programs. Government became extended and fragmented again (Endriga 2001; Hayllar 2003). President Ramos (1993–1999) made a serious attempt to bring in sweeping governance reforms but was ultimately unsuccessful (Turner 2002).

As of 1999, a total of 1.445 million personnel were employed as civil servants. Civil service in the Philippines is top-heavy and it is concentrated at the national level. About 65 percent of the civil servants were assigned to national government while only 27 percent were assigned to local government units (Asian Development Bank 2005). In 2007, Philippine civil servants staffed the country's executive agencies, the secretariats of the legislature, the judiciary, local government and the organs of the Autonomous Muslim Region of Mindanao. Out of the 1.3 million government staff, some 18,000 are non-career political appointees. This figure excludes elected officials and contractual employees, who bring the total number of government employees up to around 1.4 million

*Table 6.6* Profile of the Philippine civil service, 1997–2001

| Year | Central government | Local government | Government-owned corp. | Total | Personnel expend. as % of gov total expend. |
|---|---|---|---|---|---|
| 1997 | 913,951 | 367,551 | 97,142 | 1,378,644 | 36.4 |
| 1998 | 913,593 | 365,437 | 126,498 | 1,405,528 | 38.2 |
| 1999 | 959,966 | 390,561 | 94,971 | 1,445,498 | 37.1 |
| 2000 | NA | NA | NA | NA | 34.5 |
| 2001 | NA | NA | NA | NA | 35.0 |

Source: Asian Development Bank (2005: 28, 30).

(Hodder 2009). Table 6.6 provides a profile of the Philippine civil service from 1997 to 2001. We found that more than 35 percent of the total government expenditure was spent on personnel payment.

The Philippine civil service is affected by a number of severe problems, including political interference in appointments, promotions and discipline, poor training and corrupt practices. The civil service has a rigid and centralized job description and classification system. Like the situations in Vietnam, Laos and Indonesia, the Philippine civil service remains vulnerable to political influence. Appointments and promotions to senior and other key positions are influenced by patronage politics. A study cites the Philippines as the only country where political appointees in the public bureaucracy extend down to the director level (Asian Development Bank 2005).

Both the quality of the civil service and its reform efforts have been weak in the Philippines. Constraints on the Philippine civil service quality stem largely from the politicization and clientelism in a wide range of civil service practices. Although the systems of merit-based recruitment, promotion and discipline are largely in place, they are ineffective in practices. The Career Executive Service, for example, establishes meritocratic criteria for appointment and advancement, but less than 40 percent of appointees meet eligibility requirements (Nunberg 2002: 18). Civil service pay was historically compressed and not attractive compared with alternative career paths in the private sector. As a result, qualified professionals are hard to attract and retain. Fragmented management responsibilities between the Civil Service Commission and the Department of Budget Management have also hindered coordinated reform efforts.

In general, civil servants in the Philippines lack the required managerial and technical capabilities to successfully carry out their duties. Existing qualifications standards barely ensure their competence. Low compensation level makes it difficult to recruit competent and qualified people to join the civil service and for them to stay. Low morale persists in the civil service. Performance standards and appraisal systems are not working to encourage performance. Good performance is rewarded in the same manner as poor performance. Behaviors such as arbitrariness, self-interest and even misconduct and dishonesty are tolerated. There is no incentive to perform and to deliver high quality service to the public.

## Discussion

In summary, both the quality of the civil service system and current reform efforts have been weak in the four countries examined. Their civil services do not function under a uniformed legal and institutional framework. As shown, the civil service systems have inadequate systems of establishment control, personnel information management and manpower planning. Moreover, they cannot provide sufficient incentives to motivate staff performance given that civil service salaries are low and promotions are mainly based on seniority. Last but not least, appropriate career development and training programs for civil servants are almost non-existent.

It is also important to note that civil service reform initiatives were undertaken on a limited, pilot basis and were sometimes stymied by the difficulties. In reforming their civil services, these countries usually confront the following problems. Due to resource scarcity and weak institutionalization of merit rules, the pay system of their civil services is dysfunctional. Compared with the private sector and taking into account the average cost of living, civil servants' salaries are not high. The devolution of personnel authority to local governments caused bloated payrolls. Salary structures are compressed and, hence, cannot provide sufficient motivation for performance. The lack of discipline is evident in all of the four civil services examined since civil servants look for additional sources of income. Another problem is that civil service management and reforms in these countries cannot be easily insulated from political interference. Political patronage is the main feature of the appointments and promotions system in all four countries. In effect, the politicization of the civil service created the pressure to inflate their civil service system.

Corruption remains a very serious problem in these countries. There are ample opportunities for corruption within the public sectors, but few opportunities and tools for the detection and punishment of corrupt offenders. Many civil servants abuse the power of their positions by being involved in corrupt practices and obtaining additional income illegally. A number of reasons account for the rampant corruption in these countries, including low salaries of civil servants, erring political leadership, the lack of legal and institutional framework for anticorruption as well as the lack of useful strategies and instruments to fight corruption.

Why is China's experience suitable for these Asian countries? There is generally an accepted rule for civil service (public sector) reforms in developing countries, namely to do things by stages and in the right order (Painter 2006). A World Bank study suggests that developing countries should choose their civil service reform initiatives in line with their national capacities and initial conditions (World Bank 2004: 194). Schick (1998) discussed the limited transferability of New Zealand public sector reforms to developing countries. He argued that developing countries need a rule-bound, professional, centralized, Weberian-style bureaucracy with firmly established basic public sector budgeting and accounting procedures before they can safely introduce more decentralized, market-mimicking models of public service delivery. In particular, the first stage of reform should aim to achieve or strengthen 'formality, discipline, and compliance with the rules'. The second stage of reform should aim for 'flexibility and local discretion' (Painter 2006; Schick 1998; World Bank 2004).

The Chinese government implemented the first stage of the reform first, followed by the second stage of the reform. This made China's experience suitable for other development countries in Asia. First, China has a uniformed legislative framework and a centralized institutional arrangement for civil service management and reforms. The *Civil Service Law*, approved in 2005, is the blueprint for civil service management and reforms in China. A number of supplementary and trial regulations, implementation methods as well as policy directives were promulgated by the government. The Chinese Communist Party (CCP) exercises tight control through party regulations over senior civil servants. These documents form the legal context of the civil service reforms. As for the institutional framework, the central Organization Department of the CCP (under the leadership of the Politburo) is in charge of the public personnel management policy. Civil service bureaux are being established at various government levels to manage civil servants. Senior civil servants occupying leading positions are managed by the *nomenklatura* authority. Management and administration in China are performed largely in accordance to the law. All of the four countries in this study should make note of this point. A centrally managed and merit-based personnel management has not been established in Vietnam yet. Public personnel management authorities have been delegated to provincial and district governments. Decentralization in personnel management in Vietnam brought about negative consequences such as secretive recruitment and political patronage. As well, when civil service pay determinations have been delegated to local government, negative consequences followed such as civil service wage bills inflation and the increase in public service fees. Laos is a poor country with a highly scattered population and negligible infrastructure. It proved to be difficult to establish a uniformed and centralized civil service management framework. Indonesia also has a fragmented management structure for civil service.

Another important lesson is the importance of improving the quality of the civil service. Before decentralizing too much personnel management authority to local governments, developing countries in Asia should establish a national scheme for civil service recruitment and selection. As I mentioned above, the recruitment and initial placement of civil servants are crucial determinants of the enduring quality of the civil service. China has performed well in this aspect. Civil service recruitment relies heavily on examinations and open competition. From 1993 the Chinese government set up an annual nationwide civil service entry-level selection system for persons with college or graduate school education. Entry into the civil service, to a significant extent, is determined by individual performance in competitions. In Laos, national recruitment plans or schemes do not exist. In both Vietnam and Indonesia, the recruitment process is formally carried out on a national basis but local governments are left with a high degree of authority to select people. The lack of transparency and the possibility of rent-seeking frequently lead to corruption in the selection of civil servants. Another important instrument to improve the quality of the civil service is to provide training. The two socialist regimes, Vietnam and Laos, had traditionally given priority to ideology and political education. Therefore, government employees are short of knowledge and skills of modern management. They need to strengthen the training programs by focusing on managerial and administrative technologies. Civil service training in China has an extensive national network of institutions with most of them located in local governments. Party schools have a much more political and ideological content whereas the administration schools and socialism colleges are focused almost exclusively on management, economics and applied skills. The vast majority of civil service training takes place in the vast network of local party schools, administration schools and socialism colleges throughout the country.

Third, civil service salaries in all these countries examined are depressed and, hence, the lack of manpower in the government is a serious problem. Accordingly, increasing the pay and welfare for the whole service is a critical task facing the governments. A career in the civil service sector in China is a very attractive one because the pay and welfare benefits for civil servants are comparable to the private sector. Moreover, a mechanism to ensure regular wage rises against inflation and living cost has been installed. However, raising salaries for government employees in developing countries is easier said than done. This reform initiative is constrained by many factors such as the level of economic growth, government budget deficit and the citizens' demand for a cost-effective civil service. In addition to increasing pay and welfare benefits for civil servants, governments in developing countries can also pay attention to establishment control in order to manage their civil service wage bills.

Fourth, it has proved difficult to promote a performance culture within the Chinese civil service. Corruption is rampant in the public sector. Other governments in Asia should learn from this bitter lesson. In the Philippine civil service, performance standards and appraisal systems are not working to encourage performance. Appointments and promotions to senior positions are still influenced by patronage politics. Situations in Vietnam, Laos and Indonesia are the same. Civil servants are still accustomed to the top-down environment and report minor issues to their superiors rather than make their own decisions. Civil service recruitment and promotion are vulnerable to political influence. Governments in these countries should take initiatives to change civil servants' perception of government as being a top-down hierarchy and, in turn, change their risk-averse behavior in doing their job. Creativity and efficiency should be rewarded through implementing performance-based pay and performance-based promotion. As discussed in the previous chapters, China has established an institutional framework and some useful instruments (such as *Shuanggui*) to fight corruption. However, corruption is still rampant. According to Transparency International (2009), the Corruption Perception Index of China is ranked at 79 among 180 countries all over the world. Vital to any sustainable anticorruption efforts are a committed leadership, the establishment of an independent anticorruption agency and a concerted effort to keep corruption investigations free of political interference.

In summary, governments should aim to improve the quality and efficiency of the civil service as well as to establish an ethical norm within the system. Subsequently in the second stage, reform initiatives should aim to incorporate flexibility such as the contract-based employment and decentralization into the system. This chapter first reviews the practices and reforms of the Chinese civil service management system in order to discover some lessons and insights that could be transferred to selected developing countries in Asia. An analysis of civil service reform experience in the four countries suggests that there are significant variations among them. They varied in many areas such as the initial capacity of systems to undertake modernization programs, the contextual conditions of politics and receptivity to external administrative models as well as their reform trajectories and problems. I suggest here some methods for improvement; however, we should keep in mind that China still has a long way to go before its civil service institutions are in accordance with globally competitive performance standards. In providing several general reform principles, I believe China's experience could serve as a good starting point for these developing countries in Asia.

# 7 Conclusion

This book examined the implementation and performance of the civil service reforms in China. It not only analyzed how the various reform initiatives affected the incentive structure and behavior of civil servants in the Chinese local government context, but also outlined how policy-makers tried to strengthen their political and administrative control over bureaucrats and assessed the level of success of these efforts. This book also discussed the possibility of using China's reform experience as a model for selected developing countries in Asia, whose governments are facing the dilemma of how to recruit, retain and motivate skilled staff at an affordable cost.

One of the objectives of the civil service reforms in China was to improve the quality of government employees so that the Chinese government could regulate and manage its increasingly complex economy and fast-changing society. Policy-makers also sought to strengthen their political and administrative control over local governments and bureaucrats. Their logic was that tight control of the bureaucracy would force local bureaucrats to improve their performance in public service delivery thus helping authorities to gain or regain their legitimacy and public support. Moreover, policy-makers believed that tighter control would help to combat corruption, which was a serious problem that had damaging effects on their legitimacy. Did the implementation of these reforms help to achieve these objectives?

The principal–agent theory provided an insightful framework for the analysis. The framework enabled me to make predictions before assessing the efficacy of the civil service reforms in China. From the viewpoint of the principal–agent theory, it was vital to study the multiple principal–agent relationships that were embedded in the government in order to assess the institutional changes and their impacts. Civil servants in China served multiple principals, including their immediate superiors, the local government, the central government and the public. Under the institutional arrangement of the old cadre personnel management system, bureaucratic superiors had difficulty in obtaining full compliance from their subordinates due to the problem of information asymmetry and conflict of interest. In general, the cadre system suffered from serious defects. It was a highly centralized and undifferentiated approach to personnel management. The management system was outdated and overly simple to account for the various power relations that existed within the bureaucracy. There were vague guidelines for promotion, performance appraisal and training. In addition, poor performance was tolerated while incentives for performance were insufficient to motivate cadres. The institutional design of the civil service reforms in China included elements that provided superiors solutions to mitigate these problems, which included measures to foster competition, reduce information asymmetries and align the incentives between superiors and their subordinates. However, policy design is very different from policy implementation. This book has presented a mixed picture about the effectiveness of civil service reforms.

This chapter will first summarize the empirical findings. Second, several policy implications resulting from the analysis are identified. Subsequent to a discussion on the limitations, the chapter closes with further directions for research.

## Summary of research findings

To some extent, civil service reforms in China made improvements in important areas such as transparency, predictability, accountability, participation, efficiency and effectiveness, all of which are elements of 'good governance'. First, evidence indicated that the quality and capacity of the civil service increased during the reform era. Education levels rose while the average age of government employees declined. Civil servants are now better educated and this fact may be partially caused by the expansion of higher education in China. A more important and influential factor could be the open and competitive recruitment of the civil servants that was implemented on a nationwide scale from 1993. In the old cadre system, entry into the civil service (political elites group) was determined by the 'blood line theory' (Lee 1991), especially during the period of the Cultural Revolution. Other key criteria that enabled people to become political elites at the time were the patronage and social networks (*guanxi*). As a result, public personnel management and public administration were characterized by inefficiency, secrecy, nepotism and political patronage. Open and competitive recruitment and promotion of civil servants under the new civil service system changed these practices. The Chinese government set up an annual nationwide civil service entry-level selection system from 1993. Recruitment relied heavily on examinations and open competition. Entry into the civil service, to a significant extent, is now determined by individual performance in competitions. The process of selecting and promoting civil servants in China today is undoubtedly more open, transparent and competitive than it was under the cadre system. Moreover, transparency in the promotion processes of senior civil servants (as discussed in Chapter 3) helped to reduce the opportunities for corruption. In general, the transparency and predictability of the recruitment and promotion processes helped to increase the perceived legitimacy of the selection of civil servants.

Second, civil service reforms in China induced a shift in the promotion guideline of the Chinese hierarchy towards a system that was based on work performance and

140  *Conclusion*

problem-solving ability. In order to impress their superiors through work performance, civil servants are bound to curry favor with the citizens so as to induce the citizens to engage in cooperative behaviors with them. In this study, citizens acknowledged that the performance of local governments had indeed improved since the reforms and they felt satisfied with the local governments' performance in providing basic education and in protecting the environment.

Third, this book contributed to the existing literature by examining reform implementation in various concrete local government contexts. In the analysis of the three case studies on reform implementation by local governments, Chapter 4 illustrated the positive impacts of the reforms including a more open and competitive selection process, more formalized performance evaluation, an improvement of the quality of civil service and a more citizen-friendly demeanor among government officials. However, it also suggested that these reforms in all three places were undermined by other policies being implemented at the same time, for example, the downsizing campaign and the welfare and patronage policies that required local governments to employ demobilized soldiers. The implementation of civil service reforms in the three places was also undermined by widespread informal practices such as corruption. Civil service reforms were carried out in the midst of two vigorous attempts to downsize the government (in 1998 and 2003 respectively). As a result, many government agencies were unable to implement certain parts of the civil service reforms. For example, new hiring procedures were not implemented because many government agencies were considered to be overstaffed based on the new staffing guidelines. Chapter 4 also suggested that there were considerable variations among the three places in terms of the implementation of the reforms. In particular, the reforms process across the country occurred at an uneven pace. This uneven progress was also evident in the multiple programs that were included in the reforms. Differences in economic development could account for variation in the relative size and composition of various civil service agencies. With a less developed economy, Changchun appeared to be under-resourced compared to the other two places. This condition affected its capacity to implement civil service training programs and the staffing levels of the education and environmental protection bureaux compared to population size. Still, Changchun utilized individual appraisals more effectively to rid the government of underperformers, especially in the early days of the reform. One explanation could be that there were no other options available except the termination of employees in order to meet the downsizing targets.

Fourth, the government in China tried to professionalize the civil service through human resource development initiatives, including establishing training institutions and increasing financial input for training programs. Civil service reforms also provided guidance to civil servants about their attitudes to citizens and clients through procedures such as mass evaluations (where citizens played a role in the performance evaluation process of civil servants). Reforms sought to tighten the connection between civil servants and the public by taking steps to increase transparency and accountability in public administration and public service delivery. Civil servants were required to adjust the way they treated their clients, which compelled them to be more citizen-friendly on their jobs.

Chapter 5 suggested that reforms changed the performance measurement of senior civil servants to be more comprehensive and not purely focused on local economic development. Local leaders paid more attention to non-economic policies and, as a result, local bureaux in non-economic fields were forced to be more committed in fulfilling their professional missions. The implementation of civil service reforms and other administrative monitoring mechanisms helped policy-makers in China to strengthen their political and administrative control over local governments and bureaucrats. The tightened control brought about improvement in public service delivery. Both statistical data and case studies of public service delivery illustrated this improvement. The improvement was also attested by citizens who acknowledged that the civil service does a better job now than before.

To understand the logic of Chapter 5, one point needs to be elaborated. The success of the bureaucratic control lay in the capacity of the central leadership to ensure that the substantive decisions and behaviors of the local governments remained consistent with Beijing's broad policy principles. Despite the tremendous pressures induced by the continual reforms and decentralization, the central leadership in China achieved a reasonably high degree of cohesion among civil servants. The perception data of officials and clients in Chapter 5 revealed that the actual behaviors of the local officials in providing public services largely conformed to the directives from upper-level government.

In summary, this book presented a mixed picture about the effectiveness of the civil service reforms in China. On one hand, evidence suggested that civil service quality improved. Better public service delivery and a high level of citizen satisfaction were also evident. In addition, the reforms, to some extent, were able to motivate the individual civil servant to work hard and adjusted their way of exercising discretion, a change that was welcomed by the clients and citizens. On the other hand, some negative images of the government remained after the reforms. For example, rampant and widespread corruption continues to characterize China's civil service and undermines its meritocracy. To this day, there are still ample opportunities for corruption within the public sectors, but few opportunities and tools for the detection and punishment of corrupt offenders. As discussed in Chapter 5, China has established an institutional framework and some useful instruments (such as *Shuanggui*) to fight corruption. However, corruption is still rampant. According to Transparency International (2009), the Corruption Perception Index of China is ranked at 79 among 180 countries all over the world. The bitter lessons of China's experience in fighting corruption pointed to the importance of a committed leadership, the establishment of an independent anticorruption agency and a concerted effort to keep corruption investigations free of political interference.

As for the wage reforms that were included as part of the civil service reforms, the authorities increased civil servants' salaries, subsidies and pensions remarkably in the recent years as influenced by the assumption that paying high salaries would foster a clean government. This helped to make the civil service pay level reasonably competitive with the private sector, making a career in the civil service appear very attractive. However, considering other important objectives of wage reforms such as motivating performance, eliminating financial mismanagement of local governments and tackling regional gaps of civil service welfare, the implementation of wage reforms fell short of their promise. One of the reasons that wage reforms failed to provide additional motivation to civil servants lay in the fact that performance appraisals were conducted in a highly pro forma manner. Almost all civil servants received similarly high scores in their evaluations. Moreover, linking incompetent grades with punishment were far from institutionalized.

This book also discussed the feasibility of transferring China's reform experience to other Asian contexts with similar cultural values and initial conditions to undertake reform initiatives. The civil service and reform efforts in four developing countries in Southeast Asia were examined. China's experience in managing and reforming its civil service could serve as a model for them. The transferable elements included the establishment of a uniformed legislative and institutional framework for reforms, the institutionalization of civil service recruitment and competition and merit-based promotions, the installment of transparency and predictability into the public personnel management system and the promotion of government officials' accountability as well as public participation.

## Policy implications

This book not only deepened our understanding of the rationale behind and the direction of civil service reforms, but also helped us to relate the public personnel management to the general political development in China. To understand how the institutions operate on a day-to-day basis is important, but not as important as to understand why they work the way they do. To answer why they work in certain ways requires understanding the rational design of these institutions. This book not only outlined the reform policies in China, but also examined the implementation and performance of these reforms. In assessing the efficacy of the reform design, it helped us to understand the rationale behind these reforms. Given that reform implementation consumed considerable financial and human resources and technology, evaluating the return on this investment was of great importance.

Thirty years of economic reforms and liberalization have brought great challenges to the outdated governance structure and personnel management in China. Whether the Chinese authorities can survive the tremendous pressures induced by the continual economic reforms and decentralization is a significant issue. The Chinese political system is monopolized by the CCP rule. The power of all local government officials comes from the appointment by their superiors, not from local community elections. In such a regime, how can local governments and local bureaucrats be induced to serve the citizen and, in turn, help the central leadership to gain the public support that is necessary to sustain its level of power? The answers to these questions lie in exercising tight control of the bureaucracy. The tight political and administrative control over local governments and bureaucrats would force them to improve public service delivery and, thus, rebuild the public trust.

History provides insights into the future—the descriptions, evaluations and predictions are all connected. This book shed light on the predictions on the direction of the reforms in China. Empirical findings showed that some reform efforts did not coincidently just happen. Rather, they were components of incremental changes intentionally made by the Chinese leadership. As such, the civil service reform is part of a much greater transformation that the Chinese authorities will and must go through. Where will the reforms lead China to? Observers anticipate that the continual and extensive economic reforms and decentralization will ultimately lead to fundamental regime change in China (Dickson 2003). I agree that economic reforms and decentralization have fundamentally changed the parameters of Chinese political development. Democratic elections have been gradually introduced in some local governments and grassroots organizations, mostly at the village level (O'Brien and Li 1999). However, this process is continuing at a snail's pace. In this study, I find that citizens in China today cannot yet be considered as the real principal. Even after a series of reforms, citizens are still poorly informed about governmental affairs. They are involved only in a relatively limited number of specific cases. This may be because citizens, influenced by Chinese traditional culture, are passive. But there may be two other significant reasons: the lack of an independent court system and the restriction on the formation of interest groups and powerful non-government organizations in China. The government in China currently suppresses independent groups due to its fear that these groups may become the breeding nests for dissenting individuals and, ultimately, challenge the government's authority. Moreover, the authoritarian nature of the Chinese political regime has not been fundamentally changed. The political system is still monopolized by the CCP rule. The power of all local government officials comes from the appointment by superiors and not from local residents' elections. Therefore, effective monitoring and control mechanisms are in place to hold local bureaucrats accountable for and responsive to the needs of their superiors, but not the local residents.

Given that there is no possibility for a fundamental regime change in the near future, important political developments in contemporary China that deserve close research include governance structure change and policy-makers' control over the civil service. The Chinese authorities have devoted tremendous energy to adjust the governance structure and improve their ability in order to manage and control the public personnel. The school of comparative communist politics raised an interesting question: why has the CCP survived when most of the other ruling communist parties have not (Dickson 2003)? The answer lies in the CCP's institutional adaptability (Burns 1999a; Edin 2003; Huang 2002; Yang 2004). Despite the tremendous pressure induced by the continual reforms and decentralization, the central leadership in China has achieved a reasonably high degree of cohesion among cadres by designing effective mechanisms for elite recruitment, promotion and rotation. In short, the CCP is capable of great institutional adaptability. This study demonstrated that carefully devised reforms could contribute to the gradual formation of institutional norms that were consistent with the new environment and the regime's objectives. In particular, it found that public personnel reforms helped the leadership to sustain and improve its capacity to shape, reward and control local bureaucrats, which provided better public service and, in turn, gained or regained public support. In this way, the Chinese leadership can survive the pressures that are induced by the economic reforms while maintaining its authoritarian rule.

Referring to the impacts of personnel reforms on the relationship between the central and the local governments, this study also shed some light on one continuing debate. The debate involves two predictions regarding China's future. The 'collapse' prediction argued that there is a governance crisis in China and the regime will experience an institutional collapse (Chang 2001; Pei 2006, 1994). On the other hand, the 'strong state' prediction argued that central control has not diminished, especially in the area of public personnel management (Huang 2002, 1996, 1995; Yang 2004; Naughton and Yang 2004). This study is partial to the 'strong state' prediction since the 'collapse' prediction underestimated the ability of the CCP to adapt to the changing political environment. Officials that were interviewed for this study believed that civil service reforms in China were carried out in a fashion that was broadly consistent with the central government's stated objectives. Therefore, the Chinese leaders maintained the ability to shape, reward and control the local bureaucrats.

## Limitations

First, the timing of conducting such research (examination of reform implementation and impacts) was a challenge in and of itself. The testing of most of the hypotheses of this study called for a before-and-after comparative analysis. Obviously, surveys that were administered after the reforms that had already taken place could not directly test the effect of reforms. When this study began, institutional change had already occurred nationwide, leaving no control group (local government) untouched by the reforms.

Second, using perception data as the main measure of government performance was obviously limited. I focused on perception data because objective data of Chinese government performance were not readily available. On the one hand, the Chinese government seldom carried out organizational performance measurement while on the other hand documents on this issue were considered as internal briefings and, thus, remained off-limits to researchers. Therefore, I conducted surveys and relied on interviewees' perceptions and evaluations in order to examine the impact of the reforms on local government performance. However, it is important to keep in mind that these results were likely to be biased against the subjective factors. We should remain skeptical of these findings until more objective data on government performance are available or more case studies are conducted. Moreover, I took precautions in using perception data as a main measure of public service delivery. I not only took into account every individual interviewee's views but also made sure to compare the views of related interviewees.[1] Uncovering the extent and the structure of the information that the related interviewees were willing to reveal provided valuable information on the nature of their organization. More importantly, I aimed to identify the common knowledge of a sample or a sub-sample. In other words, it was critical to measure the extent to which the information given by the interviewee was considered as common knowledge within the sample. Ultimately, more objective data of government performance in future research is warranted to avoid subjective bias of perception data.

## Future research agenda

As I cautioned in the introductory chapter, reform implementation, central control and policy learning and transfer among governments are complex political issues that warrant a multifaceted research agenda. For the next stage of the research agenda, I propose the following. China still has a long march ahead to establish a successful civil service system and make its civil service institutions in accordance with globally competitive performance standards. Civil service reforms in China aim to promote administrative efficiency and help the policy-makers in strengthening their control over the civil service. Turning these objectives into reality are not easy tasks. Successful implementation of China's civil service reforms demands improvements in governance structures: accountability, transparency, adherence to the rule of law and greater use of direct democracy in public decision-making. Great improvements in the above governance structures in contemporary China have yet to be seen. In this book, my conclusion is that civil service reforms to date are not yet entirely successful. However, I foresee there is a positive developing trend as demonstrated in my examination of the impacts of the reforms on local government performance as well as my evaluation of the rationale behind these reforms.

# Appendices

## Appendix 1 The empirical database

The empirical database of this book comprises three main parts, including 90 in-depth interviews with officials and their clients, a citizen satisfaction survey in Haidian and fieldwork research.[1]

### *In-depth interviews*

In order to investigate local implementation of civil service reforms in China and citizen evaluation on government performance in delivering public services, we carried out 90 in-depth interviews with officials and their clients of the environmental bureaux and education bureaux of Haidian, Ningbo and Changchun in 2001. Each interview was administered with the endorsement and support of the respective bureau. We observed no evidence that the leadership of the six bureaux attempted to influence the outcomes of the interviews, and we explained clearly both in our briefing and in the text of the interview questionnaire that all the data were collected solely for academic purposes and would remain strictly confidential. Thus we can believe that the responses reflect the true opinions of the respondents.

In total, 40 officials from a pool of 388 were interviewed (the size of administrative establishment of the three environmental protection bureaux of Haidian, Ningbo and Changchun is 30, 28 and 28, respectively. The corresponding figures of the three education bureaux in the three research sites are 148, 90 and 64). Officials from different bureaucratic ranks were chosen to increase the variety of responses. We also interviewed 50 clients of government environmental service and education service. A total of 90 in-depth interviews were conducted. Each lasted about 90 minutes and was conducted in Mandarin. A structured questionnaire was prepared for face-to-face interviews. Most of our questions were open-ended. These were intended to overcome the inadequacies of closed-ended questions and gather further information for result interpretation. Table A.1 provides the profile of the interviewees.

*Table A.1* Profile of interviewees

| Officials | | (N = 40) |
|---|---|---|
| Characteristics | | Number |
| Education | | |
| | University degree | 27 |
| | Master degree | 2 |
| Bureaucratic rank | | |
| | Bureau Chief and Deputy | 2 |
| | Division Chief and Deputy | 16 |
| | Section Chief and Deputy | 13 |
| | Others | 6 |
| | NA | 3 |
| Age | (Average) | 41.46 |

| Customers | | (N = 50) |
|---|---|---|
| Characteristics | | Number |
| Education | | |
| | University degree | 24 |
| | Master degree | 2 |
| Occupation | | |
| | Principal | 7 |
| | Teacher | 5 |
| | Student | 5 |
| | Parent | 6 |
| | Factory manager or worker | 14 |
| | Retired | 3 |
| | Service unit worker | 10 |
| Age | (Average) | 39.8 |

Source: 90 in-depth interviews database, 2001.

## *Haidian citizen satisfaction survey*

A large-scale random sampling citizen satisfaction survey was conducted in Haidian in 2003. The survey, conducted in collaboration with the Research Center for Contemporary China of Peking University,[2] aimed to collect data on how Haidian residences evaluate district government performance in environmental and education policy. We chose Haidian as the sample site because it is the district with the most developed education system and institutions in Beijing, which made it a good place to examine government education performance.

A random sample of 728 adults in Haidian was generated using the probabilities proportional to size sampling method. First, 25 urban residential committees (*juweihui*) were randomly chosen. Second, 29 households were randomly chosen from each of the 25 urban residential committees, producing a total of 728 households. Third, one individual aged between 18 and 66 was randomly chosen from each of the 728 households as the interviewee. During the survey, a fieldworker took the questionnaire to the randomly chosen individual respondent and then conducted the interview. An interview took 45 minutes on average. Upon completion, the fieldworker brought the questionnaire back to the survey center. Given the previous experience that, in collecting quality research data in China, the presence of research professionals is often important, all the fieldworkers of this survey were intensively trained undergraduates from the Political Science Department of Peking University. As a result of this effort, a total of 501 permanent urban residents aged between 18 and 66 were interviewed. The response rate was approximately 69 percent. The demographic information of the interviewees is shown in Table A.2. The sample was roughly divided between the two genders (48.3 percent males and 51.7 percent females). All age groups (from 18 to over 60 years old) and urban occupation sectors are represented in the sample. About 5 percent of the informants had primary schooling or below, 23.4 percent have junior middle school diplomas, 45.7 percent had a senior middle school or vocational education and 25.5 percent are holders of university degrees or above.

*Table A.2* Profile of interviewees

| Characteristics | | Number | Percentage |
| --- | --- | --- | --- |
| Gender | | | |
| | Male | 242 | 48.3 |
| | Female | 259 | 51.7 |
| Age | | | |
| | Young (18–29) | 64 | 12.8 |
| | Middle (30–49) | 301 | 60.1 |
| | Old (over 50) | 136 | 27.1 |
| Education | | | |
| | Primary school or below | 26 | 5.0 |
| | Junior middle school | 117 | 23.4 |
| | Senior middle school | 149 | 29.7 |
| | Upper middle specialized school | 80 | 16.0 |
| | University and above | 128 | 25.5 |
| Occupation | | | |
| | Party and government institutions | 32 | 6.4 |
| | State-owned enterprises and public institutions | 229 | 45.7 |
| | Private enterprises | 36 | 7.2 |
| | Foreign-funded enterprises | 15 | 3.0 |
| | Self-employed individuals | 21 | 4.2 |
| | Others (including unemployed, students, housewives and retired) | 167 | 33.3 |
| Monthly Income | | | |
| | RMB1,000 or below | 258 | 51.5 |
| | RMB1,001–2,000 | 156 | 31.1 |
| | RMB2,001–3,000 | 55 | 11.0 |
| | RMB3,000 or above | 32 | 6.4 |

Source: Haidian citizen satisfaction survey database, January–March 2003.

We considered the Chinese social and cultural context when designing the wording of the survey questionnaire. The questionnaire was pre-tested in draft form in October 2002 to test the clarity of the language, the smoothness of the flow of questions, the appropriateness of the length and the time needed to answer the questions. It was subsequently finalized in the current format. During the survey, respondents were assured confidentiality and encouraged to provide answers that best capture their true feelings. Respondents were asked to assess a variety of programs or activities that the Haidian Environmental Protection Bureau and Haidian Education Commission conducted. They also provided their perception on the overall environment situation and overall quality of basic education in Haidian. They were also asked to assess the policy responsiveness of the Haidian district government. Care was taken to minimize respondent effects and semantic confusion. Since those in our sample are permanent residents of Haidian, we do not intend to generalize our findings to the rest of China.

## *Fieldwork research*

During the fieldwork research, I visited and conducted in-depth interviews and a questionnaire survey in environmental bureaux and education bureaux of Haidian and Changchun in March and April of 2004, and in Ningbo in February of 2005. I collected data and information on the implementation of civil service reforms and performance management programs in the local government bureaux. The data also include officials' perceptions of their clients and their performance evaluation of the bureau.

*Table A.3* Profile of interviewees

| Officials | | (N = 52) |
|---|---|---|
| Characteristics | | Number |
| Gender | | |
| | Male | 29 |
| | Female | 23 |
| Education | | |
| | College degree | 6 |
| | University degree | 39 |
| | Master degree | 7 |
| Bureaucratic rank | | |
| | Division chief | 2 |
| | Deputy division chief | 5 |
| | Section chief | 10 |
| | Deputy section chief | 9 |
| | Section member | 24 |
| | NA | 2 |
| Age | (Average) | 38.6 |
| Years worked | (Average) | 9.12 |

Source: Fieldwork survey, March–April 2004.

150  *Appendices*

The survey questionnaire mainly focused on three issues: implementation of civil service reforms, evaluation of bureau performance and identification of public service clients. In general, the survey data help to address three questions: (1) How do the officials perceive and evaluate the civil service reforms in China? (2) How do they understand and evaluate the bureau performance and the sub-division performance within their bureau? (3) How do they identify and treat their clients in delivery of public service? Altogether I have 52 samples. Table A.3 provides the profile of the interviewees.

## Appendix 2  Protocol for the 90 in-depth interviews (Questions for officials)

### *Section A  Interviewee characteristics*

A1  Work unit: which government bureau/division/section do you belong to?
A2  Bureaucratic rank (Bureau Chief/Deputy Chief, Division Chief/Deputy Chief, Section Chief/Deputy Chief, Section member, Others)
A3  Year of birth
A4  Education background

| Coding | Meaning |
| --- | --- |
| 3 | Primary school |
| 4 | Junior middle school |
| 5 | Senior middle school (including middle specialized school) |
| 6 | Upper middle specialized school |
| 7 | University |
| 8 | Postgraduate |

A5  Place of birth

### *Section B  Responsibilities of position*

B1  Please list out the main responsibilities of your position.
B2  Among the listed responsibilities, which of them are associated with the directives of the upper-level governments?
B3  Among the listed responsibilities, which of them are associated with the local circumstances?
B4  Which responsibilities mentioned above are the most important in your opinion?
B6  Are you familiar with the directives from the upper-level governments?
B7  Did your organization make some adjustments to the directives from the upper-level governments?

*Section C Perception of clients*

C1  Please identify the clients of your organization.
C2  How do you communicate with your clients?
C3  Do the clients play a role in the decision-making of your organization?

*Section D Measures to fulfill the organizational missions*

D1  What regular measures have been adopted to fulfill the missions of your organization?
D2  Among the measures mentioned above, which are directives from upper-level governments, and which are initiated by your organization?
D3  What activities have been organized to fulfill the missions?
D4  Among the activities mentioned above, which are directives from upper-level governments, and which are initiated by your organization?
D5  What is your evaluation of the effects of these measures and activities?

*Section E Assessment of organizational performance*

E1  Please evaluate the performance of your organization.
E2  Please elaborate the criteria you used for the above evaluation.
E3  In your opinion, what are the main weaknesses of the existing organizational performance measurement system?
E4  Please describe the existing organizational performance measurement system, including the actors, the resources and the process.
E5  Do you think the following are the determinants of organizational performance? Please rank them according to their strength in determining organizational performance.

| Coding | Meaning |
| --- | --- |
| 1 | Increased financial input |
| 2 | Improved technology |
| 3 | Political support |
| 4 | Improved quality of civil servants as the result of China's civil service reforms |
| 5 | Perfection of relevant rules and regulations |
| 6 | Improvement of internal administrative leadership |
| 7 | Strategic planning |
| 8 | Public support |

E6  We list out some components of China's civil service reforms. Please assess their impacts on local government performance.

152  *Appendices*

| Coding | Meaning |
|---|---|
| 1 | Open and competitive selection |
| 2 | Performance appraisal |
| 3 | Pay adjustment based on appraisal results |
| 4 | Training program |
| 5 | Reward and discipline |
| 6 | Competition in the staffing process |

E7  In your opinion, what factors will hinder improvement in organizational performance?

## (Questions for clients)

### Section A  Interviewee characteristics

A1  Work unit
A2  Year of birth
A3  Education background

| Coding | Meaning |
|---|---|
| 3 | Primary school |
| 4 | Junior middle school |
| 5 | Senior middle school (including middle specialized school) |
| 6 | Upper middle specialized school |
| 7 | University |
| 8 | Postgraduate |

A4  Place of birth

### Section B  Demand and preference on public service

B1  As a citizen, what kind of public services do you want the environmental protection/education bureaux to provide?
B2  Why do you think these public services are important?

### Section C  Perception of government efforts

C1  Are you familiar with the policies and regulations of the environmental protection/education bureaux?
C2  Are you familiar with the activities of the environmental protection/education bureaux?
C3  How did you get the information regarding the above activities?
C4  Do you think the above policies, regulations or activities of the environmental protection/education bureaux cover the demands and preference of the general public?

C5 Did you contact the environmental protection/education bureaux recently? For what?

C6 Did the environmental protection/education bureaux contact you recently? For what?

## *Section D  Assessment of government performance*

D1 Do you know the criteria that the environmental protection/education bureaux used to evaluate their own performance?

D2 In your opinion, what should be the criteria to evaluate the performance of the environmental protection/education bureaux?

D3 Compared with five years ago, which of the following will be your evaluation of the performance of the environmental protection/education bureaux?

| Coding | Meaning |
|---|---|
| 1 | Apparently improved |
| 2 | Improved |
| 3 | No changes |
| 4 | Worse |
| 5 | Apparently worse |

D4 Please identify the successful jobs that the government bureaux have done.

D5 Please identify the areas where improvements are warranted in government work.

## *Section E  Determining factors of government performance*

E1 Do you think the following are the determining factors for the government performance? Please rank them according to their strength in determining government performance.

| Coding | Meaning |
|---|---|
| 1 | Increased financial input |
| 2 | Improved technology |
| 3 | Political support |
| 4 | Improved quality of civil servants as the result of China's civil service reforms |
| 5 | Perfection of relevant rules and regulations |
| 6 | Improvement of internal administrative leadership |
| 7 | Public support |

E2 In your opinion, what factors will hinder the government performance improvement?

## Appendix 3  Haidian citizen satisfaction survey questionnaire

Sex

| Coding | Meaning |
|---|---|
| 1 | Male |
| 2 | Female |
| Total | |

### Section A  Interviewee characteristics

A1  Occupation

| Coding | Meaning |
|---|---|
| 1 | Party and government institutions |
| 2 | State-owned enterprises and public institutions |
| 3 | Private enterprises |
| 4 | Foreign-invested enterprises |
| 7 | Others |
| 99 | No answer |
| Total | |

A2  Work place

| Coding | Meaning |
|---|---|
| 1 | Work place in Haidian |
| 3 | Work place outside of Haidian |
| 99 | No answer |
| Total | |

A3  Year of birth

A4  Education background

| Coding | Meaning |
|---|---|
| 1 | Illiterate |
| 2 | Lower primary school |
| 3 | Primary school |
| 4 | Junior middle school |
| 5 | Senior middle school |
| 6 | Upper middle specialized school |
| 7 | University and above |
| 9 | No answer |
| Total | |

A5 How long did you live in Haidian?
A6 No. of children

| Coding | Meaning |
|---|---|
| 0 | No child |
| 1 | 1 child |
| 2 | 2 children |
| 3 | 3 children |
| 4 | 4 children |
| 5 | 5 children |
| Total | |

A6a No. of children attending primary school

| Coding | Meaning |
|---|---|
| 0 | No child attending primary school |
| 1 | 1 child attending primary school |
| Total | |

A6b No. of children attending junior middle school

| Coding | Meaning |
|---|---|
| 0 | No child attending junior middle school |
| 1 | 1 child attending junior middle school |
| Total | |

A6c No. of children attending senior middle school

| Coding | Meaning |
|---|---|
| 0 | No child attending senior middle school |
| 1 | 1 child attending senior middle school |
| 2 | 2 children attending senior middle school |
| Total | |

## Section B  Evaluation on environment situation

B1  We list out some of the problems the world is confronting now, please rank the first three important problems in your mind.

| Coding | Meaning |
|---|---|
| 1 | Poverty |
| 2 | Education deficiency |
| 3 | Overpopulation |
| 4 | Environmental pollution |
| 5 | Natural calamity |
| 6 | Regional war |
| 88 | Do not know |
| 99 | No answer |
| Total | |

B2  We list out some of the problems China is confronting now, please rank the first three important problems in your mind.

| Coding | Meaning |
|---|---|
| 1 | Social security |
| 2 | Education deficiency |
| 3 | Overpopulation |
| 4 | Unemployment |
| 5 | Environmental protection |
| 6 | Social welfare |
| Total | |

B3  We list out some of the problems Haidian is confronting now, please rank the first three important problems in your mind.

| Coding | Meaning |
|---|---|
| 1 | Social security |
| 2 | Education deficiency |
| 3 | Overpopulation |
| 4 | Unemployment |
| 5 | Environmental protection |
| 6 | Social welfare |
| 88 | Do not know |
| Total | |

B4  We list out five important goals of China's development, please rank them according to their importance.

| Coding (goal) | Meaning |
| --- | --- |
| 1 | Economic development |
| 2 | Science and education |
| 3 | Controlling population |
| 4 | Social equity |
| 5 | Environmental protection |
| 88 | Do not know |

B6  How serious is the environment pollution situation in China?

| Coding | Meaning |
| --- | --- |
| 1 | Very serious |
| 2 | Relatively serious |
| 3 | Not very serious |
| 4 | No problem |
| 8 | Do not know |
| 9 | No answer |
| Total | |

B7  What do you think are the main problems of China's environment?

| Coding | Meaning |
| --- | --- |
| 1 | Water pollution |
| 2 | Air pollution |
| 3 | Deforestation |
| 4 | Solid waste |
| 7 | Others (please specify) |
| 8 | Do not know |
| 9 | No answer |
| Total | |

B8  Compared with five years ago, what will be your evaluation on Haidian's environmental protection performance?

| Coding | Meaning |
| --- | --- |
| 1 | Apparently improved |
| 2 | Improved |
| 3 | No change |
| 4 | Worse |
| 5 | Apparent worse |
| 8 | Do not know |
| Total | |

B8a Please elaborate the criteria you used for the above evaluation.

B9 In your mind, who should take the responsibility for Haidian's environmental protection?

| Coding | Meaning |
|---|---|
| 1 | Government |
| 2 | Enterprises |
| 3 | Social groups |
| 4 | Individuals |
| 5 | All the above roles take equal responsibility |
| 7 | Others (please specify) |
| 8 | Do not know |
| 9 | No answer |
| Total | |

B10 We list out some of the causes of environment pollution. In your mind, which of them is/are the reasons for Haidian's environment pollution?

| Reasons | Yes | No | Do not know |
|---|---|---|---|
| B10s1. People's weak environmental awareness | | | |
| B10s2. Government's regulation deficiency | | | |
| B10s3. People's weak legal awareness | | | |
| B10s4. Population grows too fast | | | |
| B10s5. Consumption increases too fast | | | |
| B10s6. Pollution introduced by the adjacent region | | | |
| B10s7. Rapid economic growth | | | |

B10a Among the above reasons, please choose three important ones and rank them according to the importance.

B11 Now we try to understand the environment problem from the legal perspective, in your mind which is the reason for environment pollution in China?

| Coding | Meaning |
|---|---|
| 1 | Rules and regulations deficiency |
| 3 | Laws and regulations are poorly implemented |
| 5 | Institutions or individuals do not abide by the law |
| 8 | Do not know |
| 9 | No answer |
| Total | |

B12 Who should take responsibility for environmental protection? And how much of the responsibility? There is a 0 to 10 equal-distance scale on the answer sheet, with '0' representing no responsibility and '10' representing most of the responsibility.

| Coding | Meaning |
| --- | --- |
| B12s1 | The central government |
| B12s2 | The local government |
| B12s3 | Enterprises |
| B12s4 | Individual |
| B12s5 | Social group |

B13 We list out some of the aspects of government's environmental protection work. Please evaluate them one by one.

| Coding | Work | Very good | Good | Bad | Very bad | Do not know |
| --- | --- | --- | --- | --- | --- | --- |
| B13s1 | Environment protection propaganda and education | | | | | |
| B13s2 | Prefect rules and regulations | | | | | |
| B13s3 | Address citizens' complaints | | | | | |
| B13s4 | Supervise enterprises | | | | | |
| B13s5 | Enforce rules and regulations | | | | | |
| B13s6 | Improve technology | | | | | |
| B13s7 | Supervise social groups | | | | | |
| B13s8 | Increase financial input | | | | | |

B13a Among the above works, which is the most urgent one that needs to be pushed?

B14 How did you access environmental protection information? Please choose three out of the following.

| Coding | Meaning |
| --- | --- |
| 1 | Broadcast |
| 2 | Work unit's education activities |
| 3 | Newspaper and magazines |
| 4 | Government education and propaganda activities |
| 5 | TV |
| 6 | Communications with others |
| 7 | Internet |
| 77 | Others (please specify) |

160    *Appendices*

## Section C  Environmental protection performance

C1  Did you ever hear the following policies and activities of the Haidian Environmental Protection Bureau?

| Coding | Meaning |
| --- | --- |
| C1a | Control air pollution |
| C1b | Blue sky and clean water project |
| C1c | Low-interest loans for environmental projects |
| C1d | Fund return policy after the installment of online-watch machine |
| C1e | Beautiful city project (clean retailers in the streets) |

C2  In your opinion, to what extent have the above policies met the citizens' need?

| Coding | Meaning |
| --- | --- |
| 1 | To a very large extent |
| 2 | To a large extent |
| 3 | To a small extent |
| 4 | Not at all |
| 8 | Do not know |
| Total | |

C8  Which of the following areas of environmental protection need to be improved?

| Coding | Meaning |
| --- | --- |
| C8b | Monitor polluting enterprises |
| C8c | Deal with citizens' complaints |
| C8e | Measure environment quality and trace the source of pollution |
| C8f | Promote technology and research |
| C8g | Environmental protection assessment |

C9  Do you know the criteria that the environmental protection bureaux use to evaluate their own performance?

| Coding | Meaning | Choose | Not | Do not know |
| --- | --- | --- | --- | --- |
| C9a | Pollution index | | | |
| C9b | No. of large-scale projects | | | |
| C9c | No. of citizen complaints | | | |
| C9d | No. of accidents | | | |
| C9e | Honors from upper-level administration | | | |

C11  What are the determinants of good government performance?

| Coding | Meaning | Yes | No | Not know |
|---|---|---|---|---|
| 1 | Increased financial input | | | |
| 2 | Improved technology | | | |
| 3 | Political support | | | |
| 4 | Improved quality of civil servants as the result of China's civil service reforms | | | |
| 5 | Perfection of relevant rules and regulations | | | |
| 6 | Improvement of internal administrative leadership | | | |
| 7 | Public support | | | |

## Section D  Evaluation on education

D2  Which of the following is the most serious problem of China's education?

| Coding | Meaning |
|---|---|
| 1 | Education quality |
| 2 | Teachers' capability |
| 3 | Equal opportunity for education |
| 4 | Schools' facility |
| 5 | Government education input |
| 6 | Lot of children cannot access education |
| 7 | Others (specify) |
| 8 | Do not know |
| Total | |

D3  Compared with five years ago, which of the following is your evaluation of Beijing's education performance now?

| Coding | Meaning |
|---|---|
| 1 | Much better |
| 2 | Better |
| 3 | No changes |
| 4 | Worse |
| 5 | Much worse |
| 8 | Do not know |
| Total | |

D3a  Please elaborate the criteria you used for the above evaluation.

## 162   Appendices

D4  Compared with five years ago, which of the following is your evaluation of Haidian's education performance?

| Coding | Meaning |
|---|---|
| 1 | Much better |
| 2 | Better |
| 3 | No changes |
| 4 | Worse |
| 5 | Much worse |
| 8 | Do not know |
| Total | |

D4a  Please elaborate on the criteria you used for the above evaluation.

D5  Who should take the responsibility for Haidian's education performance?

| Coding | Meaning |
|---|---|
| 1 | The central government |
| 2 | Haidian Education Commission |
| 3 | Schools |
| 4 | Teachers |
| 5 | Principals of school |
| 6 | Students |
| 7 | Responsibility is shared equally among these policy actors |
| 77 | Others (please specify) |
| 88 | Do not know |
| Total | |

D6  Compared with five years ago, which of the following is your general evaluation of quality of middle school graduates in Haidian now?

| Coding | Meaning |
|---|---|
| 1 | Much better |
| 2 | Better |
| 3 | No changes |
| 4 | Worse |
| 5 | Much worse |
| 8 | Do not know |
| Total | |

D6a  In your mind, who (teachers, parents, students, education commission) should take the main responsibility for the changes of graduates' quality? Please rank according to their importance.

D7 Which of the following is/are the reasons for education problems in Haidian?

| Coding | Meaning |
|---|---|
| 1 | Lack of equal opportunity for education |
| 2 | Deficient government regulation |
| 3 | Illegal charges by the schools |
| 4 | Poor ethics of the teachers |
| 5 | Poor qualifications of the teachers |
| 6 | Population growth |
| 7 | Poor schools' facility |
| 8 | Government input inadequate |

## *Section E  Education performance*

E1 Have you ever heard of the following activities of the Haidian Education Commission?

| Coding | Meaning |
|---|---|
| E1a | Year of ethics building for teachers |
| E1b | Activity serving the taxpayers |
| E1e | Modernization of archive management |
| E1f | Large-scale inspection of school facilities |
| E1h | Select teaching performers |

E3 The Haidian Education Commission made some new policies and rules over the last few years. Do you know them?

| Coding | Meaning |
|---|---|
| E3a | Regulations to combat corruption within the Haidian education system |
| E3b | Regulations to manage quality in basic education |
| E3c | Regulations to stop illegal charges by schools |
| E3d | Regulations on teachers' ethics and qualifications |
| E3e | Regulations to prevent private provision of food to students in or near campuses |
| E3f | Regulations on self-evaluation and expert supervision on the implementation of comprehensive quality education |
| E3g | Regulations on performance measurement in the Haidian education system |

164  *Appendices*

E2  How did you know about the above activities and policies?

| Coding | Meaning |
| --- | --- |
| 1 | Broadcast |
| 2 | Work unit's education activities |
| 3 | Newspaper and magazines |
| 4 | Government propaganda activities |
| 5 | TV |
| 6 | Communications with others |
| 7 | Internet |
| 77 | Others (please specify) |

E4  In your opinion, to what extent do the above policies meet the citizens' needs?

| Coding | Meaning |
| --- | --- |
| 1 | To a very large extent |
| 2 | To a large extent |
| 3 | To a small extent |
| 4 | Not at all |
| 8 | Do not know |
| Total | |

E9  Do you know the criteria that the education commissions used to evaluate their own performance?

| Coding | Meaning |
| --- | --- |
| E9a | Promotion rate and education popularization |
| E9b | No. of large-scale activities and projects |
| E9c | No. of citizen complaints |
| E9d | No. of education accidents |
| E9e | Honors from upper-level administration |

E10  Which of the following is the most successful job Haidian Education Commission has done?

| Coding | Meaning |
| --- | --- |
| 1 | Guaranteeing equal access to basic education |
| 2 | Improving the enforcement of government regulations |
| 3 | Stopping illegal charges by the schools |
| 4 | Building teachers' ethics |
| 5 | Improving teachers' professional qualifications |
| 6 | Improving schools facilities |
| 7 | Increasing financial input |
| 8 | Do not know |
| Total | |

E11 What are the determinants of good government performance?

| Coding | Meaning | Yes | No | Do not know |
|--------|---------|-----|-----|-------------|
| 1 | Increased financial input | | | |
| 2 | Improved technology | | | |
| 3 | Political support | | | |
| 4 | Improved quality of civil servants as the result of China's civil service reforms | | | |
| 5 | Perfection of relevant rules and regulations | | | |
| 6 | Improvement of internal administrative leadership | | | |
| 7 | Public support | | | |

E11a Among the above reasons leading to good performance, which are the three most important ones? Please rank according to their importance.

## G Other information

G2 Do you have an income?

| Coding | Meaning |
|--------|---------|
| 1 | Yes |
| 5 | No |
| Total | |

G2a Your total income of last month (including salary, bonus, wage of second employment, money from friends or relatives, benefit from investment, and all other means).

G3 How many of the members of your household also have an income?

G4 Total income of your family last month (including salary, bonus, wage of second employment, money from friends or relatives, benefit from investment, and all other means).

G5 How many members of your family live on the above family income?

G6 Family consumption last month.

## Appendix 4 Fieldwork questionnaire

### Section A  Interviewee characteristics

A1  Work unit: which government bureau/division/section do you belong to?
A2  Bureaucratic rank (Bureau Chief/Deputy Chief, Division Chief/Deputy Chief, Section Chief/Deputy Chief, Section member, Others)
A3  Year of birth
A4  Education background

| Coding | Meaning |
|---|---|
| 3 | Primary school |
| 4 | Junior middle school |
| 5 | Senior middle school |
| 6 | Upper middle specialized school |
| 7 | University |
| 8 | Postgraduate |

A5  How long have you worked for this bureau?

### Section B  Implementation of China's civil service reform

B1  When did your organization finish the transition program of China's civil service reforms?
B2  Did your organization recruit newcomers in year 2003? How many of them were selected through open competitive examinations?
B3  Did you receive training in year 2003? What kind of training? How many hours for each kind?
B4  Please describe the existing individual performance appraisal in your organization.
B5  Please describe the existing organizational performance measurement system in your organization, including the actors, the resources and the process.
B6  Was your pay linked to your performance?

### Section C  Perception of clients

C1  Please identify the clients of your organization.
C2  How do you communicate with your clients?
C3  Do the clients play a role in the decision-making of your organization?

### Section D  Assessment of organizational performance

D1  Please evaluate the performance of your organization.
D2  Please elaborate on the criteria you used for the above evaluation.

D3 Please describe the existing organizational performance measurement system in your organization, including the actors, the resources and the process.
D4 In your opinion, what are the main weaknesses of the existing organizational performance measurement system?

## *Section E  Assessment of sub-division performance*

E1 Do you consider organizational harmony a good thing?
E2 How would you evaluate the performance of the other sub-divisions in your bureau?

Please use a five-point scale where '5' means very good while '1' means very bad.

Insider Evaluation of Other Sub-divisions' Performance in Education (five-point scale)

|  | *Haidian education* | *Changchun education* |
|---|---|---|
| General office |  |  |
| Personnel office |  |  |
| Teaching regulation division |  |  |
| School regulation division |  |  |
| Middle-school management office |  |  |
| Primary-school management office |  |  |
| Social education regulation office |  |  |
| Budget office |  |  |

Insider Evaluation of Other Sub-divisions' Performance in Environment (five-point scale)

|  | *Haidian environment* | *Changchun environment* |
|---|---|---|
| General office |  |  |
| Personnel office |  |  |
| Environment supervising division |  |  |
| Pollution control division |  |  |
| Regulations enforcement division |  |  |
| Policy and regulation division |  |  |
| Environment monitoring station |  |  |
| Technology division |  |  |

E3 If a colleague of another sub-division asks you for a favor to fulfill his work duty, what is your response (to help, not to help, or not sure)?
E4 In your opinion, what are the factors that undermine efforts to improve organizational performance?

# Notes

## 1 Introduction

1 Morgan and Perry (1988: 84) defined the 'civil service system' as 'mediating institutions that mobilize human resources in the service of the affairs of the state in a given territory'. In this book, however, I use the term 'civil service system' in a more restricted sense to mean a government personnel system of a particular kind that is characterized by open, competitive selection and performance-based rewards. The term 'China's civil service system' is specific, referring to the current government personnel system in China.
2 For international development agencies such as the World Bank, the term 'good governance' refers primarily to institutionalizing processes for achieving effective, efficient, transparent and accountable government.
3 A copy of the *1993 Provisional Regulations* can be found in the Ministry of Personnel (1994a: 121–9).
4 A copy of the *Notice for the Implementation Plan for the Civil Service System* can be found in the Ministry of Personnel (1994a: 130–2).
5 Zhao Ziyang attempted to remove the management of vice ministers and below from the Organization Department of the CCP Central Committee to the Ministry of Personnel. If they only controlled the 'political civil servants', the Party would lose direct control over a lot of cadres in the executive branch of the government.
6 For a recent restatement of this policy, see 'Premier outlines anticorruption work; vows to build clean government', *People's Daily online* 30 April 2008. Available online: http://english.peopledaily.com.cn/90001/90776/90785/6401754.html (accessed on 23 April 2009).
7 The importance of informal norms and organizational culture is widely recognized in the China studies literature, however. See Walder (1986).
8 These figures are for urban area only.
9 Haidian Archives (*Haidian dang'an guan*), *2008 nian Haidianqu dashiji* (Haidian memorabilia 2008). Available online: www.hdda.gov.cn/dsj/dsj2008_01.asp (accessed on 16 April 2009). Haidian District Government (Haidianqu zhengfu), *Zonghe shili xianzhu zengqiang* (Capacity has been improved). Available online: www.bjhd.gov.cn/zt/hdqzzb/hdfc/hdfc_1/200903/t20090319_143727.htm (accessed on 16 April 2009).
10 The establishment of the environmental protection bureaux in Haidian, Ningbo and Changchun are 30, 28 and 28 respectively while the corresponding figures for the three education bureaux, listed here in the same order, are 148, 90 and 64. There is a larger education establishment in Haidian, under which two agencies together employ a total of 148 employees to deal with 'education work', including both the Education Commission and the CCP Education Work Committee.
11 The data for this book came in part from a CERG research project supported by the

Hong Kong Research Grants Council, entitled 'The Impact of Reform of the Civil Service Entry Selection System in China since 1993'.
12 For details see the Appendices and Wang (2006).
13 See Appendix 1 for a profile of the interviewees.

## 2 Civil service scope, structure and context for reforms

1 The system was extended to the CCP in 1993; the Youth League, the Women's Federation, the Song Qingling Foundation, the National People's Congress Standing Committee bureaucracy, the Chinese People's Political Consultative Conference National Committee bureaucracy, the All-China Federation of Trade Unions, the Science and Technology Association and the Returned-Overseas Chinese Federation in 1994; the Association of Taiwan Compatriots, the Huangpu Military Academy Alumni Association, the eight democratic parties and the All China Federation of Industry and Commerce in 1995; the All-China Federation of Literature and Art Circles, the All-China Writers' Association, the All-China Journalists' Association, the All-China Staff and Workers Political Thought Work Research Association, the public service units (*shiye danwei*) of all local party committees, the All-China Legal Studies Association, the All-China Association for Friendship with Peoples Overseas, the All-China Foreign Affairs Studies Association, the All-China International Trade Promotion Association and the All-China Red Cross in 1996; and the All-China Disabled People's Federation in 1997 (see Ministry of Personnel, various years).
2 This is a rough guess. Statistics in the *2009 Statistical Yearbook* indicate that about 12,663,000 people work for the state, including the executive, the legislature and judiciary and political parties. The statistics did not distinguish mental workers from manual workers, which made the calculation of the number of civil servants difficult.
3 The Civil Service Bureau was established in 2008 at the center; local institutions are to be established.
4 See the Ministry of Human Resources and Social Security website www.mohrss.gov.cn/mohrss/Desktop.aspx?PATH=/sy/leaders/YinWeiMin (accessed 8 May 2009).
5 A copy of the 2002 Regulations can be found in the Ministry of Personnel (2007: 78–93).
6 See the *Notice Concerning Establishment Planning in Local Governments* issued in 1988, the *Notice Concerning Temporary Establishment and Cadre Transfer for Population Census* issued in 1988 and the *Notice Concerning Increase in the Establishment for in Local Family Planning Agencies*. These three Notices can be found at the Chinese Personnel Yearbook Editorial Office (1988–1989: 666–80).

## 3 Civil service reform policy and implementation

1 Many factors, including the expansion of higher education opportunities, have contributed to this result.
2 Interview, Ministry of Personnel, June 2002.
3 Interview, Changchun Education Commission, 26 March 2004.
4 Interview, National School of Administration, March 2010.
5 In 1993, government employees were separated from party cadres and other state organs and mass organizations to constitute the civil service. The 1993 wage system applied to the newly established civil service. Because staff members of the Party and other state organs, and mass organizations were managed according to the Provisional Regulations, the 1993 wage system also applied to them.
6 Civil service positions are considered to be prestigious and desirable in China because they yield authoritative power and consequently material rewards. Much of these rewards, often classified as 'grey incomes' and unapproved by the state, are difficult

170　*Notes*

　　to capture, therefore making it difficult, if not impossible, to examine the real earnings of civil servants in China.
7　Interviews, Beijing, May 2008.
8　*People's Daily* [*Renmin ribao*] 24 March 1998 in FBIS-CHI-98–097 7 April 1998; *China Daily* in *South China Morning Post* 22 September 1998; *New China News Agency* [*Xinhua*] 29 October 1998 in FBIS-CHI-98–310 6 November 1998; *Sing Tao Daily* [*Sing Tao Jih Pao*] (Hong Kong) 13 May 1998 in FBIS-CHI-98–133 13 May 1998; *Ming Pao* (Hong Kong) 28 October 1998 in FBIS-CHI-98–301 28 October 1998; and *Outlook* [*Liaowang*] 10 March 1997 in FBIS-CHI-97–071 10 March 1997.
9　See *Wenhui bao* [Hong Kong], 1 August 2000.
10　*Qingdao News* www.qingdaonews.com/gb/content/2006–01/25/content_5949521.htm, accessed on 13 April 2007.
11　*Xinhua news*, http://news.xinhuanet.com/legal/2004–02/24/content_1329525.htm; http://news.xinhuanet.com/newscenter/2004–11/10/content_2197953.htm; www.hlj.xinhuanet.com/zfzq/2006–03/23/content_6553880.htm; http://news.xinhuanet.com/legal/2005–05/10/content_2939557.htm, accessed on 13 April 2007.
12　*South China Morning Post* 25 March 2005. See also *South China Morning Post* 29 April 2005.

## 4　Local implementation of civil service reforms

1　There were 22 urban street offices and 11 townships under the Haidian district government in 2002. Interview, Haidian Personnel Bureau, 10 June 2002.
2　Interview, Haidian Personnel Bureau, June 2002.
3　Data of education level of newcomers in 2002 were not available when I conducted the interview. This percentage is estimated by the interviewee.
4　Interviews, Haidian Personnel Bureau, June 2002.
5　Interviews, Haidian Personnel Bureau, June 2002.
6　Xu Yunhong served as the Mayor from 1993 to 1995, and as the Party Secretary from 1996 to 1999. He was an alternate member of the 15th CCP Central Committee. He was found guilty of corruption in 2000. Zhang Weiwen was appointed as the Mayor of Ningbo in March 1996.
7　Ningbo Local History Editorial Committee (2001: 358).
8　Mi Fengjun served as the Mayor from 1991 to 1995 and then as the Party Secretary of Changchun. Mi was found guilty of corruption by the Central Discipline Inspection Commission in 2008. His last position was the Chair of Jilin People's Congress, which made him the highest official who was found guilty of corruption in Jilin province. He had stayed at the vice-provincial positions for 17 years before the crime. Song Chunchang was appointed as the Mayor in 1996.
9　Interview, Haidian Personnel Bureau, June 2002.
10　Interviews, Haidian Education Commission, March 2004.
11　Interview, Ningbo Education Commission, February 2005.
12　Interview, Ministry of Personnel, March 2004.
13　I ask this comparing question only to the civil servants who began to work before 1993.
14　Interview, Ningbo Environmental Protection Bureau, February 2005.
15　Interview, Personnel Office of Haidian Education Commission, March 2004.
16　See BBC news: http://news.bbc.co.uk/2/hi/asia-pacific/455942.stm, accessed on 30 April 2007.
17　See: www.zxxw.gov.cn/donghk/htm/30/2005_2_25_3709.html, accessed on 30 April 2007.
18　*Caijing* news, www.caijing.com.cn/newcn/home/todayspec/2007–04–15/17906.shtml, accessed on 30 April 2007.
19　Interviews, Changchun Environmental Protection Bureau, 2 August 2000.

Notes 171

20 Interviews, a Division Chief and a Deputy Division Chief, Changchun Environmental Protection Bureau, 2 August 2000.
21 The administrative establishment of the three environmental protection bureaux and the three educational bureaux are 30, 28, 28, 148, 90, and 64 respectively in Haidian, Ningbo and Changchun. There is a relatively larger education establishment in Haidian district. Indeed, 148 employees staffed two agencies that dealt with 'education work', including both the Education Commission and the CCP Education Work Committee.
22 Interview, Ningbo Education Commission, 21 February 2005.
23 Interview, Ningbo Education Commission, 22 February 2005.
24 Interview, Haidian Education Commission, 20 March 2004.
25 Interview, Haidian Education Commission, 29 March 2004.

## 5 Control of the bureaucracy and reform outcomes

1 The concept of 'control of the bureaucracy' in Chinese politics refers to the CCP controlling the government and the central government controlling the local bureaucrats. The public personnel management system is an instrument used by policy-makers in China to maintain control over the political and administrative systems. For similar arguments, see Brødsgaard (2003: 209).
2 The Constitution stipulates that the NPC is the 'highest organ of the state power' of the PRC. The State Council and the Supreme Court derive their power from the NPC and are thus accountable to the NPC. Furthermore, these three state organizations—the NPC, the State Council and the Supreme Court—are ultimately subject to the leadership of the CCP. A copy of the Constitution can be found in Lieberthal (1995: 355–81).
3 Leaders of all important state organs such as the NPC, State Council, Supreme Court and the Supreme Procuratorate are usually included in the Politburo and leaders of various ministries and provinces are usually included in the Central Committee of CCP. For similar arguments, see Li (2004).
4 In practice, these are not clear-cut categories since there are no professional boundaries among governmental agencies. For example, local agents can transfer from one agency to another; they can also be promoted to the position of local leaders and local leaders can be promoted to head an agency at a higher level.
5 See Article 4 of the 2002 Regulations on Selection and Appointment of Party and Government Leading Cadres. A copy of the 2002 Regulations can be found in the Ministry of Personnel (2007: 78–93).
6 See Temporary Regulations on Performance Evaluation of Party and Government Leading Cadres. A copy of the temporary regulations can be found in Yang and Wang (2008: 191–205).
7 See *Tixian kexue fazhanguan yaoqiu de defang dangzheng lingdao banzi he lingdao ganbu zonghe kaohe pingjia shixing banfa* (Temporary Regulations on Performance Evaluation of Local Party and Government Leading Cadres in the Pursuit of a Scientific View of Development). A copy of the temporary regulations can be found in Yang and Wang (2008: 206–25).
8 See *Guojia gongwuyan zhiwei lunhuan zhanxing tiaoli* (Provisional Regulations of the Position Rotation for Civil Servants), in *Zhongguo renshi bao* (Chinese Personnel Post) 13 August 1996.
9 See *Renshibu tuixing gongwuyuan zhidu youshang xin taijie* (A Breakthrough of the Ministry of Personnel in the Implementation of Civil Service System), in *Zhongguo renshi bao* (Chinese Personnel Post), 16 April 1996.
10 See Chapter 6, Article 34 of the *Regulations on Selection and Appointment of Party and Government Leading Cadres*, issued by the Central Committee in July 2002.
11 In fact, the CDIC is the only national organ that holds a plenary session once a year in

172  *Notes*

addition to the three most powerful ones in China: the Central Committee of the Party, the National People's Congress and the National People's Political Consultative Conference.
12 Interview with an environmental protector of an enterprise in Haidian, 5 July 2001; Interview with an environmental protector of an enterprise in Ningbo, 3 August 2000.
13 Interviews, Ningbo Environmental Protection Bureau Pollution Abatement Division and Ningbo Environmental Protection Bureau Technology Division, 2 August 2000.
14 Interview with an environmental protector of an enterprise in Haidian, 5 July 2001.
15 Interview with an environmental protector of an enterprise in Ningbo, 3 August 2000.
16 Interview, Haidian Environmental Protection Bureau Law and Regulation Section, 11 June 2001.
17 Interview with an environmental protector of an enterprise in Haidian, 5 July 2001.
18 Interview with an environmental protector of an enterprise in Ningbo, 3 August 2000.
19 Interview, Ningbo Environmental Protection Bureau Technology Division, 2 August 2000.
20 There are debates on the signaling function of complaints. Do more complaints indicate poor government performance or more trust of citizens in government? In my study, interviewees argue that citizens in China raise complaints to government due to trust.
21 Interview, an Urban Residential Committee in Haidian, 23 August 2001.
22 Interview, an Urban Street Office in Changchun, 23 November 2000.
23 Interview with an environmental protector of an enterprise in Haidian, 5 July 2001.
24 Interview, an Urban Residential Committee in Ningbo, 3 August 2000.
25 Interview with an environmental protector of an enterprise in Haidian, 3 July 2001.
26 Interview, Haidian Environmental Protection Bureau, 11 June 2001.
27 Interview with an environmental protector of an enterprise in Ningbo, 3 August 2000. In China, regulatory officers are not allowed to accept benefits from the entrepreneurs, not even dinner. People think having dinner might lead to corrupt behaviors.
28 Interview with an environmental protector of an enterprise in Haidian, 3 July 2001; Interview, Haidian Environmental Protection Bureau Planning and Development Section, 11 June 2001.
29 Interview, Changchun Environmental Protection Bureau Regulation Enforcement Division, 22 November 2000.

## 7 Conclusion

1 Here 'related' refers to the interviewees in the same organization; or those which have an official-client relationship.

## Appendices

1 The data for this book came in part from a CERG research project supported by the Hong Kong Research Grants Council, entitled 'The Impact of Reform of the Civil Service Entry Selection System in China since 1993' RGC No. HKU7128/98H.
2 Conducting a good survey in China depends heavily on having a reliable Chinese partner. The Research Center for Contemporary China of Peking University in Beijing, which was set up in 1988, has conducted numerous surveys for both Chinese and foreign organizations. Their website is www.rcccpku.org/ch/index.php.

# Bibliography

'*2006 gongwuyuan gongzi gaige ziliao daquan*' (Collection of materials on 2006 civil service wage reform). Available online: http://tieba.baidu.com/f?kz=156189137 (accessed on 23 December 2007).
Alchian, A. A. and Demsetz, H. (1972) 'Production, Information Costs and Economic Organization', *American Economic Review* 62 (5), 777–95.
Asian Development Bank (2005) *Country Governance Assessment Report: Philippines*, Manila: Asian Development Bank.
Asian Development Bank (2004) *Country Governance Assessment Report: Indonesia*, Manila: Asian Development Bank.
Asian Development Bank (2001) *Key Governance Issues in Cambodia, Lao PDR, Thailand, and Vietnam*, Manila: Asian Development Bank.
Aufrecht, S. E. and Li, S. (1995) 'Reform with Chinese Characteristics: The Context of Chinese Civil Service Reform', *Public Administration Review* 55 (2), 175–82.
Baiman, S. (1990) 'Agency Research in Managerial Accounting: A Second Look', *Accounting, Organizations and Society* 15 (4), 341–71.
Baiman, S. (1982) 'Agency Research in Managerial Accounting: A Survey', *Journal of Accounting Literature* 1, 154–213.
Barnard, C. (1938) *The Functions of The Executive*, Cambridge, MA: Harvard University Press.
Barnett, D. A. (1967) *Cadres, Bureaucracy, and Political Power in Communist China*, New York: Columbia University Press.
Bates, R. A. G., Levi, M., Rosenthal, J. L. and Weingast, B. (1998) *Analytic Narratives*, Princeton: Princeton University Press.
Beijing Local History Editorial Committee (ed.) (2003) *Beijing nianjian 2002* (Beijing Yearbook 2002), Beijing: Beijing Yearbook Press.
Beijing Local History Editorial Committee (ed.) (2002) *Beijing nianjian 2001* (Beijing Yearbook 2001), Beijing: Beijing Yearbook Press.
Beijing Local History Editorial Committee (ed.) (2001) *Beijing nianjian 2000* (Beijing Yearbook 2000), Beijing: Beijing Yearbook Press.
Beijing Local History Editorial Committee (ed.) (2000) *Beijing nianjian 1999* (Beijing Yearbook 1999), Beijing: Beijing Yearbook Press.
Beijing Local History Editorial Committee (ed.) (1999) *Beijing nianjian 1998* (Beijing Yearbook 1998), Beijing: Beijing Yearbook Press.
Beijing Local History Editorial Committee (ed.) (1998) *Beijing nianjian 1997* (Beijing Yearbook 1997), Beijing: Beijing Yearbook Press.

## 174 Bibliography

Bekke, H. A. G. M., Perry, J. L. and Toonen, T. A. J. (eds) (1996) *Civil Service Systems in Comparative Perspective*, Bloomington: Indiana University Press.

Bernstein, T. P. and Lu, X. (2000) 'Taxation Without Representation: Peasants, the Central and the Local States in Reform China', *The China Quarterly* 163, 742–63.

Bian, Y. (1994) 'Guanxi and the Allocation of Urban Jobs in China', *The China Quarterly* 140, 971–99.

Bianco, W. and Bates, R. (1990) 'Cooperation by Design: Leadership, Structure, and Collective Dilemmas', *American Political Science Review* 84, 133–48.

Bo, Z. (2004) 'The Institutionalization of Elite Management in China', in B. Naughton and D. L. Yang (eds) *Holding China Together: Diversity and National Integration in the Post-Deng Era*, Cambridge: Cambridge University Press, 70–100.

Bo, Z. (2002) *Chinese Provincial Leaders: Economic Performance and Political Mobility since 1949*, Armonk, NY; London: M.E. Sharpe.

Bo, Z. (1999) 'Selection and Appointment of Leading Cadres in Post-Deng China', *Chinese Law and Government* 32 (1), 45–61.

Boyne, G. A. (2003) 'Sources of Public Service Improvement: A Critical Review and Research Agenda', *Journal of Public Administration Research and Theory* 13 (3), 367–94.

Brehm, J. and Gates, S. (1999) Working, *Shirking, and Sabotage: Bureaucratic Response to a Democratic Public*, Ann Arbor: The University of Michigan Press.

Breton, A. and Wintrobe, R. (1986) 'The Bureaucracy of Murder Revisited', *Journal of Political Economy* 94, 905–26.

Breton, A. and Wintrobe, R. (1982) *The Logic of Bureaucratic Conduct: An Economic Analysis of Competition, Exchange and Efficiency in Private and Public Organizations*, Cambridge, MA: Cambridge University Press.

Brødsgaard, K. E. (2003) 'China's Cadres and Cadre Management System', in G. Wang and Y. Zheng (eds) *Damage Control: The Chinese Communist Party under the Jiang Zemin Era*, Singapore: Eastern Universities Press, 209–31.

Burns, J. P. (2007) 'Explaining Civil Service Reform in Asia', in J. C. N. Raadschelders, T. A. J. Toonen and F. M. Van der Meer (eds) *Comparing Civil Service Systems in the 21st Century*, Basingstoke: Palgrave Macmillan, 65–81.

Burns, J. P. (2006) 'The Chinese Communist Party's Nomenklatura System as a Leadership Selection Mechanism: an Evaluation', in K. E. Brødsgaard and Y. Zheng (eds) *The Chinese Communist Party in Reform*, London: Routledge, 33–58.

Burns, J. P. (2005) 'Civil Service Reform in China', in *Governance in China*, Paris: OECD, 51–74.

Burns, J. P. (2004a) *Government Capacity and the Hong Kong Civil Service*, Hong Kong; New York: Oxford University Press.

Burns, J. P. (2004b) 'Governance and Civil Service Reform', in J. Howell (ed.) *Governance in China*, New York: Rowman & Littlefield Publishers, Inc., 37–57.

Burns, J. P. (2003a) 'Downsizing the Chinese State: Government Retrenchment in the 1990s', *The China Quarterly* 175, 775–802.

Burns, J. P. (2003b) 'Rewarding Comrades at the Top in China', in C. Hood and P. B. Guy with G. Lee (eds) *Reward for High Public Office: Asian and Pacific Rim States*, London: Routledge, 49–69.

Burns, J. P. (2001) 'The Civil Service System of China: The Impact of the Environment', in J. P. Burns and B. Bowornwathana (eds) *Civil Service Systems in Asia*, Cheltenham: Edward Elgar Publishing Ltd., 79–116.

Burns, J. P. (1999a) 'The People's Republic of China at 50: National Political Reform', *The China Quarterly* 159, 580–94.

Burns, J. P. (1999b) 'Changing Environmental Impacts on Civil Service Systems: The Cases of China and Hong Kong', in H. K. Wong and H. S. Chan (eds) *Handbook of Comparative Public Administration in the Asia-Pacific Basin*, New York: Marcel Dekker, Inc, 179–218.

Burns, J. P. (1994a) 'Strengthening Central CCP Control of Leadership Selection: The 1990 Nomenklatura', *The China Quarterly* 138, 458–91.

Burns, J. P. (1994b) 'Civil Service Reform in China', *Asian Journal of Political Science* 2, 44–72.

Burns, J. P. (1993a) 'China's Administrative Reforms for a Market Economy', *Public Administration and Development* 13 (4), 345–60.

Burns, J. P. (1993b) 'Administrative Reform in China: Issues and Prospects', *International Journal of Public Administration* 16 (9), 1345–69.

Burns, J. P. (1989a) 'China's Governance: Political Reform in a Turbulent Environment', *The China Quarterly* 119, 481–518.

Burns, J. P. (1989b) 'Chinese Civil Service Reform: The 13th Party Congress Proposal', *The China Quarterly* 120, 739–70.

Burns, J. P. (1989c) *The Chinese Communist Party's Nomenklatura System: A Documentary Study of Party Control of Leadership Selection, 1979–1984*, New York: M.E. Sharpe.

Burns, J. P. (1987a) 'The Chinese Civil Service System', in I. Scott and J. P. Burns (eds) *The Hong Kong Civil Services and Its Future*, Hong Kong: Oxford University Press, 204–26.

Burns, J. P. (1987b) 'Civil Service Reform in Contemporary China', *Australian Journal of Chinese Affairs* 18, 47–83.

Burns, J. P. (1987c) 'China's Nomenklatura System', *Problems of Communism* 36, 36–51.

Burns, J. P. and Wang, X. (2010) 'Civil Service Reform in China: Impacts on Civil Servants' Behavior', *The China Quarterly* 201, 58–78.

Cabestan, J. P. (1992) 'Civil Service Reform in China: The Draft Provisional Order Concerning Civil Servants', *International Review of Administrative Sciences* 58 (3), 421–36.

Carino, L. V. (1989) 'A Dominated Bureaucracy: An Analysis of the Formulation of, and Reactions to, State Policies on the Philippine Civil Service', Occasional Paper no. 89-4, Publications Office College of Public Administration, University of the Philippines.

Chan, H. S. (2004) 'Cadre Personnel Management in China: the *Nomenklatura* System 1990–1998', *The China Quarterly* 179, 703–34.

Chan, H. S. (2003) 'The Civil Service under One Country, Two Systems: The Case of Hong Kong and the People's Republic of China', *Public Administration Review* 63 (4), 405–17.

Chan, H. S. (2001) 'In Search of Performance Profile in the People's Republic of China', *Public Administration Quarterly* 24 (4), 469–90.

Chan, H. S. and Lam, T. C. (1995) 'Designing China's Civil Service System: General Principles and Realities', *International Journal of Public Administration* 18 (8), 1301–21.

Chan, H. S. and Li, S. (2007) 'Civil Service Law in the People's Republic of China: A Return to Cadre Personnel Management', *Public Administration Review* 63 (7), 383–98.

Chan, H.S., Wong, K., Cheung, K. C. and Lo, J. (1995) 'The Implementation Gap in

## 176  Bibliography

Environmental Management in China: The Case of Guangzhou, Zhengzhou and Nanjing', *Public Administration Review* 55 (4), 333–40.
Chan, K. M. (1999) 'Corruption in China: A Principal–agent Perspective', in H. K. Wong and H. S. Chan (eds) *Handbook of Comparative Public Administration in the Asia-Pacific Basin*, New York: Marcel Dekker, Inc., 299–324.
Chang, G. (2001) *The Coming Collapse of China*, New York: Random House.
Changchun Local History Editorial Committee (ed.) (2001) *Changchun nianjian 2000* (Changchun Yearbook 2000), Changchun: Changchun Yearbook Press.
Changchun Local History Editorial Committee (ed.) (2000) *Changchun nianjian 1999* (Changchun Yearbook 1999), Changchun: Changchun Yearbook Press.
Changchun Personnel Bureau (ed.) (1997) *Changchun shi jigou gaige yu gongwuyuan zhidu gaige wenjian ziliao huibian* (Collection of Documents on Changchun's Implementing Institutional Reform and China's Civil Service Reform).
Chen Q. (ed.) (1994) *Shijian yu tansuo* (Experimental Implementation of Civil Service System in Haidian), Beijing: China Personnel Press.
Cheung, A. B. L. (2005) 'The Politics of Administrative Reforms in Asia: Paradigms and Legacies, Paths and Diversities', *Governance* 18 (2), 257–82.
Cheung, A. B. L. and Poon, K. K. (2001) 'The Paradox of China's Wage System Reforms: Balancing Stakeholders' Rationalities', *Public Administration Quarterly* 24 (4), 491–521.
Cheung, A. B. L. and Scott, I. (eds) (2003) *Governance and Public Sector Reform in Asia: Paradigm Shifts or Business as Usual*, London: Routledge.
Chew, D. (1990a) 'Civil Service Pay in China, 1955–1989: Overview and Assessment', *International Review of Administrative Sciences* 56, 345–64.
Chew, D. (1990b) 'Recent Developments in Civil Service Pay in China', *International Labour Review* 129(6), 773–82.
Chinese Personnel Yearbook Editorial Office (ed.) (1988–1989), *Zhongguo renshi nianjian 1988–89* (Chinese Personnel Yearbook 1988–89), Beijing: China Personnel Press.
Chou, K. P. (2009) *Government and Policy-making Reform in China*, London and New York: Routledge.
Chou, K. P. (2008) 'Does Governance Matter? Civil Service Reform in China', *International Journal of Public Administration* 31 (1), 54–75.
Chou, K. P. (2004) 'Civil Service Reform in China, 1993–2001: A Case of Implementation Failure', *China: An International Journal* 2 (2), 210–34.
Chou, K. P. (2003) 'Conflict and Ambiguity in the Implementation of the Civil Service Reform in China, 1993–2000', unpublished Ph.D. dissertation, The University of Hong Kong.
Chow, K. W. (1993) 'The Politics of Performance Appraisal', in M. K. Mills and S. S. Nagel (eds) *Public Administration in China*, Westport, CT: Greenwood Press, 109–15.
Chow, K. W. (1991) 'Reform of Chinese Cadre System: Pitfalls, Issues, and Implications of the Proposed Civil Service System', *International Review of Administrative Sciences* 57, 25–44.
Chow, K. W. (1988) 'The Management of Cadre Resources in Mainland China: The Problems of Job Evaluation and Position Classification, 1949–1987', *Issues and Studies* 24(8), 18–28.
Chow, K. W. (1987) 'Political Succession in the People's Republic of China: Politics and Implication of Cadre Assessment (1949–1984)', *Asian Profile* 15(5), 396–401.
Chung, J. H. (2010) 'The Evolving Hierarchy of China's Local Administration: Tradition and Change', in J. H. Chung and T. C. Lam (eds) *China's Local Administration: Traditions and Changes in the Sub-national Hierarchy*, London and New York: Routledge.

## Bibliography 177

Chung, J. H. (1995) 'Studies of Central-Provincial Relations in the People's Republic of China: A Mid-Term Appraisal', *The China Quarterly* 142, 487–508.

Civil Service Bureau (2010a) Reports on dealing with civil service examinations abuse cases. Available online: www.scs.gov.cn/Desktop.aspx?path=Desktop.aspx?PATH=gjgwyj/gjgwyjsy/xxllym&gid=8f2990eb-e641-4299-b248-2a6c5579b37d&tid=Cms_Info (accessed on 23 January 2010).

Civil Service Bureau (2010b) *Cong lunzi paibei dao jingzheng shanggang* (From Seniority to Internal Competition for Posting). Available online: www.scs.gov.cn/Desktop.aspx?path=Desktop.aspx?PATH=gjgwyj/gjgwyjsy/xxllym&gid=59190658-19b9-479e-86d7-8b789c6d62c2&tid=Cms_Info (accessed on 23 January 2010).

Civil Service Bureau (2009) Announcements on 2009 national civil service examinations. Available online: www.gov.cn/gzdt/2008-10/12/content_1118206.htm (accessed on 23 January 2010).

Cooke, F. L. (2005) *HRM, Work and Employment in China*, London and New York: Routledge.

Cooke, F. L. (2003) 'Seven Reforms in Five Decades: Civil Service Reform and Its Human Resource Implications in China', *Journal of the Asia Pacific Economy* 8 (3), 380–404.

Dai, G. (1994) 'The Establishment of an Examination and Recruitment System with Chinese Characteristics in the People's Republic of China', in J. P. Burns (ed.) *Asian Civil Service Systems: Improving Efficiency and Productivity*, Singapore: Times Academic Press, 190–6.

Das, S. K. (1998) *Civil Service Reform and Structural Adjustment*, Oxford: Oxford University Press.

Deng, X. (1984) *Deng Xiaoping wenxuan* (Selected Works of Deng Xiaoping), Beijing: People's Publishing.

Dickson, B. J. (2003) *Red Capitalists in China: The Party, Private Entrepreneurs, and Prospects for Political Change*, Cambridge: Cambridge University Press.

Dong, L. (1994) 'The Establishment of the Chinese Civil Service System: A Delayed Political Reform Program', in L. Dong (ed.) *Administrative Reform in the People's Republic of China since 1978*, Leiden: IIAS, 43–61.

Eaton, S. and Zhang, M. (2010) 'A Principal–agent Analysis of China's Sovereign Wealth System: Byzantine by Design', *Review of International Political Economy* 17(3), 481–506.

Edin, M. (2003) 'State Capacity and Local Agent Control in China: CCP Cadre Management from a Township Perspective', *The China Quarterly* 173, 35–52.

Endriga, J. N. (2001) 'The National Civil Service System of the Philippines', in J. P. Burns and B. Bowornwathana (eds) *Civil Service Systems in Asia*, Cheltenham: Edward Elgar Publishing Ltd., 212–48.

Fewsmith, J. (1996) 'Institutions, Informal Politics and Political Transition in China', *Asian Survey* 36(3), 230–45.

Film, D. and Lindauer, D. L. (2001) *Does Indonesia Have a Low-pay Civil Service?* World Bank Policy Research Working Paper 2621.

Frederickson, G. H. and Smith, K. B. (2003) *Public Administration Theory Primer*, Boulder, CO: Westview Press, 185–207.

Gigerenzer, G. and Selten, R. (2001) *Bounded Rationality: The Adaptive Toolbox*, Cambridge, MA: MIT Press.

Gong, T. (2009) 'The Institutionalization of Party Discipline Inspection in China: Dynamics and Dilemmas', in T. Gong and S. K. Ma (eds) *Preventing Corruption in Asia: Institutional Design and Policy Capacity*, London and New York: Routledge, 64–80.

## Bibliography

Gong, T. (2008) 'Objective Responsibility vs. Subjective Responsibility: A Critical Reading of the CCP's Internal Supervision Regulation', *China Review* 8 (2), 77–102.

Gong, T. (2006) 'Corruption and Local Governance: The Double Identity of Chinese Local Governments in Market Reform', *The Pacific Review* 19 (1), 85–102.

Gong, T. (1994) *The Politics of Corruption in Contemporary China: An Analysis of Policy Outcomes*, Westport, CT: Praeger.

'Gongwuyuanfa banbu wuzhounian' (2010) (Civil Service Law promulgated five years), *Xinhua news agency*. Available online: www.gov.cn/jrzg/2010–01/05/content_1503896.htm (accessed on 23 January 2010).

Government of Vietnam General Statistics Office (2003) *Statistical Yearbook 2003*, Hanoi: Statistical Publishing House.

Grindle, M. (1997) *Getting Good Government: Capacity Building in the Public Sectors of Developing Countries*, Boston: Harvard University Press.

Gu, B. (1991) 'Beijing Municipal Bureau Chiefs Performance Appraisal Plan and Implementation', *Chinese Law and Government* 23(4), 74–89.

Gunn, C. (2007) 'Laos in 2006: Changing of the Guard', *Asian Survey* 47 (1), 183–8.

Guo, Y. (2008) 'Corruption in Transitional China: An Empirical Analysis', *The China Quarterly* 194, 349–64.

Haidian Personnel Bureau (ed.) (2002) *Beijing shi Haidian qu guojia gongwuyuan guanli wenjian huibian* (Collection of Documents on the Management of Civil Servants in Haidian).

Haidian Personnel Bureau (ed.) (1998) *Haidian qu guanyu guojia gongwuyuan zhidu zhifa jiancha de zicha baogao* (Interval Investigation on the Implementation of Civil Service System in Haidian District).

Harding, H. (1981) *Organizing China: The Problem of Bureaucracy 1949–1976*, California: Stanford University Press.

Hayllar, M. R. (2003) 'The Philippines: Paradigm Lost or Paradigm Retained?' in A. B. L. Cheung and I. Scott (eds) *Governance and Public Sector Reform in Asia: Paradigm Shifts or Business As Usual?*, London: Routledge Curzon, 248–71.

Hodder, R. (2010) 'Informality in the Philippine Civil Service', *Asian Studies Review* 34, 231–51.

Hodder, R. (2009) 'Political Interference in the Philippine Civil Service', *Environment & Planning C* 27 (5), 766–82.

Holmstrom, B. and Milgrom P. (1991) 'Multitask Principal–agent Analysis: Incentive Contracts, Asset Ownership, and Job Design', *Journal of Law, Economics, and Organization* 7, 24–52.

Horn, M. J. (1995) *The Political Economy of Public Administration: Institutional Choice in the Public Sector*, Cambridge: Cambridge University Press.

Hou, J. (2007) *Gongwuyuan zhidu fazhan jishi* (The History of Civil Service Establishment and Development), Beijing: China Personnel Press.

Hou, J. (1997) 'Building up a Personnel System Compatible with Socialist Market Economy', in IIAS (ed.) *New Challenges for Public Administration in the Twenty-First Century*, Brussels: International Institute of Administrative Sciences, 119–26.

Hu, A. (2001) *Zhongguo: tiaozhan fubai* (China: Fighting Against Corruption), Hangzhou: Zhejiang renmin chubanshe.

Huang, Y. (2002) 'Managing Chinese Bureaucrats: An Institutional Economics Perspective', *Political Studies* 50, 61–79.

Huang, Y. (2001) 'Political Institutions and Fiscal Reforms in China', *Problems of Post-Communism* 48(1), 16–26.

Huang, Y. (1996) *Inflation and Investment Controls in China: The Political Economy of Central-Local Relations during the Reform Era*, Cambridge: Cambridge University Press.

Huang, Y. (1995) 'Administrative Monitoring in China', *The China Quarterly* 143, 828–43.

Huang, Y. (1990) 'Web of Interests and Patterns of Behavior of Chinese Local Economic Bureaucracies and Enterprises during Reforms', *The China Quarterly* 123, 431–58.

International Monetary Fund (2008) *World Economic Outlook 2007*, International Monetary Fund.

Jahiel, A. R. (1998) 'The Organization of Environmental Protection in China', *The China Quarterly* 156, 757–87.

Jensen, M. C. and Meckling, W. H. (1976) 'Theory of the Firm: Managerial Behavior, Agency Costs and Ownership Structure', *Journal of Financial Economics* 3, 305–60.

Jonsson, K. (2010) 'Laos in 2009: Recession and Southeast Asian Games', *Asian Survey* 50 (1), 241–6.

Kampen, T. (1993) 'The CCP's Central Committee Departments (1921–1991): A Study of Their Evolution', *China Report* 29(3), 299–317.

Klauss, R. (2001) 'Laos: Civil Service System in a Transitional Economy', in J. P. Burns and B. Bowornwathana (eds) *Civil Service Systems in Asia*, Cheltenham: Edward Elgar Publishing Ltd., 183–211.

Kreps, D. (1990) *A Course in Microeconomics*, Princeton: Princeton University Press.

Kristiansen, S. and Ramli, M. (2006) 'Buying an Income: The Market for Civil Service Positions in Indonesia', *Contemporary Southeast Asia* 28 (2), 207–33.

Kwong, C.L., and Lee, P. K. (2000) 'Business-government Relations in Industrializing Rural China: A Principal–agent Perspective', *Journal of Contemporary China* 9(25), 513–34.

Lam, T. C. and Chan, H. S. (1996a) 'China's New Civil Service: What the Emperor Is Wearing and Why', *Public Administration Review* 56(5), 479–84.

Lam, T. C. and Chan, H. S. (1996b) 'Reforming China's Cadre Management System: Two Views of a Civil Service', *Asian Survey* 36 (8), 772–81.

Lam, T. C. and Chan, H. S. (1995) 'The Civil Service System: Policy Formulation and Implementation', in C. K. Lo, S. Pepper and K. Y. Tsui (eds) *China Review 1995*, Hong Kong: The Chinese University Press, 2.1–2.43.

Lam, T. C. and Cheung, K. C. (1998) 'The Rise and Challenge of Administrative Reform in China: Post-Mao and Beyond', in J. Y. S. Cheng (ed.) *China in the Post-Deng Era*, Hong Kong: The Chinese University Press, 137–70.

Lam, T. C. and Perry, J. L. (2001) 'Service Organizations in China: Reform and Its Limits', in P. N. Lee and C. W. H. Lo (eds) *Remaking China's Public Management*, Westport, CT: Quorum Books, 19–40.

Lampton, D. M. (1987) 'The Implementation Problem in Post-Mao China', in D. M. Lampton (ed.) *Policy Implementation in Post-Mao China*, Berkeley: University of California Press, 3–24.

Lan, Z. (2001) 'Understanding China's Administrative Reform', *Public Administration Quarterly* 24(4), 437–69.

Landry, P. F. (2008) *Decentralized Authoritarianism in China: The Communist Party's Control of Local Elites in the Post-Mao Era*, Cambridge; New York: Cambridge University Press.

Landry, P. F. (2004) 'Informal Responses to Formal Decentralization in China', paper presented at the annual meeting of the Midwest Political Science Association.

## 180  Bibliography

Lee, H. Y. (1991) *From Revolutionary Cadres to Party Technocrats in Socialist China*, Berkeley: University of California Press.

Lee, P. N. S. and Lo, C. W. H. (2001), 'Remaking China's Public Management: Problem Areas and Analytical Perspectives', in P. N. S. Lee and C. W. H. Lo (eds) *Remaking China's Public Management*, Westport, CT: Quorum Books, 1–18.

Li, C. (2004) 'Political Localism Versus Institutional Constraints: Elite Recruitment in the Jiang Era', in B. Naughton and D. L. Yang (eds) *Holding China Together: Diversity and National Integration in the Post-Deng Era*, Cambridge: Cambridge University Press, 29–69.

Li, D. D. (1998) 'Changing Incentives of the Chinese Bureaucracy', *American Economic Review* 88 (2), 393–7.

Li, R. and Zeng, Y. (1994) *Ganbu xiang gongwuyuan guodu shiwu* (A Practical Handbook of Civil Service Transition), Beijing: China Personnel Press.

Li, W. (1990) 'Reform in the Chinese Public Personnel System', *Public Personnel Management* 19 (2), 163–74.

Lieberthal, K. G. (2004) *Governing China: from Revolution through Reform* 2nd edn. New York: Norton.

Lieberthal, K. G. (1995) *Governing China: From Revolution through Reform*, New York: W. W. Norton & Company, Inc.

Lieberthal, K. G. and Lampton, D. M. (eds) (1992) *Bureaucracy, Politics and Decision Making in Post-Mao China*, Berkeley: University of California Press.

Lieberthal, K. G. and Oksenberg, M. (1988) *Policy Making in China: Leaders, Structures and Processes*, Princeton, NJ: Princeton University Press.

Liou, K. T. (1997) 'Issues and Lessons of Chinese Civil Service Reform', *Public Personnel Management* 26, 505–14.

Liu, M. (2001) *Administrative Reform in China and Its Impact on the Policy-making Process and Economic Development after Mao*, Lewiston, NY: Edwin Mellen Press.

Lo, C. W. H., Yip, P. K. T. and Cheung, K. C. (2000) 'The Regulatory Style of Environmental Governance in China: The Case of EIA Regulation in Shanghai', *Public Administration and Development* 20 (4), 305–18.

Lu, X. (2000) *Cadre and Corruption: The Organizational Involution of the Chinese Communist Party*, Stanford, CA: Stanford University Press.

Ma, S. K. (2009) '"Policing the Police": A Perennial Challenge for China's Anticorruption Agencies', in T. Gong and S. K. Ma (eds) *Preventing Corruption in Asia: Institutional Design and Policy Capacity*, London and New York: Routledge, 81–96.

Ma, S. K. (1999) 'Man of Efficiency and Man of Ethics: Can China's Administrative Reform Produce Both for Her Economic Development', *Policy Studies Review* 16 (2) 133–46.

Ma, S. K. (1996) *Administrative Reform in Post-Mao China: Efficiency or Ethics*, Lanham, MD: University Press of America.

Manion, M. (2004) *Corruption by Design: Building Clean Government in Mainland China and Hong Kong*, Cambridge, MA: Harvard University Press.

Manion, M. (1993) *Retirement of Revolutionaries in China: Public Policies, Social Norms, Private Interests*, Princeton: Princeton University Press.

Manion, M. (1985) 'The Cadre Management System, Post-Mao: The Appointment, Promotion, Transfer and Removal of Party and State Leaders', *The China Quarterly* 102, 203–33.

McCubbins, M. and Schwartz, T. (1984) 'Congressional Oversight Overlooked: Political Patrols versus Fire Alarm', *American Journal of Political Science* 28 (1), 165–79.

Milgrom, P. and Roberts, J. (1992) *Economics, Organization and Management*, Englewood Cliffs, NJ: Prentice Hall.

Miller, G. J. (1992) *Managerial Dilemmas: The Political Economy of Hierarchy*, Cambridge: Cambridge University.

Ministry of Personnel (ed.) (various years) *Renshi gongzuo wenjian xuanbian* (Selection of Personnel Work Documents, 1994, 1995, 1996, 1997 and 1998), Beijing: China Personnel Press.

Ministry of Personnel (ed.) (2007) *Renshi guanli changyong fagui xuanbian* (A Collection of Regulations on Public Personnel Management), Beijing: China Personnel Press.

Ministry of Personnel (ed.) (1994a) *Guojia gongwuyuan zhidu quanshu* (A Collection of Documents on State Civil Service System), Changchun: Jilin Literature and History Press.

Ministry of Personnel (1994b) *Guojia gongwuyuan zhidu shishi fang'an* (Implementation Plan of China's Civil Service Reform), Beijing: Ministry of Personnel.

Moe, T. (1984) 'The New Economics of Organization', *American Journal of Political Science* 28 (4), 739–77.

Mok, K. H and Forrest, R. (2008) (eds) *Changing Governance and Public Policy in East Asia*, London and New York: Routledge.

Morgan, P. E. and Perry, J. L. (1988) 'Re-orienting the Comparative Study of Civil Service Systems', *Review of Public Personnel Administration* 8 (3), 84–95.

National Bureau of Statistics (ed.) (2010) *Zhongguo tongji nianjian 2009* (China Statistical Yearbook 2009), Beijing: China Statistics Press.

National Bureau of Statistics (ed.) (2009) *Zhongguo laodong tongji nianjian 2008* (China Labour Statistical Yearbook 2008), Beijing: China Statistics Press.

National Bureau of Statistics (ed.) (2008) *Zhongguo chengshi nianjian 2007* (Urban Statistical Yearbook of China 2007), Beijing: China Statistics Press.

National Bureau of Statistics (ed.) (2005) *Zhongguo chengshi nianjian 2004 (Urban Statistical Yearbook of China 2004)* Beijing: China Statistics Press.

National Bureau of Statistics (ed.) (2001) *Zhongguo tongji nianjian 2000* (China Statistical Yearbook 2000), Beijing: China Statistics Press.

National Bureau of Statistics (ed.) (1996) *Zhongguo tongji nianjian 1995* (China Statistical Yearbook 1995), Beijing: China Statistics Press.

National Environmental Protection Bureau (2000) *Zhongguo huanjing nianjian 1999* (China Environment Yearbook 1999), Beijing: Zhongguo huanjing kexue chubanshe.

National Environmental Protection Bureau (1999) *Quanguo gongzhong huanjing yizhi diaocha baogao* (National Public Environmental Knowledge Survey Report), Beijing: Zhongguo huanjing kexue chubanshe.

National Environmental Protection Bureau (1996) *Zhongguo huanjing nianjian 1995* (China Environment Yearbook 1995), Beijing: Zhongguo huanjing kexue chubanshe.

Naughton, B. and Yang, D. L. (2004) *Holding China Together: Diversity and National Integration in the Post-Deng Era*, Cambridge: Cambridge University Press.

Ningbo Local History Editorial Committee (ed.) (2002) *Ningbo Yearbook 2001* (Ningbo Yearbook 2001) Ningbo: Ningbo Yearbook Press.

Ningbo Local History Editorial Committee (ed.) (1998) *Ningbo Yearbook 1997* (Ningbo Yearbook 1997) Ningbo: Ningbo Yearbook Press.

Ningbo Personnel Bureau (ed.) (1999) *Ningbo shi guanyu shixing guojia gongwuyuan zhidu de zicha baogao* (Interval Investigation on the Implementation of China's Civil Service System in Ningbo City).

Nunberg, B. (2002) 'Civil Service Quality after the Crisis: A View of Five Asian Cases', *Asian Journal of Political Science* 10, 1–20.

## 182  Bibliography

Nunberg, B. (1995) *Managing the Civil Service: Reform Lessons from Advanced Industrialized Countries*, Washington DC: World Bank.

Nunberg, B. (1992) *Managing the Civil Service: What LDCs Can Learn From Developed Country Reforms*, Washington DC: World Bank.

O'Brien, K. J. and Li, L. J. (1999) 'Selective Policy Implementation in Rural China', *Comparative Politics* 31 (2), 167–86.

OECD (1996a) *Integrating People Management into Public Service Reform*, Paris: OECD.

OECD (1996b) *Performance Management in Government: Contemporary Illustrations*, Paris: OECD.

OECD (1996c) *Putting Citizens First: Portuguese Experience in Public Management Reform*, Paris: OECD.

OECD (1994) *Performance Management in Government: Performance Measurement and Result-oriented Management*, Paris: OECD.

Organization Department of CCP (1999) *Dangzheng lingdao ganbu tongji ziliao huibian 1954–1998* (Collection of Statistical Information on Party and Government Leading Cadres 1954–1998), Beijing: Dangjian duwu chubanshe.

Painter, M. (2006) 'Sequencing Civil Service Pay Reforms in Vietnam: Transition or Leapfrog?' *Governance* 19 (2), 325–46.

Painter, M. (2004) 'The Politics of Administrative Reform in East and Southeast Asia: From Gridlock to Continuous Self-improvement?' *Governance* 17 (3), 361–86.

Painter, M. (2003a) 'Public Administration Reform in Vietnam,' in A. B. L. Cheung and I. Scott (eds) *Governance and Public Sector Reform in Asia: Paradigm Shifts or Business As Usual?*, London: Routledge Curzon, 208–26.

Painter, M. (2003b) 'Public Administration Reform in Vietnam: Problems and Prospects', *Public Administration and Development* 23, 259–71.

Pei, M. (2006) *China's Trapped Transition: The Limits of Developmental Autocracy*, Cambridge, MA: Harvard University Press.

Pei, M. (1994) *From Reform to Revolution: The Demise of Communism in China and the Soviet Union*, Cambridge, MA: Harvard University Press.

Peters, G. B. (2005) *Institutional Theory in Political Science: The New Institutionalism*, London; New York: Printer.

Peters, G. B. and Savoie, D. J. (1994) 'Civil Service Reform: Misdiagnosing the Patient', *Public Administration Review* 54 (5), 418–25.

Quah, J. S. T. (2009) 'Combating Corruption in the Asia-pacific Countries: What Do We Know and What Needs To Be Done?' *International Public Management Review* 10 (1), 5–33.

Quah, J. S. T. (2003) 'Causes and Consequences of Corruption in Southeast Asia: A Comparative Analysis of Indonesia, the Philippines and Thailand', *Asian Journal of Public Administration* 25 (2), 235–66.

Rees, R. (1985) 'The Theory of Principal and Agent', *Bulletin of Economic Research* 37, 4–28.

Reischauer, E. O. and Fairbank, J. F. (1960) *East Asia: The Great Tradition*, Boston: Houghton Mifflin.

Ren, J. (2007) '*Zhangjiajie moshide shinian lunhui* (The ten years of the Zhangjiajie model)', *Juece (Decision-making)*, 3–4.

Rosser, A. (2003) 'What Paradigm Shift? Public Sector Reform in Indonesia since the Asian Crisis,' in A. B. L. Cheung and I. Scott (eds) *Governance and Public Sector Reform in Asia: Paradigm Shifts or Business As Usual?*, London: Routledge Curzon, 227–47.

Ryan, J. D. and Wandel, J. C. (1996) 'Vietnam's Reform Experience—The Quest for Stability During Transition', UNDP Program Staff Paper.

Sapio, F. (2008) '*Shuanggui* and Extralegal Detention in China', *China Information* 22 (1), 7–37.

Schiavo-Campo, S. (1998) 'Government Employment and Pay: The Global and Regional Evidence', *Public Administration and Development* 18, 457–78.

Schick, A. (1998) 'Why Most Developing Countries Should Not Try New Zealand Reforms', *The World Bank Research Observer* 13, 1123–31.

Schurmann, F. (1968) *Ideology and Organization in Communist China*, Berkeley: University of California Press.

Shambaugh, D. (2008a) *China's Communist Party: Atrophy and Adaptation*, Berkeley; Los Angeles; London: University of California Press.

Shambaugh, D. (2008b) 'Training China's Political Elite: The Party School System', *The China Quarterly* 196, 827–44.

Shirk, S. (1994) *How China Opened Its Door: the Political Success of the PRC's Foreign Trade and Investment Reforms*, Washington DC: Brookings Institution.

Shirk, S. (1993) *The Political Logic of Economic Reform in China*, Berkeley: University of California Press.

Simon, H., Thompson, V. and Smithburg, D. (1991) *Public Administration*, New Brunswick, NJ: Transaction Publishers.

Simon, H. A. (1985) 'Human Nature in Politics: the Dialogue of Psychology with Political Science', *American Political Science Review* 79, 293–304.

Simon, H. A. (1981) *The Sciences of the Artificial* 2nd edn. Cambridge: MIT Press.

Simon, H. A. (1947) *Administrative Behavior*, New York: The Free Press.

Sun, Y. (2009) 'Cadre Recruitment and Corruption: What Goes Wrong?' in T. Gong and S. K. Ma (eds) *Preventing Corruption in Asia: Institutional Design and Policy Capacity*, London and New York: Routledge, 48–63.

Sun, Y. (2004) *Corruption and Market in Contemporary China*, Ithaca, NY: Cornell University Press.

Swanson, K. E., Kuhn, R. G. and Xu, W. (2001) 'Environmental Policy Implementation in Rural China: A Case Study of Yuhang, Zhejiang', *Environmental Management* 24 (4), 481–91.

Tirole, J. (1994) 'The Internal Organization of Government', *Oxford Economic Papers* 46 (1), 1–29.

Tirole, J. (1986) 'Hierarchies and Bureaucracies: On the Role of Collusion in Organization', *Journal of Law, Economics and Organization* 2, 181–200.

Tjiptoherijanto, P. (2007) 'Civil Service Reform in Indonesia', *International Public Management Review* 8 (2), 31–44.

Tong, C. H., Straussman, J. D. and Broadnax, W. D. (1999) 'Civil Service Reform in the People's Republic of China: Case Studies of Early Implementation', *Public Administration and Development* 19, 193–206.

Transparency International (2009) *Corruption Perception Index 2009*. Available online: www.transparency.org/policy_research/surveys_indices/cpi/2009 (accessed on 8 May 2010).

Tsao, K. K. and Worthley, J. A. (1995) 'Chinese Public Administration: Change with Continuity during Political and Economic Development', *Public Administration Review* 55 (2), 169–74.

Turner, M. (2002) 'Choosing Items from the Menu: New Public Management in Southeast Asia', *International Journal of Public Administration* 25, 1493–1512.

## Bibliography

United Nations (2005) *Lao People's Democratic Republic: Public Administration Country Profile*, United Nations.

Walder, A. G. (1995) 'Career Mobility and the Communist Political Order', *American Sociological Review* 60 (3), 309–28.

Walder, A. G. (1986) *Communist Neo-traditionalism: Work and Authority in Chinese Industry*, Berkeley: University of California Press.

Wang, S. and Hu, A. (1999) *The Political Economy of Uneven Development: The Case of China*, Armonk, NY: M.E. Sharpe.

Wang, X. (2006) *China's Civil Service Reform and Local Government Performance: A Principal–agent Perspective*, Ph.D. dissertation, University of Hong Kong.

Wedeman, A. (2000) 'Budgets, Extra-budgets and Small Treasuries', *Journal of Contemporary China* 9, 489–511.

Wedeman, A. (1999) 'Agency and Fiscal Dependence in Central-provincial Relations in China', *Journal of Contemporary China* 8, 103–22.

Whiting, S. H. (2004) 'The Cadre Evaluation System at the Grass Roots: The Paradox of Party Rule', in B. Naughton and D. L. Yang (eds) *Holding China Together: Diversity and National Integration in the Post-Deng Era*, Cambridge: Cambridge University Press, 101–19.

Whiting, S. H. (2000) *Power and Wealth in Rural China: The Political Economy of Institutional Change*, Cambridge: Cambridge University Press.

Wildavsky, A. (1975) *Budgeting: A Comparative Theory of Budgetary Processes*, Boston: Little Brown.

World Bank (2004) *World Development Report 2004: Making Service Work for Poor People*, Washington DC: World Bank.

Wu, Z. (2009) *Woguo gonggong bumen renli ziyuan guanli gaige* (Public Sector Human Resource Management Reforms in China), Shanghai: Jiaotong University Press.

Xi, L. (2002) *Zhongguo gongwuyuan zhidu* (Chinese Civil Service System), Beijing: Tsinghua University Press.

Yan, H. (1995) 'Establishing a Public Service System', in C. L. Hamrin and S. Zhao (eds) *Decision-Making in Deng's China: Perspectives from Insiders*, Armonk, NY: M.E. Sharpe, 169–75.

Yang, D. L. (2004) *Remaking the Chinese Leviathan: Market Transition and Politics of Governance in China*, Stanford, CA: Stanford University Press.

Yang, S. and Wang, J. (eds) (2008) *Gongwuyuan kaohe* (Performance Evaluation for Civil Servants), Beijing: China Personnel Press.

Yin, W. (2003) '*Ganbu renshi zhidu zhongda gaige*' (Great reforms on cadre personnel management system), *Zhongguo gongwuyuan* (Chinese public servants), June 2003, 8–11.

Zhang, B. (2006) *Tuijin ganbu renshi gongzuo kexuehua, minzhuhua, zhiduhau de zhongda jucuo* (Great Measure to Make Cadre Personnel System more Scientific, Democratic and Institutionalized: Understanding and Implementing Civil Service Law of PRC). Available online: www.mop.gov.cn/Desktop.aspx?PATH=rsbww/sy/xxll&Gid=36796243-b120–477e-9c3e-bcab0545fd88&Tid=Cms_Info (accessed on 8 April 2006).

Zhong, Y. (2003) *Local Government and Politics in China: Challenges from Below*, Armonk, NY; London, England: M.E. Sharpe.

Zhou, X. (1995) 'Partial Reform and the Chinese Bureaucracy in the Post-Mao Era', *Comparative Political Studies* 28, 440–68.

Zhu, G. (2008) *Gongwuyuan guimo wenti zhengfu jigou gaige* (The civil service scope and institutional reforms in China), Beijing: Renmin University Press.

Zhu, G. (1998) *Dangdai zhongguo shehui ge jieceng fenxi* (Analysis of social strata in contemporary China), Tianjin: Tianjin People's Publishing House.

# Index

Page numbers in *italics* denote tables, those in bold denote figures.

1956 system 52
1985 system 53–4
*1993 Provisional Regulations* 3–5, 36, 54
1993 system 54
1998 downsizing campaign 43, 78
*2002 Regulations* 36, 46, 97

administrative expenses 25, *28*
administrative reforms 1, 4, 7, 33
adverse selection 2, 9, 38, 41, 44, 47
All-China Association for Friendship with People's Overseas 169n1
All-China Disabled People's Federation 169n1
All-China Federation of Literature and Art Circles 169n1
All-China Federation of Trade Unions 169n1
All-China Foreign Affairs Studies Association 169n1
All-China Journalists' Association 169n1
All-China Legal Studies Association 169n1
All-China Writers' Association 169n1
alternate members of the Politburo 32
anticorruption 5, 19, 33, 35, 93–4, 103–7
Aquino, President 132
Asian Development Bank 118
Association of Taiwan Compatriots 169n1
Autonomous Muslim Region of Mindanao 133
avoidance 73, 101–3

behavioral paradigm 10–11
Beijing 15–16
Beijing Personnel Bureau 68
bounded rationality 10–12

boundedly rational 8, 10–12
buying and selling of government posts 3, 18, 41, 63–6

cadre personnel management system 2, 3, 8, 17, 18, 21, 37–40
cadres 20–4
Central Discipline Inspection Commission 33–5, 87, 105–7
central leadership 19, 93–7
Central Party School 35–6, 52
centrally planned economy 52
Changchun 15–16
Changchun Administration School 83
Changchun Education Commission 49–50
Changchun Environmental Protection Bureau 89, 111–12
Cheng Kejie 64
Chinese Communist Party (CCP) 2, 21, 93, 135, 13th national congress 4, 14th national congress 4, 16th national congress 107; Central Committee 18, 32–3, 36, 46, 67, 94–6; General Secretary of the CCP 4, 30; *nomenklatura* system 33; Organization Department 18, 32, 46, 67, 95–6, 99
Chinese leadership *see* central leadership
Chinese People's Political Consultative Conference 97
Chinese political system 94, 142
citizen satisfaction surveys 108
civil servants: generalists 29–30; officers for regulation enforcement 29; political civil servants 4; professionals and technicians 29–30; professional civil servants 4

# Index

civil service system: civil servant recruitment 25; civil service *entry-level* selection 43–5; competitive selection 43–7; performance appraisal 48–9
*Civil Service Law* 1, 2, 5, 22, 36–7
'collapse' prediction 144
collective leadership 104
Communist Party of Vietnam 122
Communist Party Secretariat 32
Communist revolutionary period 2, 21
comparative case studies 16
conflict of interest 8–10
consistency of behavior 11–12
contexts for the reforms 17, 32–5, 36–7
control by the policy-makers 17
control mechanisms 8–11
control over the bureaucracy 1, 4–6, 97–101
conventional principal-agent model 9–11
corruption 63–6
Corruption Perception Index 121, 136, 141
county party committee 103–5; standing committee of the county party committee 104
credible commitment 12, 50

decentralization 6, 18, 67, 93–4
demobilized soldiers 38, 44, 70–2, 78, 82
democratic recommendation (*mingzhu tuijian*) 45–6
Deng Xiaoping 4, 98
Deng Xiaoping Theory 32
discipline policy 63–6
Doi Moi renovation 122
dual leadership system 105

eight democratic parties 21–2, 169n1
establishment planning 68, 83
ethnic diversity 122
extra-budgetary funds 62

financial mismanagement 18, 42, 60
five sets of the local authorities 104
F-Ratio *115*, *117*

good governance 2, 139
government expenditure 17, 20, 25, *28*, **29**, 52
grade (*jibie*) wage system 52; *see also* 1956 system
grassroot-level positions 45
Guizhou 25, *27*

Haidian district 15–16

Haidian Education Commission 69, 84, 89, 91, 114–15
Haidian Personnel Bureau 68, 72, *75*
hardship allowances 56, 63
Hebei 63
Hu Jintao 35, 100
Huangpu Military Academy Alumni Association 169n1

incentive alignment 3, 9–10, 18, 41, 49–50
incentive-compatible mechanism 9
in-depth interviews 16, *109*, 146
Indonesia 118, 121, 128–30
induction training 51–2, 71
informal norms 11–12, 66
information asymmetry 8–9
institutional adaptability 7, 93–4, 143–4
internal competition for posting (*jingzheng shanggang*) 46–7
*Internal Supervision Regulation* 106
International Monetary Fund 118, *121*

Jiangxi 63–4
Jilin People's Congress 87

kinship avoidance 102

Lao People's Revolutionary Party (LPRP) 125
Laos 125–8
leading cadres 97–9
leading cadres responsibility system 99–101
leading positions 29–33
Li Peng 4
life-tenure system 40, 53
local leadership groups 46
local party secretaries 46, 103–5

Mao Zedong Thought 32
Marcos, President 131–2
Marxism-Leninism 32
Marxist-Leninist ideology 35
mass evaluations (*minzhu pingyi*) 46–7
mass organizations 21–2, 54
Mi Fengjun 81, 87
Ministry of Human Resource and Social Security 5
Ministry of Personnel 18, 46, 67, 96
Ministry of Supervision 33, 35
moral hazard 9, 38, 48

National Environmental Protection Bureau 108

National People's Congress 1, 5, 36, 94; standing committee of National People's Congress 30, 32
National School of Administration 35–6, 51
new public management movement 13
Ningbo 15–16
Ningbo Education Commission 47, **79**, 84, 91
Ningbo Environmental Protection Bureau *80*, 84, 86–7, 110–12
Ninth Five-Year Plan 109–10
non-government organizations 22, *26*, 143
non-leading positions 29–33

Organization for Economic Co-operation and Development (OECD) 3, 120
one-level-down system 95, 103
open recruitment (*gonkai xuanba*) 46–7
open-ended questions 109
organization culture 2, 12–13
organization theory 10
organizational compliance 10

'Party controls cadres' 36, 97
party core group (*dangzu*) 33–4, 43
payroll expenditure 25
People's Liberation Army 38
People's Republic of China (PRC) 21
performance contracts 49–50, 100, 107
performance culture 19, 120, 136
performance targets 50
performance-based rewards systems 9
personal rapport (*guanxi*) 39
Philippines 118, 121, 131–3
Politburo 4, 32–3, 94; standing committee of the Politburo 30
political loyalty 39–40, 98–9
political regime type 118, 122
position allowances 56, 60
position classification 30, 68
position exchange 101
positions and ranks 30
post and grade wage system 54; *see also 1993 system*
post-Mao authorities 1, 4, 103
post-Suharto governments 128
Premier 30, 32
pre-promotional qualification training 51
pre-service training 51
President of the PRC 30
primary stage of socialism 32
principal-agent framework 8–15
probabilities proportional to size sampling method 16, 147

Procurator General 32
procuratorate 22
propaganda department 103
*Provisional Regulations on State Civil Servants* 3–5, 36, 54; *see also 1993 Provisional Regulations*
public employees supported by the state budget 20, 23
public notification (*gongshi zhidu*) 46–7
public service units 21–5, 38
Purchasing Power Parity (PPP) *121*

questionnaire survey 16, 149

rank-in-person 52, 55
regional allowances 56
regional gaps of civil service welfare 42, 142
*Regulations on Selection and Appointment of Party and Government Leading Cadres* 36, 46, 97; *see also 2002 Regulations*
Returned-Overseas Chinese Federation 169n1
risk-sharing contractual arrangement 9

sabotage 8, 10–12
Science and Technology Association 169n1
secret bank accounts (*xiao jinku*) 62
seeking social proof 11–12
separation of the Party from the government 4
Shaanxi *27*, 63
Shanxi *27*, 63
Shenzhen 4
shirking 8, 10–12
*shuanggui* 106–7, 136, 141
social class background 39–40, 98–9
social organizations 21–6
socialism colleges 35–6, 136
Southeast Asia 5, 19, 118, 123, 142
staff and workers of the state organs 21–3
State Council 18, 33–6
State-Owned Enterprises (SOEs) 23
'strong state' prediction 144
structural wage system 53–4; *see also 1985 system*
Suharto 128–9
Sukarno 128
Supreme People's Court 32, 97
Supreme People's Procuratorate 32, 97

Tenth Five-Year Plan 110
three-actor games 94

Three Represents 32
Tiananmen Incident 4
Tibet 25, *27*, 62, *63*
top-down control mechanisms 9–12
township and village enterprises (TVEs) 14
Transparency International 119, *121*, 130, 136, 141
two-level-down cadre management system 95, 103

United Front Work Department 36
United Nations 118
urban residency permit 43
urban residential committees 16, 147
urban street offices 68–9
utility maximizers 8

vice-provincial-level cities 15
Vietnam 122–5
Vietnam's political system 122

wage reforms 52–62
wage structure 5; grade wage 71, 73; post and grade structure 56; post wage 71, 73
Weberian principles 119
Women's Federation 22, 169n1
World Bank 118, 134

Xi Jinping 35
Xinjiang *27*, 63
Xu Yunhong 76, 87

Youth League 22, 43, 169n1

Zeng Qinghong 35
Zhangjiajie 106
Zhao Ziyang 4
Zhou Liangluo 88
Zhu Rongji 43
zone of acceptance 10–11